Remembering Iosepa

REMEMBERING IOSEPA

*History, Place, and Religion
in the American West*

Matthew Kester

OXFORD
UNIVERSITY PRESS

OXFORD
UNIVERSITY PRESS

Oxford University Press is a department of the University of Oxford.
It furthers the University's objective of excellence in research, scholarship,
and education by publishing worldwide.

Oxford   New York
Aucklandm   Cape Town   Dar es Salaam   Hong Kong   Karachi
Kuala Lumpur   Madrid   Melbourne   Mexico City   Nairobi
New Delhi   Shanghai   Taipei   Toronto

With offices in
Argentina   Austria   Brazil   Chile   Czech Republic   France   Greece
Guatemala   Hungary   Italy   Japan   Poland   Portugal   Singapore
South Korea   Switzerland   Thailand   Turkey   Ukraine   Vietnam

Oxford is a registered trademark of Oxford University Press in the UK
and certain other countries.

Published in the United States of America by
Oxford University Press
198 Madison Avenue, New York, NY 10016

© Oxford University Press 2013

Library of Congress Cataloging-in-Publication Data
Kester, Matthew, author.
Remembering Iosepa : history, place, and religion in the American West / Matthew Kester.
     pages cm
Publication of the author's dissertation, University of California, Santa Barbara, 2008.
Includes bibliographical references and index.
ISBN 978–0–19–984491–3 (hardcover : alk. paper)
1. Iosepa (Utah)   2. Immigrants—Utah.   3. Hawaiians—Utah.   4. Church of Jesus Christ
of Latter-day Saints—Missions—Hawaii—History—19th century.   5. Mormon Church—
Missions—Hawaii—History—19th century.   I. Title.
F835.H3K47 2013
979.2'43—dc23
2012030728

ISBN 978–0–19–984491–3

9 8 7 6 5 4 3 2 1
Printed in the United States of America
on acid-free paper

CONTENTS

ACKNOWLEDGMENTS

I am grateful for the help and support of a great number of people and institutions that made the research and writing of this book possible. First off, I would like to thank all of my colleagues at Brigham Young University Hawai'i, especially Jim Tueller, Cynthia Compton, Chad Compton, David and Yifen Beus, Chad Ford, Marynelle Chew, Anna Kaanga, Becky Demartini, Zoia Falevai, Ed Kinghorn, Isaiah Walker, Jeff Burroughs, Norman Fuali'i Thompson III, Aaron Schade, Ken Wright, Ethan Yorgasen, Michael Aldrich, Tevita Ka'ili, Rose Meno Ram, Anna-Marie Christiansen, Kali Fermantez, and Terry Pane'e. Special thanks must go to Riley Moffat and Phillip McArthur, both mentors and friends of many years, and the late Lance Chase. William Kauaiwiuaokalani Wallace III, who passed away in the spring of 2009, was an endless source of wisdom and inspiration, in every way possible. From the University of Hawai'i, I received invaluable friendship, support, and good advice from Hokulani Aikau and the late Karen Peacock. Anapesi Ka'ili and Matt Basso, from the American West Center at the University of Utah, have had a positive influence on me from afar. Special thanks also to David Rich Lewis at Utah State University and the rest of the editorial staff at the *Western Historical Quarterly*. A modified version of the third chapter of this book appeared as an article in that publication, and I remain honored at the support they offered me in that endeavor.

As an archivist myself, I realize perhaps more than most that without the conscientious work and support of archives and curatorial staff, very little research in this world would be possible. The staff at the Church Historical Department in Salt Lake City, especially Brad Westwood and Chad Orton, are most appreciated. I would also like to thank Reid Neilsen and Benjamin Pykles for their interest in and support of this project. From the L. Tom Perry Special Collections at Brigham Young University in Provo, I would like to thank Gordon Daines, Russ Taylor, and Tom Wells, as well as Fred Woods from the Department of Religion. Sam Passey at the University of Utah's Marriott Library is an excellent resource and a pleasure to work with. The State Archives of Hawai'i is a first-class place to conduct research thanks to the efforts of Gina Vergara-Bautista and Susan Shaner. I offer my thanks also to the staff of the Research Center at the Utah State Historical Society for their assistance in obtaining photographs of Iosepa. A great deal of material for this book also came from the Joseph F. Smith Library Archives and Special Collections at Brigham Young University Hawai'i, where I am the archivist. Any breach of service or organization in those collections falls squarely on my shoulders.

This project began and took shape during my years as a graduate student at the University of California Santa Barbara, and the faculty of the history department there were exceptional in every way. I thank James Brooks, now the director of the School of American Research in Santa Fe, New Mexico, for his direction and encouragement. This project would have been impossible without the guidance and support of Zaragosa Vargas (now at the University of North Carolina at Chapel Hill), Randy Bergstrom, and Rudiger Busto. The phrase "thank-you" is truly inadequate when applied to my longtime mentor and friend Paul Spickard; had he not intervened at so many critical junctures in my life, things would have turned out much differently for me. My cohort at UCSB was the best; a special thank-you to David Torres-Rouff, Rudy Guevarra, Jeff Moniz, and Sharleen Levine. And from beyond UCSB thanks go to the rest of the *hui*. You know who you are.

Thanks to my mother, Cynthia Kester, and my father, Ron Kester, for teaching me well, encouraging and supporting my education every step of the way, and just generally being everything one would want one's family to be. My mother instilled in me a love and passion for the power of the written word, and my father passed on to me a love and thirst for knowledge. Are there two better gifts to give? I will always be indebted to my brother C. J. for knowing I am a nerd and not treating me like one, and my three sisters, Amy, Libby, and Melissa, just for putting up with me. I have a huge extended family in the Ko'olauloa community, especially in the towns of Lā'ie, Hau'ula, and Sunset Beach, but I would like to especially recognize the love and friendship of the Pualoa family, the Soren family, the Stant family, the Wright family, and Marsha Taylor and family. My hanai sister Alana Barrera continues to be a much needed dose of levity and reality, and I offer her my thanks.

I also want to thank Cory Ho'opi'iaina and his family for their time, patience, and acceptance of my intrusive visits at the annual Memorial Day celebrations at Iosepa in Skull Valley. And I extend my thanks to all of the attendees at those celebrations, who were without exception so generous with their time, thoughts, and knowledge. Of all the descendants of

Iosepa settlers, few have worked as tirelessly and passionately as Dawn Wasson to preserve the history and memory of her ancestors. She is an inspiration to me, for her work as a historian and for her willingness to stand and be heard, and I thank her deeply for her guidance and example. To the many descendants of Iosepa pioneers, the Kekauoha and Chang families, the Alapa and Worthingtons, the Christiansens and Hubbells, the especially the Wallaces, thank you.

The final and most heartfelt love and thanks must go to my wife, Summer, and my three children, Kainoa, Isabella, and Tosh. They have been a constant source of love and support and have made this journey worthwhile. They are my life and my inspiration.

Matt Kester
Ka'a'awa, Hawai'i

Remembering Iosepa

Introduction
Connections

It was mid-November in Salt Lake City, and the cloudless, midday sky shone bright blue. Clear skies in November on the Wasatch Front mean cold, and it was freezing. I was in Salt Lake City doing research and staying at a hotel near the University of Utah and had arranged for the hotel shuttle to drop me off at the university library. A few moments later a white van with the hotel logo on it pulled up. I hopped in and thanked the driver for the ride. "No problem," he replied. "Where are you visiting from?" "Hawai'i," I told him. "I am here doing some work." "Hawai'i, huh?" he replied. "Where in Hawai'i?" "On O'ahu," I said, "the northeastern side, a little town called Lā'ie." "Lā'ie? Oh, I have family there!" I asked him what his family's name was. He told me; I knew two of his uncles quite well. He was Tongan, born and raised in West Salt Lake City. Our brief conversation turned to the subject of Hawaiian high school football, which was how I was acquainted with one of his uncles. It was something we were both clearly passionate about. The local Hawaiian team from my area, Kahuku High School, had traveled to Utah earlier in the season to play an exhibition game with one of Salt Lake City's better teams, from Highland High School. Kahuku had lost, a disappointment to us both. "After that loss," the driver told me, "I scraped all the Kahuku stickers off my car and didn't wear my Red Raiders shirts or sweatshirts for a while. I just didn't want to hear it. All of us Polys were pissed off." It was a short ride to the library; we caught each other's names, I thanked him for the ride, and we said good-bye. He gave me a card with the hotel phone number on it to call if I needed a shuttle ride back. I spent the rest of the afternoon poring over the records of the Iosepa Agricultural and Stock Company.

I looked out the fifth floor window of the library. It was now dusk. Probably a lot colder too, I thought. I found the hotel shuttle card and called to request a pickup, then walked outside and waited. The view from the base of the Wasatch Range into the valley below in the twilight was beautiful, even with temperatures in the low twenties. After about fifteen minutes the shuttle arrived, with a different driver at the wheel. I said hello and thanked the young man for picking me up. "Where are you from?" he asked. I told him. "Wow," he replied, "that must be nice." He said he had lived in Utah all of his life. The driver of the earlier shuttle was his cousin.

Walking into the hotel lobby, I noticed a sea of red shirts and large people. The hotel was hosting the University of Utah football team for a pregame banquet. They were going to play New Mexico the next evening, and I had tickets. Walking through the throng of players, I saw a familiar face. I called his name, and he looked over and smiled when he saw me. Our families are next-door neighbors in Hawai'i, although he had been away at school since we moved in. We shook hands and talked a bit, then I wished him luck and told him I would tell his family hello, of course.

In the space of about six hours, I had bumped into three people connected with the community I call home. One of them shares this home with me, and the other two have a vague but palpable connection to my community. They have made it *their* community, too. Because I am in Utah, none of this seems odd at all, even though I am three thousand miles away from home. If I were staying in West Valley, I would no doubt run into many more people I knew from home. West Valley is where most of the Polynesians live; everybody knows that.

"About two thousand years ago—perhaps three hundred years more or three hundred years less—there occurred the most remarkable voyage of discovery and settlement in all human history." This passage refers to the voyages of Oceanian discoverers into the sea of islands that is the Pacific Ocean, the voyages that peopled all of Oceania. What makes these travels so remarkable is their deliberateness. The voyaging canoe, or *va'a*, made them possible. The *va'a* is a remarkable and ingenious piece of technology. At the same time that continental peoples on the other side of the earth were tentatively venturing out of sight of dry land, these Oceanian voyagers traversed the largest geographic feature on the planet on deliberate and calculated settlement expeditions. The success of the first fantastic journey was as much a matter of belief as it was of skill. People do not sail willingly to their deaths. If these voyagers did not believe it could be done, the voyage would never have been attempted. The fact that it *had* been done, and the knowledge of *how* it had been done, fostered in them a belief that it could be done again. As Greg Dening, the author of the quote above, also stated, these

voyages, and the tools that made them possible, were the product of "the cultural DNA of two millennia through all the Pacific."[1] Perhaps the only question on the minds of these voyagers was not whether there were more islands awaiting them, but how many there were. What were the borders of this seemingly boundless realm? Were there more islands, populated by strangers? Such questions must have animated the ambitions of countless Oceanian voyagers.

Sometime between approximately 1830 and 1850, a Native Hawaiian named Richard Mahoui decided to board a foreign ship bound for foreign shores. Like those of the Oceanian voyagers two millennia before him, we can only guess at his motives. The world that informed his decision, the Hawaiian Islands of the early nineteenth century, is more familiar to us. It is unlikely he was a voyager against his will, but his choice to make the journey might have been made at the behest of kin or a chief. Still, he could as easily have made the decision to satisfy his own wanderlust, to act on the prompting of a dream, or maybe just to follow a hunch: the nagging feeling that this was an opportunity not to be missed. We cannot know whether this was a permanent move, or if he left on a journey with a specified route or duration, or with the assurance that he could return home if he so desired. But we know he left. Like the voyagers who departed scores of other islands in search of a new home, he left a record of his travels, an imprint in time testifying about his journey. Richard Mahoui appears in 1850 records in Washington State, one of at least twenty-five Native Hawaiians (listed in the census records as "Sandwich Islanders") residing in Clark County. He lived in the "Kanaka Village" at Fort Vancouver. Mahoui didn't have to build his own va'a. A ship came to him, built and sailed by Haole (white foreigners). He climbed aboard, and his journey began. In the years that followed, hundreds of Native Hawaiians left their homes as sojourners and settlers.[2] Although many eventually returned to Hawai'i, the vast majority of those who stayed settled in western North America. The focus of this book is a small minority of those Native Hawaiian settlers: the nineteenth-century Mormon colonists in Utah, who were drawn east by the dictates of their new religion. Their history, like the history of Native Hawaiian settlers in the Pacific Northwest or the Sierra Nevada foothills, is an often overlooked part of Hawai'i's story.

The story of these Native Hawaiian settlers is also an integral part of the history of western North America, and telling it provides an opportunity to bring these histories together. By acknowledging the importance of these histories for both Hawai'i and the American West, we recognize the interconnectedness of the regional histories in and around Oceania in the nineteenth and twentieth centuries. By emphasizing the ideological (in this case religious) motivations that create and sustain diasporic communities globally, we acknowledge the variety of factors that motivate human action and the agency of individuals in the context of the larger structures that shape their lives. By stressing the importance of place for those whom we so often see as displaced, we demonstrate the centrality of communities in shaping their own histories. For a variety of reasons, Native Hawaiians have been settling in western North America since the early nineteenth century. In the twenty-first century they have been joined by other Pacific Islanders, creating a transnational diaspora that connects islands and continents. I argue for continuity between these seemingly different stories that span two very different eras.

This recent growth in a complex and transnational "Pacific diaspora" that spans Oceania from Sydney to Anchorage has been the subject of a prodigious amount of scholarship. Scholars from various disciplines have estimated its effects and mapped its relationships across borders and boundaries; they have lamented "brain drains" and the reliance of home nations on the money that their family members remit; and they have explored the root causes and disparate effects of this diaspora on families, individuals, nations, and cultures. Although much of this scholarship has focused on the negative or deleterious effects of this movement across the Pacific,[3] recently there have been efforts to rethink this dispersion in the context of the broader history and culture of Oceania. This shift in thinking began with the 1993 publication of Epeli Hau'ofa's groundbreaking essay "Our Sea of Islands," an instant classic that generated an academic upheaval of such magnitude that it is fair to think of Pacific Islands' scholarship in terms of pre- and post- "Our Sea of Islands." In this essay Hau'ofa narrates his own epiphany, a new paradigm in thinking about Oceanian cultures, communities, and economies:

> Smallness is a state of mind. There is a gulf of difference between viewing the Pacific as 'islands in a far sea' and as 'a sea of islands.' The first emphasizes dry surfaces in a vast ocean far from the centers of power. When you focus this way you stress the smallness and remoteness of islands. The second is a more holistic perspective in which things are seen in the totality of their relationships.... [I]t was continental men, Europeans and Americans, who drew imaginary lines across the sea, making the colonial boundaries that, for the first time, confined ocean peoples to tiny spaces.... The difference between the two perspectives is reflected in the first two terms used for our region: Pacific Islands and Oceania. The first term, 'Pacific Islands,' is the prevailing one used everywhere; it connotes small areas of land surfaces sitting atop submerged reefs or seamounts.... "Oceania" connotes a sea of islands with their inhabitants. The world

of our ancestors was a large sea full of places to explore, to make their homes in, to breed generations of seafarers like themselves.... The world of Oceania may no longer include the heavens and the underworld; but it certainly encompasses the great cities in Australia, New Zealand, the USA, and Canada. And it is within that expanded world that the extent of the people's resources must be measured.[4]

Immediately the past, present, and future movement of Pacific Islanders across Oceania was conceptualized in new ways. Gone were the notions of isolation and smallness, and the economic models that emphasized relationships between "core" and "peripheral" nations. Hau'ofa offered a new vision of Oceania that was as radical and revolutionary in its ideology as it was humble and self-effacing in its presentation. Although Hau'ofa's theoretical model is still challenged by some in its particulars,[5] its vision of an ideological shift as determined by the participants themselves in this vast global diaspora ranks among the most profound changes in regional postcolonial theory, made all the more powerful by its rhetorical clarity and sense of purpose.[6] Like many studies in the post-Hau'ofa era of scholarship in Oceania, the pages that follow are influenced by his thinking about the Pacific diaspora in the twenty-first century.

I can't remember at what point I decided to write this story this way. My initial goal was to write a detailed history of Iosepa, a small community of Native Hawaiian Latter-day Saints established in 1889 at a ranch in Skull Valley, seventy-five miles southwest of Salt Lake City. Residents there had gathered, as faithful nineteenth-century Mormons did, to join other Latter-day Saints from around the world to prepare for Jesus Christ's prophesied return. The community was christened "Iosepa" in honor of Joseph F. Smith, the prophet and president of the Church of Jesus Christ of Latter-day Saints from 1901 to 1918. He had been a missionary in Hawaii in his younger years. Community members worked on the ranch, which was established as a joint stock corporation. In 1915, at the height of its prosperity, Joseph F. Smith announced that a temple would be built in Hawaii, and the community was abandoned. Today Iosepa is known primarily to three groups of people: historians of late nineteenth-century Utah (and then only those working on Mormon-related topics); descendants of the original Iosepa settlers; and, increasingly, Pacific Islanders living in close proximity to the Iosepa "ghost town" (the number of folks in this last category is large and growing each year).

I had heard the name Iosepa before I knew its full story or grasped the breadth of its connections to the community in Hawaii that I call home. I lived for a short time on Iosepa Street; so named, I discovered later, because along it were the homes of those families who had returned from living in Utah. I had seen a brief recollection of life in Iosepa in an oral history collection, along with a short documentary produced for Utah television. The grandmother of a close friend arranged to be buried there, alongside her kin. I had listened, in our church meetings, to older people recounting the stories of the sacrifices and faith of their ancestors who settled in Utah at Iosepa. I had attended dinner at a friend's family reunion and heard aunties and uncles and grandmothers and grandfathers recount the stories they had heard about that place. Faith, sacrifice, and diligence. Poverty and discrimination. These were pioneers.

It occurred to me that the public memory of this community was at least as interesting and important as the history of the community itself. And of course the various commemorative activities surrounding Iosepa also make up the "real" history of the community, a history far more lasting and influential than an outsider's flawed rendering. As I learned more about the Hawaiian Mission of the Church of Jesus Christ of Latter-day Saints, the history of Mormon settlement and colonization throughout the Great Basin, and the reverence accorded to the story of Iosepa among the Pacific Islanders in Utah today, I began to think that a simple retelling of Iosepa's twenty-eight years was inadequate, that the story of Iosepa transcends its short history in both directions. Looking westward, it began with the arrival of Mormon missionaries in Hawaii in 1850. Looking eastward, it began with the first communities of Native Hawaiians who came as settlers and sojourners to western North America. And from the perspective of contemporary communities of Pacific Islanders in the West, many of whom see in Iosepa a historical metaphor for their lived experience, it is a story that continues to unfold. Just as Native Hawaiian voyagers to western North America took advantage of opportunities provided by the vibrant Pacific trade network, Mormon missionaries' choice to seek converts in Hawai'i took advantage of the connections between the western United States and the Hawaiian islands. Both groups were traveling well-worn routes, made possible by the development of trade and transportation networks that linked Honolulu and Lahaina with places like San Francisco, Vancouver, and Salt Lake City. Seen from this perspective, the similarities between Iosepa and the communities that both preceded and followed it become sharper.

The Pacific diaspora is not limited to the western United States. Communities of diasporic Pacific Islanders are an important demographic component of Aotearoa/New Zealand (the Maori are hosts to a slew of migrants and settlers, both European and other Pacific Islanders) and Australia. Within Oceania itself there is a great deal of movement between rural communities, generally concentrated in low-lying atolls, and the urban enclaves that have developed in places like Suva, Fiji, and Honolulu, Hawai'i.[7] But the western United States is host to some of the largest communities of Pacific Islanders in the world. Salt Lake City has the largest concentrated population of Pacific Islanders outside of Honolulu, and cities in the west such as Los Angeles, San Francisco, Seattle, and Las Vegas have large, geographically distributed populations of Native Hawaiians and Pacific Islanders.[8] The history of Pacific Islanders in the American West has been overshadowed by a focus on historical studies of East Asian and Eastern European migrants, and contemporary communities have been eclipsed more recently by a concentration on immigration from Latin American nations.[9] This has been exacerbated by a persistent practice among many historians of the American West of all but ignoring Hawai'i, Guam, Samoa, and Micronesia in their discussion of US imperialism and expansion in the late nineteenth and early twentieth centuries. Regardless of its absence in many histories of the American West, however, the Pacific diaspora remains a vibrant and growing story in the urban West and shows no sign of abatement.

The story that I tell in the following chapters provides evidence of the deep ties between the Far West and Hawaii in the nineteenth and twentieth centuries, but also depicts Hawai'i as part of Oceania, the region with which it has far deeper and more lasting cultural and historical ties.[10] Scholars who argue for including Hawai'i in the regional history of the American West fail to address important movements of people in the opposite direction: the migration of Native Hawaiians (and in the postwar twentieth century, other Pacific Islanders) east as settlers and sojourners in the western United States. Without their stories, it is impossible to imagine a perspective in which Hawai'i exists not on the edge of empire, but in the center of a Pacific world that met the expansionist West full force.

Most histories of Hawai'i in the modern period make specific connections between Hawai'i's political economy and concurrent developments in western North America.[11] Although nearly all of these works are centered in Hawai'i, it is impossible to ignore the myriad connections in trade and immigration that developed among Honolulu, the western United States, and British Columbia. Most authors have felt it sufficient to document those relevant pieces of US economic and political history that directly affected the Hawaiian economy in the sandalwood, whaling, and sugar eras. In addition, the economic and political development that led to the overthrow of the Hawaiian monarchy by US forces in 1893 and Hawai'i's subsequent annexation to the United States in 1898 has clearly demanded historians' attention. The two most obvious developments in the nineteenth-century American West with a direct impact on Hawaiian economic, political, and social life were the growth of the British and American fur trade in the Pacific Northwest prior to 1850 and the discovery of gold in California, leading to the growth of modern San Francisco.[12] Generally only passing mention is made in many otherwise excellent histories of Hawai'i to the substantial emigration of Hawaiian subjects to western North America and their employment in the American whaling industry.[13] Although many synthetic histories of Hawai'i acknowledge the existence of Native Hawaiian emigration, few mention the experiences of the emigrants abroad, the ratio of sojourners to settlers, and other issues pertaining to Native Hawaiian emigrants. A story that receives far greater attention, for many reasons, is the immigration of Asian contract laborers to Hawai'i from the mid-nineteenth to the mid-twentieth centuries and their experiences as laborers on Hawaiian sugar plantations. There are, however, several studies that focus on Hawai'i as a way station to the American West for these same East Asian laborers.[14]

Beginning in the early 1990s Native Hawaiian scholars began to reclaim Hawai'i's history, creating new interpretations of Hawai'i's past from an indigenous perspective. These scholars have understandably focused on the political and social history of the illegal overthrow of and subsequent annexation of Hawai'i to the United States in the late nineteenth century.[15] Other works concentrate on the events leading up to the massive loss of land by Native Hawaiians in the Māhele of 1848 to 1854, rather than on Native Hawaiian emigration to western North America during that period. Although there has been a slew of articles over the years providing both firsthand accounts of Native Hawaiians abroad in the nineteenth century and general surveys of Native Hawaiians emigrating either as whalers or laborers in the fur trade,[16] only recently have historical monographs taken Native Hawaiian emigration in the nineteenth century as their primary subject.[17]

In addition to asserting continuity between communities of diasporic Pacific Islanders in the West in the nineteenth and twentieth centuries, this book addresses the role of religion (in this case Mormonism) in creating and sustaining diasporic communities over time. The history of Mormonism in Hawai'i is the subject of several books, articles, and dissertations.[18] Many Native Hawaiian converts to the Church of Jesus Christ of Latter-day Saints retained a large portion of their traditional beliefs and practices, a fact that vexed many a Mormon missionary well into the twentieth century.[19] It is nearly impossible to define the process of religious conversion, let alone quantify it, so it must suffice to say that Native Hawaiian

Mormons in the nineteenth and early twentieth centuries continued, and many today continue, to practice and believe strongly in certain aspects of indigenous Hawaiian spirituality. Because this was frowned on and considered *hewa*, evil or sinful, to white missionaries from the Church of Jesus Christ of Latter-day Saints, it was practiced largely outside of their view and rarely if ever described in detail. However, some Native Hawaiians also believed in the gods of foreigners and incorporated Mormon religious beliefs into their everyday lives. I use the term "Native Hawaiian Saints" to reflect the idea of Saints as a self-referential social category within Mormonism. Saints in the nineteenth century gathered to Zion, adhered to the Word of Wisdom, believed *The Book of Mormon* to be the word of God revealed through the prophet Joseph Smith, and so forth. Certainly many Native Hawaiian Mormons did and believed in all of these things, and many considered themselves Saints because of it. But this in no way implies that they had effectively abandoned all allegiances to or belief in indigenous spirituality. Rather, Native Hawaiian Mormons, like all religious converts, held their new and old belief systems in a productive tension, often creating spiritual crosswalks between the old and new that served to strengthen faith in both, as many do to this day.

This book also looks at the collective memory of Iosepa among Pacific Islander Mormons in Utah today and draws heavily on the literature in the field of public history on commemoration, collective memory, and place. The graveyard at Iosepa in Skull Valley has become host to at least one important annual event commemorating the "Polynesian Pioneers" of Iosepa that draws impressive crowds from all areas of the United States. Beginning as early as the 1950s, before the restorative work to erect monuments and pavilions, rebuild access roads, and install kitchens and bathrooms, Native Hawaiian students at Brigham Young University regularly visited the site to clean graves, pull weeds, and *mālama*, or preserve, the dignity of the site. I address the reasons why the site has become so important to the substantial Native Hawaiian and Pacific Islander community in the West today and how the reinterpretation and remembering of the site adds a new chapter to the history of Iosepa and the Pacific diaspora in the American West, connecting Pacific Islander communities in the nineteenth and early twentieth centuries to the growing communities of Pacific Islanders in the West today.

Iosepa was the result of the intersection of social, economic, and political forces that connected Hawai'i and the American West throughout the latter half of the nineteenth century. Mormonism in the American West and Hawai'i, and the migrations and communities that it fostered, demonstrate the dual role of economic, political, and religious forces in creating and sustaining diasporic communities globally. Ignoring the religious motivations behind the emigration of Native Hawaiian Mormons to the Salt Lake Valley obscures them as historical subjects for whom Mormonism was an important marker of individual and group identity. At the same time, ignoring the economic and political developments that made Mormon missionary activity in Hawai'i in the nineteenth century possible also obscures an important part of the same story. The story of Iosepa is an example of the Pacific diaspora to the western United States that needs to be told with all of these important forces in mind. As I present the story in the chapters that follow, I hope to do just that.

The basic organization of the book is as follows: Chapter 1 provides a context for the early connections that took Native Hawaiian emigrants east and Mormon missionaries west in the nineteenth century. It begins by examining the movement of Native Hawaiians to western North America starting in the early nineteenth century and the concurrent movement westward of Americans to Hawai'i. The Native Hawaiians took advantage of the vibrant and growing Pacific trade network that connected Hawai'i with the growing ports and cities of western North America. They reacted to the radical changes in Hawai'i that resulted from the expanding population of foreign settlers by exercising the options that the new social landscape provided. For a people with a seafaring history, such a course of action was hardly surprising, and their experiences abroad reverberated throughout Hawaii and laid the groundwork for subsequent voyages to the east.

Chapter 2 connects the actions of both Mormon missionaries and Native Hawaiian converts in Hawai'i to the economic and political situation from 1850 to 1889. I examine the political and social changes in Hawai'i from the arrival of the first American missionaries to the period of the Māhele and the Mortgage Act of 1874. I argue that these changes made it possible for Mormon missionaries to acquire land in Hawai'i where they could settle Native Hawaiian converts to prepare them to migrate to the Salt Lake Valley. Native Hawaiians who converted to Mormonism, however, used Mormon collectivism in the Palawai Valley and Lā'ie as a means to re-create the *ahupua'a* system of production and distribution, which was being eroded by land speculation in the post-Māhele years. In addition, chapter 2 addresses the development of religious ideologies within Mormonism that justified and strengthened Mormon leaders' commitment to a prolonged missionary presence in Hawai'i throughout the late nineteenth century.

Chapter 3 tells the story of Native Hawaiian Mormons' early migration to the Salt Lake Valley in Utah and the events leading up to their removal to Skull Valley in 1889. In the first section of this chapter I examine popular representations of Native Hawaiians and Pacific Islanders in Utah and the West.

I also explore the economic, political, and social conditions in Utah that created a community divided along religious as well as ethnic and racial lines. I focus on how Native Hawaiian Mormons negotiated their position vis-à-vis white Mormons, who marginalized them based on race, and non-Mormons, who used their presence in Salt Lake City to attack Mormon emigration policies. The final section of this chapter looks at the Utah Supreme Court case that denied citizenship to Native Hawaiian applicants based on their race and church leaders' decision to settle Native Hawaiian Saints in Skull Valley.

Chapter 4 focuses on the community of Iosepa in Skull Valley, Utah, now a ghost town (in)famous throughout both Hawaii and Utah as the home of a ranch established by LDS church leaders and funded through a joint stock company to settle Native Hawaiian converts removed from Salt Lake City in the summer of 1889. The community lasted until approximately 1917, when it was abandoned following president of the Church of Jesus Christ of Latter-day Saints Joseph F. Smith's announcement that a temple was being built in Lāʻie, Hawaiʻi. Smith advised community members to leave Skull Valley and the community they had built and return to Hawaiʻi. By 1917 all but a handful of Iosepa's 228 residents had tearfully left Skull Valley and returned to Hawaiʻi. I address the history of Iosepa in the ideological context of its founding as well as in the social and economic history of the Great Basin and the American West. Although the church managed Iosepa according to a modified model of the sugar plantation that it operated on Oʻahu, the religious motivation behind Iosepa helped mitigate the difficulties and hardships of the settlement's early years. Eventually it was the religious faith of the settlers that led them to abandon the community at the height of its prosperity.

My final chapter looks at the contemporary Native Hawaiian and Pacific Islander community in the Salt Lake Valley. The story of Iosepa provides an important link to the regional history, which connects Pacific Islander Mormons in Utah to a larger pioneer history, an important narrative for defining peoplehood in Mormon communities. Commemorative activities at Iosepa in Skull Valley and elsewhere laud the original settlers as "Polynesian pioneers." Redefining the Iosepa town site as sacred space metaphorically and symbolically links contemporary Pacific Islander communities in the Salt Lake Valley to the broader history of Mormons in Utah. This chapter demonstrates how remembering Iosepa collectively has become an important part of asserting religious identity for Pacific Islander Mormons in Utah and Hawaiʻi.

CHAPTER 1

"The Pacific World"

Between 1800 and 1850, Oceania and the world on its borders grew closer as foreign ships sailed the Pacific in increasing numbers to hunt and trade. The development of this maritime trade in the first half of the nineteenth century changed the social, economic, and political landscape of Hawaii and provoked a variety of responses and adaptation strategies from everyone involved. This chapter explores the paths both east and west that were established in this era and some of the people who traveled them. These are the routes that brought Native Hawaiians east and Mormon missionaries west to Hawaii and laid the foundation for communities that followed.

PART I—PATHS EAST

The Kingdom of Hawaii profited from the opportunities that accompanied the development of the Pacific maritime trade and created a foreign policy that fostered limited and controlled commerce. Foreign traders and their goods were incorporated into existing cultural frameworks that regulated the economic, political, and social meanings typical of the changing times.[1] Before 1840 the real devastation among native peoples throughout the Pacific was silent and invisible: the rapid and catastrophic population loss caused by foreign microbes. By the time European and American military and government officials arrived as settlers, intent on protecting (and exploiting) the livelihoods of their citizens, they faced indigenous populations severely crippled by the demographic catastrophe that disease wrought. Their numbers thus reduced, Pacific Islanders were less able to mount prolonged, open, armed resistance to aggressive foreigners. The demand for foreign goods and the protracted nature of foreign settlement (waves of explorers, merchants, missionaries, and finally the colonial state) often overwhelmed populations that were fractions of their former numbers.

Despite these daunting and complex changes, however, indigenous Pacific Islanders in the early nineteenth century sought to benefit from the increased foreign presence. In this context, the rising number of Oceanians who chose to leave on foreign ships is hardly surprising. The decision to leave their islands, for whatever period of time, was a strategy of negotiating changing situations common throughout Oceania. Like other Pacific Islanders, Native Hawaiians seized the opportunities that foreign vessels offered and sought to work them to their own advantage. Through their travels they extended the known borders of Oceania and created new paths that would be followed by others throughout the nineteenth and twentieth centuries. These experiences were the precursors to the journeys of Native Hawaiians in subsequent decades. The three stories that follow represent some of the paths followed by Native Hawaiians in the late eighteenth and early nineteenth centuries, the first of many that followed in this mold.

"His Original Design and Inclination Was to Proceed to England"

In the fall of 1787 John Meares recorded an account of Kaiana (Tianna), who sailed with Meares aboard the *Nootka*.[2] The brother of Kauai's sovereign, Kaumuali'i, Kaiana was "a chief of illustrious birth and high rank."[3] Whether he was appointed at the behest of his brother or simply claimed the privilege of his rank is unknown, but the desire of his fellow Kauaians to accompany the ship "to Brittannee" was unmistakable.[4] Kaiana was indeed a chief of high birth, a descendant of the Keawe line, one of Keakealani's sons and a "noted ruler of Hawai'i."[5] As a young chief, Kaiana received the education reserved for those of his rank, not only in the arts of war, politics, and statecraft, but also as a builder and an "orator" and in the genealogy of the island's chiefly families.[6] Meares recognized Kaiana's uncommon talent and royal lineage, and he was subsequently held in high esteem by both Meares and the ship's crew. Kaiana traveled with Meares as a passenger to China, after first visiting the Pacific Northwest Coast (present-day Vancouver Island), where he remained several months, until the fall of 1787. Kaiana then sailed to China, where he spent the remainder of 1787, departing there for Hawai'i with Meares in January 1788 aboard the *Felice*. During his stay in China Kaiana undoubtedly witnessed the arrival and departure of various European ships and some of the intricacies of international trade in the region in and around Canton. He had the opportunity to observe different kinds of trade goods and their subsequent value in the regional market. Kaiana was fascinated and intrigued by Canton's shipyards.[7] He collected for himself various objects of trade, including a portrait of himself done by "Spoilum, a celebrated artist of China."[8] After procuring new vessels and outfitting them with provisions and a crew in China, Meares's expedition prepared to sail southwest to the Hawaiian Islands. Kaiana, "with his mind enlarged by the new scenes and pictures of life which he beheld, and in the possession of various articles of useful application," readied himself to return to Kauai. Meares described Kaiana's reaction to the prospect of going home:

> His reflection had often sickened at the thought of his family and his country.... When, therefore, he was assured of his approaching return to Atooi, the idea that he should again embrace the wife whom he loved, and the child on whom he doted, with all the added consequence which would accompany him, from the knowledge he had acquired, the wealth he possessed, and the benefits he should communicate to the place of his nativity, produced those transports which sensible minds may conceive, but which language is unable to describe.[9]

The *Felice* sailed from Canton on January 22, 1788, bound for Hawai'i.[10] Kaiana was to be returned to Kauai by Captain Douglas of the *Iphigenia*, the second vessel in Meares's expedition, after a short stay in Prince William's sound on the Northwest Coast. By this time Kaiana had had two opportunities to visit the Northwest Coast and observe the region and its inhabitants, whom Kaiana thought poorly of because of their small stature.[11]

After their brief visit to the Northwest Coast, Kaiana returned with Douglas to the island of Hawai'i. Fearing that the prestige he had gained through his experiences and possessions would induce his brother to murder him, Kaiana chose not to disembark on Kauai and continued southwest. Finding Hawai'i and Maui in a state of war, and with his suspicions that danger awaited him on his home island confirmed, he chose to accompany Meares back to the Northwest Coast for a short trip, returning to the Hawaiian Islands later in 1788. By this time Kaiana had been gone from Hawai'i for almost a year. His one short visit home had offered no safe haven, and he contemplated a strategy for negotiating the political strife to which he was bound to return.[12] Kaiana first went with Douglas to Maui, where he received a warm welcome from his brother-in-law, and from there went on to Hawai'i, sending advance notice to Kāmehameha, the ranking chief of that island, of their impending arrival at Kealakekua.[13] Kāmehameha received both Kaiana and Douglas warmly, and Kaiana presented him with "a quantity of muskets and cannon," a gift valuable not only for its practical use but having symbolic value not lost on Kāmehameha.[14] After several days Douglas prepared to sail for O'ahu, leaving Kaiana on Hawai'i after honoring him with a seven-gun salute.[15]

The departure of the *Iphigenia* marked the end of Kaiana's experience as a guest of British captains aboard their ships. A chief with a ready nose for political advantage and the potential to increase his own *mana* in Hawai'i's competitive political landscape, Kaiana's ambition and rank had secured his place as a passenger on a foreign vessel. His expert manipulation of the *Haole* captains, whom he persuaded to ferry him between both islands and continents, had paid off handsomely. Traveling as a guest of Meares and Douglas, he had gained valuable knowledge and possessions, including money and weapons. Finding political conditions unstable upon his return, he not only avoided a situation that was potentially deadly for himself, but parlayed his newfound wealth and knowledge into a valuable position as a favorite of Kāmehameha, whose ascendance to power Kaiana would also exploit. Kāmehameha gave Kaiana land and subjects and placed him in command of his army. Like the king's *Haole* advisors, John Young and Isaac Davis, Kaiana's knowledge of European weaponry and tactics proved valuable. Unlike Young and Davis, Kaiana's royal lineage, combined with the knowledge he had gained abroad, gave him privileged status in both worlds. Leading Kāmehameha's forces to battle against his own brothers, Kaiana's leadership and foreign gifts contributed to a decisive victory for Kāmehameha that secured all of the island of Hawai'i under his rule.[16] The fruits of Kaiana's voyage helped usher in a new era in Hawaiian history.

"A Bold and Trustworthy Fellow"

In the early years of the nineteenth century the son of a young Kona chief named Naukane followed his father to the court of their sovereign, Kāmehameha, in Honolulu. Entranced by the stories told by the men who had sailed with the *Haole* on their many voyages to and from foreign lands, the boy watched the ships sailing in and out of Honolulu harbor with intense curiosity. Leaving their home ports in the northeastern United States with the minimum number of sailors they needed to round Cape Horn, American ships recruited Hawaiians as *hana* (workers) for the nascent Northwest Coast fur trade. The *Tonquin*, an American vessel under the command of Jonathan Thorne, arrived in Honolulu harbor in the late winter of 1811. The *Tonquin* was funded by American millionaire John Jacob Astor in an effort to break into the potentially lucrative fur trade, a venture popularized by the recently published works of British explorer

Alexander MacKenzie and descriptions from the Lewis and Clark expedition.[17] With the approval of Kāmehameha, Thorne recruited Hawaiians to be sailors and laborers at the post Astor intended to build near the mouth of the Columbia River. Kāmehameha, fearing for the safety of his subjects and determined to ensure they would be fairly treated while abroad, appointed Naukane to accompany them.

Although the voyage of the *Tonquin* was merely the beginning of Naukane's experiences in the fur trade, the other Hawaiians aboard were not so fortunate. Astor's initial expedition was ill-equipped, understaffed, and plagued with bad luck from the beginning. The initial party had only thirty-one men, including eleven Hawaiians, far fewer than the more successful British expeditions. Eight crewmen, including one of the Hawaiian sailors, were lost with two of the whaleboats in the rough waters at the mouth of the river. The unnamed Hawaiian perished from exposure after diving into the icy ocean waters to assist a drowning Scottish sailor. Naukane, the ranking *ali'i* (chief) of the Hawaiian group, "acted as a priest and led the others in burial rites." The remainder of the crew was divided, one group being sent to help build the fort at Astoria while the rest stayed with the *Tonquin*, trading for furs on the coast. Naukane accompanied the group to the site chosen to build Astoria, several miles east at a wide point on one bank of the Columbia River. It proved to be a fortunate assignment. The *Tonquin* was destroyed in a fiery explosion when the indigenous inhabitants of Clayoquot ignited one of the ship's kegs of dry powder. The entire crew was lost with the vessel, including the Hawaiians.

Despite this catastrophe, Naukane and the remainder of the crew continued to labor at Astoria. Several days later a survey team from the British Northwest Company, under the command of a man named David Thompson, arrived at the fort and was hosted by David Stuart, Astoria's post commander. Apparently Thompson and Stuart negotiated a swap of sorts. Naukane, who "was looked upon by Mr. Thompson as a prodigy of wit and humor," was traded for a Canadian laborer.[18] From that point forward, Naukane worked the interior fur trade as an employee not of the Americans, but of the British. This fortuitous turn of events undoubtedly broadened the scope of Naukane's travels. The British Northwest Company and the Hudson Bay Company (HBC) merged into one organization. Prior to this event, however, furs were transported overland using a variety of methods, including horses, dog sleds, and canoes, to the HBC forts in the east. Naukane traveled with Thompson's group east until they arrived at Fort William on Lake Superior in 1812, where they discovered that the British were at war with the Americans. Thompson and a small crew, Naukane included, were immediately ordered to return to the Northwest, "to seize Astoria." To Naukane's apparent wit was now added another asset: knowledge of the Astoria fort and the mouth of the Columbia River. The crew sailed to England, outfitted a retinue of vessels as men of war and supply ships, and headed south and west to Brazil, where Naukane and his group changed vessels and made for Cape Horn and around to the Northwest Coast in July 1813. Despite a nearly devastating fire caused by an explosion on board, Naukane's vessel arrived at the Columbia River in November ready for a battle that never happened. The Astorians, weak and outclassed by their British opponents, agreed to peacefully transfer the company's assets to the Northwest Company. Astoria officially became Fort George in December 1813. The Hawaiians who had been employed by the Pacific Fur Company, including Naukane, were returned to Fort George aboard British vessels.[19] Despite the failure of this venture, Astor's innovative practice of hiring contract laborers in Hawai'i was adopted by the Northwest and Hudson Bay Companies in subsequent years.[20]

In 1815 Naukane returned to a kingdom in transition. Attached as an *ali'i* courtier to Kāmehameha's son Liholiho, Naukane, like Kaiana before him, enjoyed the prestige that his vast experience with *Haole*, both British and American, had won him. Unlike Kaiana, he was not of high enough rank to pose a threat, so he enjoyed a secure position in Liholiho's court. Naukane continued in his service to Liholiho whose mounting debts and excessive drinking were a growing source of consternation to the *Haole* community, merchants and missionaries alike. The *ali'i*'s mass consumption of European consumer goods, financed by exporting sandalwood, placed burdens on the *maka'ainana* (commoners), although they remained unwavering in support of their king. The lavish consumption of Liholiho's entourage, which likely included Naukane, further increased the king's debt.[21] In 1823 Liholiho departed on a diplomatic mission to England. Naukane, well-accustomed to ocean voyages, went with him. During the journey an outbreak of measles infected nearly all of the Hawaiians in Liholiho's retinue and eventually claimed the lives of the king and queen. On September 11, 1824, Naukane met King George IV of England at Windsor Palace. He returned to Hawai'i in 1825 to an icy welcome from his countrymen, their suspicions aroused by his failure to protect the king. Naukane made hasty preparations to leave again for the Columbia River area. Finding employment as a laborer for the Hudson Bay Company at Fort Vancouver, Naukane worked for several more years, then retired on a plot of land granted to him near the fort. By this time Fort Vancouver was developing into a picturesque and diverse community that included several Hawaiian and part-Hawaiian families.[22] Naukane continued to work part time raising stock; eventually he contracted tuberculosis and died at Fort Vancouver in 1838.[23]

Sometime in 1807 three young Hawaiian boys left Hawaiʻi with an American sea captain to "receive an education" in the northeastern United States. One was the twelve-year-old son of Kāmehameha, king of the newly united islands of Hawaiʻi. The other boys, Thomas Hopu and Henry Opukahaʻia, were "selected to be attendants of the young prince." Captain Caleb Brintnall's ship, the *Triumph*, left Hawaiʻi for the Northwest Coast to obtain furs and returned to Hawaiʻi before sailing north for Canton. Fearing that he would never see his son again, Kāmehameha forbade the boy to leave again. His two attendants, however, "having our expectations excited, and having a strong curiosity to see America," continued on with Brintnall to China. On the voyage north young Hopu fell overboard in high seas while drawing a bucket of water. Although he was spotted by a shipmate, in the time it took for the ship to come around, he lost sight of it in the large ocean swells. Fearing he was lost at sea, Hopu turned to his *akua* (god). "I cried to my god, Akooah, for help, and made my vow to him ... that if he would save me out of the great and mighty waters, and I might reach the ship, I would devote to my god, Akooah, a fine jacket, which I had received from my Captain, as a present." After what must have been many long minutes passed, Hopu began to lose hope. "While I was thinking in this situation, I saw a bird from God.... I then talked to him these words, 'If you are a bird of God, please go back to your master, and tell him I have already given a jacket to your master and come quickly and save me, that I perish not in this deep water, where there is no bottom'." Immediately following his prayer, the ship was upon him, and he was pulled onto the deck.[24]

Hopu remained in China for six months. From there he went to New York, arriving in the fall of 1809. After a short stay in New York both Hopu and Opukahaʻia were taken in by prominent families in New Haven, Connecticut, Hopu into the home of a Doctor O. Hotchkiss. A few weeks after his arrival in Hotchkiss's home, the doctor made known to Hopu his belief in "the true God, and Jesus Christ whom he has sent into the world to die for sinners." Hopu listened intently to Hotchkiss's sermon, after which they traded questions regarding each other's beliefs. Interested but ultimately unconvinced, Hopu remained in New Haven for a few more years with Hotchkiss. In time he found that his "disposition seemed inclined rather to rove to sea, than to stay on land," and he chose "the life of a sailor." Hopu then "went to sea, about twelve voyages, out of New Haven, in several vessels: And during the late war,[25] more frequently to the West India Islands." Hopu's ship was seized by the British navy, and he and his shipmates were imprisoned on St. Kitts, where his firsthand observation of the cruelties of chattel slavery in the Caribbean produced in him "a great desire to return to America." Eventually he was able to board an American vessel back to New Haven and resume his life as a sailor.

While sailing again in the West Indies, his boat capsized forty miles from land. Seeing their desperate situation, Hopu implored his shipmates to "look to your God for help, while danger is near, rather than cry out. At all times, in your troubles, if you know the Bible is the word of Christ, you ought to pray to the God of heaven, more than the heathen." In the end Hopu saved his life and the lives of his shipmates by roping a lifeboat and fashioning a sail from a jacket. They elected him their captain. Naked, hungry, and navigating by the stars, the men made landfall after six days and nights. Famished and near death, the crew came upon "three Negroes fishing on the east part of the island," who gave them fish and water and led them to town. There, to Hopu's astonishment, he ran into his former captain, and together they sailed for America.

Once again Hopu was caught up in the dicey relationship between Britain and the United States. Briefly imprisoned off the coast of Nantucket, Hopu was released, took a job as a coachman in New Haven, and eventually followed his employer to Whitestown, New York. During his nine-month stay there, he had a dream:

> I dreamed one night, that God, in whom I live, and move, and have my being, was going to destroy the earth by a flood. I saw, in my dream, that the windows of heaven were opened, and the waterspouts were descending from heaven upon the earth. Then I heard the voice of the people saying, "Now this world is coming to an end." At the same time, I thought that I would escape to the mountains: but I found no place to escape to, or to hide my face from the eyes of the Almighty God. So I awake from my sleep, at the middle of the night, with great fear and distress of mind. I felt that I was a very wicked sinner, in the sight of God. But before this time, I thought that I was good enough to go to heaven, as well as those who called themselves real Christians. . . . This was the first means, in leading me to embrace that Savior, who hath died for sinners, and awakened my sleeping mind.

Hopu left for New Haven in September 1815 with the intention of boarding a ship back to Hawai'i, but he was persuaded by his Christian friends to remain in America to obtain an education. He also attended Protestant services weekly. After a powerful prayer meeting one night, Hopu returned to the minister's home, where he was questioned about the depth of his love for God and the depth of his hatred for his "wicked heart." Finding Hopu's loathing for his former ways sufficiently sincere, the minister came to his final and, apparently, most important question. "Well, friend Thomas," queried the minister, "let me ask you one more question, and then I will not ask...again: Are you afraid to go home and tell about the Saviour to your bewildered countrymen? And what is your chief object?" "No," replied Hopu, "I am not afraid to go back to Owhyhee and tell them about the Saviour; for Christ has commanded all his true followers should go into the world and preach his gospel to old and young, bond and free, and to every rational creature upon earth.... Thus my chief object for time and eternity is to glorify Christ Jesus."

Hopu remained in Connecticut for three more years. In February 1818 Henry Opukaha'ia contracted typhus, died, and was buried in Cornwall, Connecticut. Hopu returned to Hawai'i in 1819, traveling with the first party of Christian missionaries back to his native islands. His memoir, "Written by himself and transmitted to the corresponding secretary by the Reverend Joseph Harvey," appeared in 1822. The memoir closes with an exhortation, ostensibly to his fellow Hawaiian converts in New England: "Weep then but not because we go to our native Isle dear friends; Perhaps we may go with joy; weep for the heathen world who do not know the Saviour you enjoy. At the command of our Heavenly Father, may we on earth part again to meet in heaven where there is no farewell."[26]

Although much of the conversion part of Hopu's memoir was probably penned posthumously by Harvey, the profoundly spiritual nature of his experiences while he was a traveler is difficult to ignore. Written years after the events he described and likely embellished by a foreign voice, Hopu's memoir is a conversion narrative after the fact, and as in all histories, the present intrudes on the meanings we make of the past. But Hopu's telling of his story is still instructive; he constructs a carefully coded narrative, infusing his own history with a significance gained by writing himself into the center of global events and processes out of his immediate control. And although our stories of Kaiana and Naukane come to us only through multiple layers of representation, one imagines that they both at some point made sense of their histories, much like Hopu.

A similar set of global forces shaped the histories of the protagonists of these three stories, but their experiences led them along very different paths. All three were either *ali'i* or enjoyed close connections to *ali'i*, a fact that also shaped their experiences. Certainly a common seaman would never have commanded a captain's favor or enjoyed a bed in a Victorian New England home. Their experiences also reflect a uniquely male perspective; none participated in the sex trade with foreign sailors, for instance. And yet even within the small demographic of the Hawaiian population they represent, their fates were very different.

These stories illustrate the difficulty of creating a truly representative picture of Hawaiian experiences abroad in the late eighteenth and early nineteenth centuries. In the period between 1790 and 1840 Hawai'i became completely integrated into an emerging world economic system. Relationships between governments and communities based on capitalist exchange went through a brief period when the balance of social, economic, and political power did not resemble contemporary circumstances. The common thread in the three stories presented is the situational nature of power. All three of our protagonists find themselves in situations of power and powerlessness, often marked as they cross borders that are real, imagined, and contested. All three make sense of these situations in unique ways. Together they reveal a few of the many ways that global history played out locally in Oceania and the changing nature of the region in the eighteenth and nineteenth centuries.

An international maritime trade network linking western North America, China, and Hawai'i developed in the latter years of the 1780s. Roughly a decade before, in 1778, British ships had landed in Hawai'i for the first time, and in their search for a northwestern route between the Atlantic and Pacific Oceans had landed in the Pacific Northwest as well. These voyages hinted at the potential of trans-Pacific maritime trade, but it was left to later voyagers, primarily British and American, to work out the particularities of profitable regional trading schemes. By 1830 a vigorous and complex international trade network spanning the Pacific had begun to develop, and it would continue to expand and change through the beginning of the twentieth century. This transformation of the region helped give birth to the new contexts and constraints Native Hawaiians found as they continued to traverse their seas. Voyagers in subsequent decades operated in equally transformative contexts that continued to shape the tenor of their experiences.

In the nineteenth century Hawai'i truly became the crossroads of the Pacific, hosting hundreds of visiting ships annually and a small but rapidly growing population of foreign merchants, missionaries, laborers, and ne'er-do-wells. Like many Pacific Islanders, Hawaiians availed themselves of the opportunities the foreign vessels presented and eagerly lobbied foreign captains for passage.[27] The earliest Hawaiian voyagers on European ships were passengers on interisland journeys, guests aboard two vessels, the *King George* and the *Queen Charlotte*, which spent several months at Hawai'i in 1786 and 1787 in the course of voyages between Nootka and Canton. According to historian F. W. Howay, these two British vessels were "the first maritime trading vessels to visit the Hawaiian Islands."[28] In the following year several Hawaiians with a strong sense of curiosity and wanderlust sailed on the *Prince of Wales* to Canton. One traveled for the next four years, making his way to the Northwest Coast and England and returning to Hawai'i in 1792.[29] Subsequent Hawaiian voyagers, many of whom left the islands in the late eighteenth and the earliest years of the nineteenth centuries, visited Boston, Connecticut, New York, Brazil, and England, circumnavigating the globe. These eighteenth-century voyagers are the earliest examples of what became a much more common phenomenon in the nineteenth century: Native Hawaiian participation in the Pacific maritime trade.

The Pacific trade emerged in the last decade of the eighteenth century and was dominated by England and the United States beginning around 1830. Early efforts by French, Russian, and Spanish entrepreneurs were ambitious but less successful; those traders ultimately failed to link goods and markets among eastern, western, and central Pacific ports. Hawai'i entered this trade network as a supplier of agricultural products as well as a market for manufactured and luxury goods from Europe and China. The United States and Britain struggled to dominate emerging markets in Canton, California, Mexico, South America, and Hawai'i. The Hudson Bay Company (HBC) purchased American John Jacob Astor's failed Pacific Fur Company in 1813. The HBC dominated the interior Columbia River fur trade of the Northwest Coast, and under the direction of George Simpson it expanded into exporting salmon and lumber from the region. Its trappers worked the Columbia and Snake Rivers east to the Rocky Mountains through a network of forts and agents, eventually ranging as far south as northern California and north into present-day British Columbia. Fort George, Fort Victoria, and Fort Vancouver all emerged as the HBC's regional hubs and major settlements, and the HBC managed transactions through local agents in Honolulu and Yerba Buena. American traders took a different approach, working the coastal fur trade from Vancouver Island north to the Russian Fur Company outpost at Sitka, while they diversified their commercial activities with whaling and sandalwood operations in Hawai'i and the southern Pacific and maintained relationships in China. The HBC's weak presence in East Asian ports opened the way for American dominance of the trade among the Northwest Coast, Honolulu, and China. The HBC's activities in Canton were discouraged by the provincial nature of the East India Company and its jealous protection of the London market for East Asia's regional commodities. After Mexican independence in 1821, California emerged as a market for American and British food and manufactured products and as a source of hides and tallow; the hide-and-tallow trade remained the mainstay of California's export economy until 1846. Spanish ports in San Blas, Acapulco, Lima, and Valparaiso were also common stops for ships sailing back and forth from Cape Horn.[30]

The hub of all these commercial ventures in the Pacific became Hawai'i. The American north Pacific whaling fleet wintered there annually, and visiting ships could easily obtain provisions year-round. Following a period of warfare in the islands between about 1782 and 1794, the Hawaiian government emerged as a stable and hospitable polity that spanned all of the major islands except Kauai. Under the leadership of Kāmehameha I, Hawai'i eagerly participated in foreign trade, exporting raw materials like sandalwood and supplying provisions for foreign ships.[31] And Native Hawaiians eagerly participated by availing themselves of the opportunity to work and settle abroad.

Trade, Travel, and Settlement in Oceania

Using the phrase "Pacific maritime trade" to refer to the commercial activity that connected the eastern and western Pacific Rim is somewhat misleading. Maritime trade in Oceania predates European entry into the Pacific world by centuries. In addition to open-ocean settlement expeditions, Pacific Islanders maintained trade and kinship relationships across vast distances. The histories and genealogies of various Pacific archipelagos attest to centuries of prolonged contact between major islands and atolls. For these voyagers, the Pacific Ocean was not a barrier but a bridge, an integral and familiar extension of the terrestrial realm of their island ecosystem.[32]

These were deliberate voyages of settlement, often preceded by exploratory journeys that gathered information about the duration and difficulty of the trip, as well as about potential rewards. The practice of sailing *against* the prevailing winds dictated much of the pattern for the settlement of Central and Remote Oceania; the ability to sail back quickly with the winds should the vessel be faced with an emergency or fail to make landfall dictated this essential element of early Oceanian blue-water seafaring. One scholar suggests that long voyages were difficult more "as tests of endurance rather than especially difficult navigational exercises." In the case of the "Tahiti/Hawai'i leg," the journey was probably "not very difficult navigationally." Both island groups were "substantial targets" that a well-equipped voyaging canoe could reach in "three to four weeks."[33] Once the navigational markers were established, including the identification of specific constellations and stars in their relation to the horizon, the trip could be made with relative confidence. Although the frequency of these voyages ebbed and flowed, the arrival of Europeans inaugurated an era of renewed possibility for long-distance voyaging in a new context.

Hawai'i's place in the Pacific fur trade began to take shape even before Hawaiian resources like sandalwood and salt became valuable export commodities. Foreign vessels engaged in trade and other maritime enterprises in the Pacific continued to stop in Hawai'i for fresh supplies and shelter from winter storms. The search for a Northwest Passage to facilitate trade with China continued to motivate British capitalists to fund voyages of exploration.[34] In 1790 eleven ships wintered in Hawaiian waters as they evaluated the possibilities of trade between the Northwest Coast and Canton.[35]

Hawaiian participation in the Pacific maritime trade of the nineteenth century varied widely, from official, state-sponsored economic activity to individual contract labor for foreign commercial interests. Now that it appeared on European and American charts, Hawai'i became a regular port of call for both trade and whaling vessels in the North Pacific. The period between 1778 and 1790 saw only a few foreign ships in Hawaiian waters, but by the mid-1790s British, French, and American vessels were visiting Hawai'i to trade various goods for provisions, including hogs, potatoes, salt, and fresh water.[36] Although the introduction of foreign goods and a cash-based economy proved disruptive to the Hawaiian economic system, the greatest disadvantage of the Pacific maritime trade to the Hawaiian government was the political machinations of American and British merchants and traders who had set up shop in the growing port of Honolulu. Racism and ethnocentrism toward Native Hawaiians, both *ali'i* (chiefs) and *makā'ainana* (commoners), created an environment that pitted Hawai'i's political leaders against formidable foreign rivals bent on forcing Native Hawaiians to submit to foreign rule. This issue preoccupied Hawaiian domestic and foreign policy throughout the nineteenth century.[37]

The introduction of foreign diseases ravaged the Hawaiian population in the initial years following contact with Europeans, slashing Hawai'i's population from nearly a million inhabitants prior to Cook's arrival to around 50,000 by the mid-nineteenth century. This trend would continue until the latter half of the nineteenth century, as foreign visitors and residents increased and as shorter and more frequent voyages from ports within the Pacific Rim provided opportunities for disease to travel even faster. Smallpox epidemics continued to kill Hawaiians in alarming numbers well after 1850, both in Hawai'i and the western United States.[38] Hawai'i was forced to negotiate its position in the Pacific maritime trade in an environment of upheaval and demographic catastrophe. In this environment, Hawaiian officials scrambled to stem the tide of Hawaiian men willing to leave the islands to work on foreign vessels.

Seaman, Laborers, Mercenaries, Settlers

The presence of Europeans and Americans in Oceania was both a destructive and a creative force. It was destructive in the sense that foreign goods, religions, ideologies, diseases, and people all disrupted existing social, economic, and political systems throughout Oceania, often with disastrous consequences for the region's indigenous peoples. Yet it was creative in the sense that those Oceanians who survived foreign diseases strove to find their place in a rapidly changing world and attempted to shape it to their ultimate advantage. The story of Oceania in the nineteenth century cannot be seen as a simple process of conquest or colonization; rather, it should be understood as a negotiation between competing and often contradictory systems of living that changed the lives of settlers and indigenous peoples alike. Colonization did not proceed along patterned and predictable lines throughout Oceania. Understanding cultural contact and colonization as heterogeneous and multifaceted reveals the complexities that illuminate the lives of all those involved. Hawaiians responded to the presence of *Haole* in various ways, and their interactions with different foreigners necessarily produced different results.[39]

Hawaiians and the British Fur Trade

The story of Naukane illustrates the experiences of one Hawaiian involved in the British fur trade in the Pacific Northwest, which lasted from the late 1700s until roughly 1840. The focus of that trade in North America was the Pacific Northwest, an area with a diverse population of competing language and cultural groups operating regional trade networks based on hunting and fishing. Historical geographer Richard Mackie notes that, "[t]he fur trade...embraced all or part of no less than five culture areas of North America and dozens of separate language families,"[40] although during this period few permanent Hawaiian settlers ventured too far from the coast. The development of the fur trade in this region was dominated by the British North West and Hudson Bay Companies, with sporadic but ultimately unsuccessful competition in the early nineteenth century from John Jacob Astor's Pacific Fur Company. The HBC's dominance lasted until the establishment of Fort Victoria in 1843, which signaled the beginning of American settlement and the development of US-dominated timber industries.[41] Hawaiian "Kanakas"[42] were eagerly sought by American and British companies and agents as both skilled and unskilled farmers, contract laborers, and seamen.[43] Although Hawaiians worked as contract laborers for both the American and British companies, the HBC's domination of the interior fur trade was labor intensive, and the vast majority of the Hawaiians who worked in the Pacific Northwest interior did so as HBC employees. Many Hawaiians eventually settled in the Pacific Northwest, primarily around Fort Vancouver, Fort Victoria, and Fort Langley. Beginning in the mid-1840s Hawaiian settlers in the region experienced a sharp decline in political, economic, and social status as American settlers brought their well-defined racial hierarchies west with them.[44] Before the 1840s, however, Hawaiian laborers and settlers in the Pacific Northwest from present-day Oregon to British Columbia negotiated their respective positions vis-à-vis a small number of white settlers, HBC employees, military officers, and the region's many indigenous groups.

Between 1815 and 1830 the North West and Hudson Bay Companies built a series of forts along the Columbia and Snake Rivers, expanding their operations in the interior. More Native Hawaiians were recruited as contract laborers in 1817, along with "large numbers" of Iroquois as trappers. In 1821 the companies merged under the name Hudson Bay Company. The HBC operated ten forts and employed up to 230 trappers and laborers.[45] Teams arrived at the coast from the forts by canoe twice a year, in the spring and fall, to deliver furs and pick up provisions. Iroquois manned the company's canoes, and the Native Hawaiians were employed as laborers at the forts and posts. As they became accustomed to the more skilled work of trapping, many accompanied the trapping parties into the interior. In addition, the difficulties of transporting supplies to the forts meant that it was necessary to grow crops to supplement the diet of fish and venison. This task in many cases fell to Native Hawaiian workers.[46]

Native Hawaiians continued to sign on as contract laborers for the HBC in increasing numbers. By 1830 the company had expanded its exports to include salmon and timber and employed between forty and sixty Native Hawaiian laborers.[47] By 1838 between four and five hundred barrels were sent to Oahu annually. In addition, Columbia River salmon found ready markets in California, Lima, Valparaiso, Callao, and Atlantic ports. Throughout the 1830s the HBC dominated salmon exports from the Columbia River region, despite attempts by American firms to compete in the salmon market. One American company hoped to transport Columbia River salmon to the East Coast market, but found that salmon could not be caught, packed, and transported east quickly enough to remain fresh for sale. To solve this problem, company officials sought to overcome their reliance on indigenous fishermen by recruiting Hawaiian laborers. In 1835 thirty Hawaiian men were employed by the newly formed Columbia Fishing and Trading Company to fish salmon on the Columbia River. An unknown number of men from this group were accompanied by their wives, and possibly children.[48] It is unclear whether these men had been recruited from Hawai'i or had completed labor contracts elsewhere in the region. New recruits from Hawai'i often brought wives from home, whereas those signing new labor contracts might have taken local women as wives, a common practice.[49] Fort George, an outpost of the British North West Company, and Fort Okanogan were staffed by a labor force that consisted of roughly equal numbers of Indians and Hawaiians. The difficult work of clearing land for the fortified locations in the face of hostile and often violent opposition from indigenous groups made occasional defense of the forts necessary as well. Hawaiian laborers proved adept at both these tasks.[50]

Between 1810 and 1840 the opportunities for Hawaiian laborers to work in the ranks of the HBC and its subsidiaries (and other commercial ventures) increased alongside Hawai'i's importance as a hub in the increasingly profitable Pacific trade. The trade itself had expanded far beyond the original goals of British and American merchants of direct shipment of furs to China in exchange for goods like tea, silk, and porcelain. The integration of Hawai'i as a market for goods, a source of labor, and a port for wintering and supplying ships meant greater ease in shipping goods across the Pacific as well as south to emerging markets in California, Mexico, and South America. Salmon, timber, and other items from the Columbia area, as well as Chinese consumer goods, all sold in Hawai'i and California. In 1829 the Sandwich Islands Agency was founded by the HBC, and by 1834 the agency headquarters had supplanted Canton as the original destination for Columbia produce and other goods. By 1846 the agency's Honolulu headquarters was "one of the seven leading business houses" in Hawai'i.[51] Through the agency, goods could be ordered and received from various sources throughout the trade network and sold to departing vessels. Labor was procured for the Pacific Northwest forts as well as for company vessels. One of the most important items for the company, salt, was mined and sold from Honolulu, as was sandalwood, often shipped to China and manufactured into boxes, incense, and curios, popular as trade goods on the Northwest Coast. Its central location guaranteed a steady variety of goods and services were available in Honolulu. Products ranging from "salt, molasses, tea, paint oil, treacle, cocoa, cordage, soap, rum, black camlet, [and] linseed oil" to Hawaiian-grown sugar cane, tobacco, cotton, coffee, arrowroot, indigo, rice, ginger, and mulberry silk were readily available through various agents newly established in Honolulu and Lahaina's growing business districts.[52] The British fur trade and its continuous presence in Hawai'i contributed to the patterns of Hawaiian settlement that appeared in the Pacific Northwest. Between the end of the eighteenth century and

1865 more than a thousand Hawaiians left the islands to settle permanently in the Pacific Northwest, the vast majority beginning as laborers in the British fur trade.[53] Adding to the vibrant commercial activity of Honolulu's port district was the increasing number of American whaling vessels that wintered and resupplied there. They also provided an avenue for Hawaiians to work aboard foreign vessels in the mid-nineteenth century.

Hawaiians on American Vessels—Whaling and the California Trade

The American whaling trade in the Pacific began in earnest at the close of the eighteenth century and peaked between 1835 and 1855. The first American whaling vessels arrived in Honolulu in 1820; during whaling's peak years, an average of more than four hundred whaling ships visited Honolulu harbor each year. Many ships spent the better part of the North Pacific winter in the islands.[54] The southern whale fisheries off South America, the western fisheries near the Tasman Sea, and the North Central Pacific fisheries from the Aleutian Islands to Japan and the eastern Philippines were all full of American whaling vessels by the early 1840s. Most spent time in Honolulu to refit and recruit sailors. Whale oil was an important fuel and lubricant; whalebone, ambergris, and other whale products were used to make an array of popular consumer products, including brushes, corsets, and cosmetics. The breadth of the Pacific whaling grounds and the length of the voyages (initially three years, but often expanded to four or even five) made whalers a common sight in Pacific ports.[55] American whaling in the north and central Pacific began to flourish just as the Pacific fur trade began to dwindle. This situation left the British to dominate the trade in goods like lumber and salmon from the interior of the Pacific Northwest, while Americans dominated whaling in the region, as well as the hide-and-tallow trade along the California coast.[56] Many Oceanian crew members must have spent years away from their homelands, and they probably often signed onto successive voyages from adopted home ports in Boston and New Bedford. The Pacific maritime trade provided new contexts, connections, and opportunities for such endeavors.

By the late 1840s Hawaiians had traveled to and in some cases settled in areas up and down the North American coast from San Diego to Vancouver. British- and American-dominated commerce in the Pacific included the California coast, a market that the HBC recognized as early as the late 1820s. American ships involved in the hide-and-tallow trade at the California ports of San Diego, Santa Barbara, Monterey, and Yerba Buena also frequented the California coast. California ships in that trade also relied on Native Hawaiian crew members. Unlike those Hawaiians who found employment in the Northwest fur trade, labor on American ventures in the Pacific revolved around a life at sea. It is likely that estimates of the number of Hawaiians working aboard whaling vessels also included those who were working the hide-and-tallow trade along the California coast. Regardless, the numbers were substantial. In 1846 a report by the minister of the interior to the king listed the official number of Native Hawaiians who had left the islands in that year at 651. With an estimated three thousand Native Hawaiians already working aboard foreign ships, this means approximately one-fifth of Hawaiian males between the ages of fifteen and thirty were gone from the islands.[57]

Richard Henry Dana's memoirs from his time as a sailor on a hide-and-tallow ship on the California coast in 1835 and 1836 contain many descriptions of his experiences with Native Hawaiian sailors and provide clues to both the perceptions of European and American whites by their Oceanian counterparts and the various ways Hawaiians especially used foreign captains and ships to their advantage. Dana was a young Harvard graduate from a middle-class New England family who shipped as a sailor aboard the ship *Pilgrim*, a hide-and-tallow vessel out of Boston bound for California. His two years in the Pacific maritime trade familiarized him with the entire gamut of participants in this cosmopolitan endeavor. His observations of his Native Hawaiian shipmates and companions illuminate the lives of common laborers and seamen "before the mast" in the Pacific. Dana's description of the community of Hawaiians in Mexican California reveals the complex negotiations shaped by the demands of labor and the hierarchies of race between Hawaiian sailors and American sea captains and their crews.

Dana's initial impression of Hawaiians is unmistakable. His subtle disdain for "Sandwich-Islanders" or "Kanakas" echoes prevailing early nineteenth-century New England notions of white supremacy. Their "outlandish language and assertive, gregarious behavior, prodded, no doubt, by the confidence of experience," left Dana a grudging admirer of Hawaiian seafaring and ocean skills, which could scarcely be denied. Dana's initial impression of California, which he swore he would "never forget," consisted of a lesson on beaching a crew boat at dusk in heavy autumn surf near Santa Barbara. Waiting outside for a break between the pounding sets:

> We lay our oars in the swell, just outside of the surf, waiting for a good chance to run in, when a boat, which had just put off from the Ayacucho, came alongside of us, with a crew of dusky Sandwich Islanders, talking and hallooing in their outlandish tongue. They knew that we were novices in this kind of boating, and waited to see us go in. The second mate, however, who steered our

boat, determined to have the advantage of their experience, and would not go first. Finding, at length, how matters stood, they gave a shout, and taking advantage of a great comber which came swelling in, rearing its head, and lifting up the sterns of our boats nearly perpendicular, and again dropping them in the trough, they gave three or four strong pulls, and went in on the top of the great wave, throwing their oars overboard, and as far from the boat as they could throw them, and, jumping out the instant the boat touched the beach, they seized hold of her by the gunwale, on each side, and ran her up high and dry upon the sand. We saw, at once, how the thing was to be done.[58]

Reflecting upon the incident later, Dana recalled the "disagreeable" impression of California—"anchoring three miles from shore; running out to sea before every southeaster; landing in a high surf; with a dark looking town; a mile from the beach, and not a sound to be heard, or anything to be seen, but Kanakas, hides, and tallow bags."

In early May 1835 Dana fell in with a group of Hawaiian beachcombers in San Diego, "a dozen or twenty in number, who had worked for other vessels, and been paid off when they sailed, [and] were living on the beach, keeping up a grand carnival." Well-supplied by weekly trips to the San Diego pueblo, a "bullock once a week...kept them in meat, and one of the them went up to town every day to get fruit, liquor, and provisions. Besides this, they had bought a cask of ship-bread, and a barrel of flour from the Lagoda, before she sailed." Buoyed up by a steady supply of provisions, adequate shelter, and exceptional company, "there they lived, having a grand time, caring for nobody." With their labor in high demand and their wants supplied, "idleness" (as Dana disparagingly described it) in fact allowed these Hawaiians to negotiate terms for voyages, including duration, and to support one another in comfort as a community rather than through individual efforts:

> I once heard [a Hawaiian sailor] say, with the highest indignation, to a Yankee trader who was trying to persuade him to keep his money to himself—"No! We no all 'e same a' you!—Suppose one got money, all got money. You;—Suppose one got money—lock him up in chest.—No good!—Kanaka all 'e same a' one!" This principle they carry so far, that none of them will eat anything in the sight of others without offering it all around. I have seen [one of] them break a biscuit, which had been given to him, into five parts, at a time when I knew he was on a very short allowance, as there was but little to eat on the beach.[59]

Hawaiians working abroad in the Pacific maritime trade also found ways to resist the hierarchical implications of wage labor. In a region where labor was scarce but a vital necessity, many with seafaring skills found themselves with a measure of bargaining power, often undertaken collectively to secure favorable terms of employment or in some cases choosing to remain unemployed. This seems to have been the case with the crew of Native Hawaiians temporarily settled in southern California in 1835 that Dana described:

> Captain Thompson wanted to get three or four more of them to come on board the Pilgrim, as we were so much diminished in numbers...and tried to negotiate with them. One of them, a finely built, active, strong, and intelligent fellow, who was sort of a king among them...acted as a spokesman. He was called Mannini,—or rather, out of compliment to his known importance and influence, *Mr.* Mannini, and was known all over California. Through him, the captain offered them fifteen dollars a month, and one month's pay in advance; but it was like throwing pearls before swine, or, rather, carrying coals to Newcastle. So long as they had money, they would not work for fifty dollars a month, and when their money was gone, they would work for ten.[60]

For this middle-class New England observer, the behavior of these "Kanakas" fit prevailing cultural stereotypes and provided evidence of their unwillingness to work and behavior that hardly served what Dana felt to be their long-term best interests. However, these Hawaiians chose a more intelligible arrangement in which a community shared resources and the necessity of labor and distributed them equally under the direction of a recognized *ali'i*. Mannini is identified here by his role as a "spokesman" or a "king among them." He may have been recognized by his companions as the legitimate leader or spokesman by virtue of his rank in Hawaiian society. In this capacity, Mannini would certainly be responsible for the conditions under which his companions worked. An unwillingness to work according to the whim and schedule of *Haole* captains, along with a lack of interest in Western patterns of consumption, reveals not laziness or irrationality but a conscious effort to manipulate a unique situation (wage labor in the California hide-and-tallow trade) in a new context (the developing Pacific maritime trade) according to Hawaiian, not Western, cultural values.

The Gold Rush

In 1850 Walter Griffith Pigman described a saloon scene at the Winters Hotel in the town of Culloma, California:

> Filling up the far side of the room was the gaudy and well-stocked bar where four spruce young fellows in shirt sleeves and flowing collars were busily engaged

dealing out horrible compounds to the thirsty customers strung along the whole length of the counter. The other three sides of the saloon were crowded with monte tables, each one of which was surrounded with a crowd of young and old so that it was almost impossible to obtain a glimpse of the dealers or their glittering banks. There was a perfect babel of noise! English, French, Spaniards, Portuguese, Italians, Kanakas, Chilians[sic], all were talking their respective languages. Glasses were jingling, money was rattling, and, crowning all, two fiddlers in a distant corner were scarping furiously on their instruments, seemingly the presiding divinities of this variegated pandemonium![61]

The discovery of gold reverberated globally, and the news spread throughout the Pacific as quickly as it did to the eastern United States. Opportunities to travel to California by sea via the connections between Europe, the eastern United States, China, and Hawai'i brought a polyglot mix of fortune seekers. Among them were an unknown number of Hawaiians. Like the defunct fur trade in the north and the American whaling industry, the search for gold in California attracted Hawaiians east to the foothills of California.

Even before the discovery, northern California was well known to Hawaiians working the hide-and-tallow trade. Hawaiians comprised some 10 percent of the population of Yerba Buena in 1847.[62] But on June 25, 1858, the Honolulu newspaper *Polynesian* alerted Hawaiian residents to the discovery of gold in California. "An exceedingly rich gold mine has been discovered in the Sacramento Valley, and all classes and sexes have deserted their occupations and rushed *en masse* to make their fortunes.... We can assure our readers there is no hoax in this; for we have seen the gold with our own eyes, and it really benefited our optics."[63] Less than a month later, the exodus that had already taken place was the subject of another article: "The little city of Honolulu has probably never before witnessed such an excitement as the gold fever has created. Probably not less than 200 will leave for California in the course of two months if passage can be procured."[64] Native Hawaiian participation in California settlement and gold mining is documented through frequent references in firsthand accounts to "Kanakas," a term that failed to distinguish between other Pacific Islanders who might have made their way to the California hills.

John Sutter, the quintessential California settler, frequently mentioned his Hawaiian laborers and companions. Like many travelers in and around the Pacific, Sutter passed through Hawai'i on his way from Fort Vancouver to Yerba Buena in December 1838. Sutter had dreams of a colony in California and a personality convincing and affable enough to charm the officials at Fort Vancouver as well as Kauikeauoli, the Hawaiian *Mō'ī* (king). During his five-month stay in Hawai'i, Sutter gained an audience with the king, who offered Sutter the opportunity to "take charge of his military establishment." Sutter wisely turned down the job (he had no military experience, but spun masterful tales of a glorious and decorated military career.) What Sutter did manage to do in Honolulu was outfit himself to create the "California colony" he originally envisioned. He acquired tools, supplies, and a crew of "5 White men and 8 Kanacas [sic]" and left Hawai'i for Yerba Buena. Carrying them westward, the brig *Clementine* left first for Sitka, Alaska, where it traded supplies with Russian fur trappers, then proceeded south to Yerba Buena. Severe winds and seas plagued the *Clementine*'s journey south, and the ship limped into the port of San Francisco with Sutter and crew in tow on July 2, 1839.[65]

Upon their arrival, Sutter and his crew headed up the Sacramento River, making their first encampment at a place he called "New Helvetia." Sutter's initial party of settlers included him, three white men, an Indian youth, and twelve Native Hawaiians (ten men and two women). It is unclear whether Sutter recruited more Hawaiians over the course of his journey from Honolulu or if the initial number he recruited in Honolulu was recorded incorrectly. It also appears that one of the Hawaiian women lived with Sutter as a common-law wife. They pitched their camp on August 14, 1839. In an interview with Sutter by Hubert Howe Bancroft in 1876, Sutter recalled their arrival at New Helvetia: "From the landing place I went back about a quarter of a mile to the spot where the Fort subsequently stood....The Kanakas first erected two grass houses after the manner of their houses on the Hawaiian Islands; the frames were made by white men and covered with grass by Kanakas. The houses were very comfortable." In the accounts of the discovery of gold at Sutter's fort in 1848, no Native Hawaiian laborers are mentioned, and it is likely that by that time they had all been replaced by Indian labor. In any case, the role of Native Hawaiians in establishing California's most famous settlement has been overlooked, to the detriment of our collective understanding of the shifting relationships between Hawai'i and western North America in the early to mid-nineteenth century.

Although the disappearance of Sutter's "Kanakas" from the historical record remains a mystery, perhaps they eventually joined one of the several growing communities of Hawaiians in California during the gold rush. The search for gold prompted many Native Hawaiians to head east immediately to seek their fortunes. In October 1848 Hawaiian newspapers reported: "Not less than three-hundred foreign residents, plus a good number of natives, have left the islands for California since the discovery of gold there."[66] That same month another article claimed that, "the natives appear to be quite as anxious to go as the foreigners; some have gone, and many more would go if they had the means."[67] Between 1849 and 1868 several American missionaries living in Hawai'i traveled to California and recorded their observations of Hawaiian communities they visited there. Their accounts reveal the diversity of experience among the Hawaiians who worked in and around the California goldfields. Richard H. Dillon's 1955 article "Kanaka Colonies in California" in the *Pacific Historical Review* compiles several of these accounts. In 1849 Reverend Samuel Damon camped with Hawaiians in a small mining camp on the Sacramento River. When they heard that he had come from Hawai'i, Damon was treated kindly and was given "quantities of gold dust for their families and friends in the islands."[68] Damon was appalled by the actions of the white Christians there, some of whom, he observed, were actively selling liquor to the Hawaiians, many of whom were also Christians. Damon and his companions rebuked the offenders, demonstrating the paternalism so common among American missionaries in Hawai'i at the time. The memoirs of Prentice Mulford, published in 1889, describe a cosmopolitan camp at the "Red Mountain Bar" of Scotsmen, English, and "'Old Harry,' an aged negro, a skilled performer on the bugle and a singer, who offered at times to favor us with what he termed a 'little ditto.' He was the Ethiopic king of a knot of Kanakas gathered about him."[69] Other Native Hawaiian settlers in California suffered from the increasing racism and xenophobia directed toward foreign miners working claims in the Sierra foothills.[70] Few first-person accounts from these Hawaiian voyagers have emerged, whether they were employed in the Pacific Northwest as seamen on foreign vessels or as independent prospectors searching for gold in streambeds in California's foothills. Historian David Chappell has suggested that they are "double ghosts," known to us primarily through the representations of others who undoubtedly misconstrued the meanings of their words and the purposes behind their actions.[71] Hawaiians abroad, whether they traveled as passengers, labored in foreign lands, or worked as seamen on foreign ships, entered a diverse world that not only brought them to new places but introduced them to people from all over the globe: British and Americans, other Pacific Islanders, Portuguese, Chileans, Native Americans from a variety of cultural groups, and many others.

They understood their experiences, however, from a perspective unique to their own cultural milieu. From this perspective, Hawaiian participation in the Pacific maritime trade may be seen as both accommodation and resistance to the changes in their world. Such experiences no doubt forged a more cohesive and unified identity of Hawaiianness, as Hawaiians were forced to define themselves against an array of *malihini*, or foreigners, with whom they came into contact.[72] Both the increasing number of

Hawaiians leaving the islands, if only as sojourners, on foreign ships, and the even more rapidly increasing number of foreigners arriving as settlers, in Hawai'i, in addition to Hawai'i's recent political unification, contributed to a more robust national consciousness among Hawaiians throughout the nineteenth century.[73]

In the late eighteenth and early nineteenth centuries regional and local trade networks throughout Oceania were integrated into a global trade system that spanned the Pacific. Hawai'i emerged during this period as an integral part of this trade network that offered goods and services to foreigners and in turn provided markets for foreign goods. These global events created new contexts and shaped the potential actions of individuals and communities whose power over these events was for the most part limited. Even had they wanted to, neither Kaiana, Naukane, nor Thomas Hopu could have halted or even substantially altered many of these events. But like so many others around the globe, their leaders included, they recognized a shift in the spectrum of possibility and sought not only to make sense of it but to shape it to their advantage. For Native Hawaiians at least, the first few decades of the nineteenth century offered opportunities that would be far more limited in later years. They were the advance guard of generations of voyagers who would come after them. In subsequent years some Native Hawaiians who made the choice to voyage abroad, whether on *Haole* or native vessels, arrived at their decision based on a different set of worldviews and constraints, and their experiences abroad took place in an equally complex and unpredictable landscape.

PART II—PATHS WEST

The histories of Hawai'i and California, and indeed the American West as a whole, had become inseparable by 1850. Economic ties between Honolulu and San Francisco, the movement of Chinese labor east through Honolulu into the western territories, the movement of Hawaiians east to the California goldfields, and the movement of Mormon missionaries west to preach their religion in Hawai'i all illustrate the processes of colonization that brought Hawai'i under American influence by force at the close of the century. The rapid influx of eastern capital into the Hawaiian kingdom and the western territories and its attendant effects on labor migration and resource allocation transformed Hawai'i and the West physically, politically, and demographically.[74] Mormon missionaries to Hawai'i followed not only existing routes but paths made possible by their own quest to establish a religious empire.

Even before his death, Joseph Smith, the founder and prophet of the Church of Jesus Christ of Latter-day Saints (whose members are colloquially known as "Mormons" in most areas of the country), had planned colonization missions in western North America, "beyond United States boundaries."[75] Intense persecution at the hands of the residents and governments of Missouri, as well as their non-Mormon (or "Gentile" in Mormon parlance) neighbors in the new Mormon stronghold of Nauvoo, Illinois, undoubtedly influenced his decision. After Smith was murdered in 1844 by an Illinois mob and opposition to the Mormon presence in Illinois continued to mount, church leaders quietly made more serious plans to relocate the Mormons in the West and abandon the United States entirely.[76] Beginning in September 1845 direct attacks on Mormons' farms and homesteads resulted in hundreds of homes being burned and families being displaced. Although Smith's successor, Brigham Young, advocated a policy of nonretaliation, the attacks continued, and Mormons had little hope that any local authorities would assist them. After considering several locations for settlement in the West, including Oregon and Vancouver Island, Young's careful study of published exploration reports convinced him to settle his followers near the Rocky Mountains. An expedition west to San Francisco via ship, led by Samuel Brannan, held out the prospect of a California settlement as well.[77]

Gathering the Saints

Mormon settlements in Missouri and Illinois especially reflected the church's religious commitment to a concept known, at least by contemporary scholars and church members, as "the gathering." Mormon sacred texts provide the religious impetus for this concept. "Gather ye out from among the nations, from the four winds, from one end of heaven to the other. Send forth my elders of my church unto the nations, which are afar off; unto the islands of the sea."[78] All converts were encouraged to participate in this gathering and to build an egalitarian religious society in preparation for the second coming of Jesus Christ. This was to be accomplished, after the converts had physically gathered in a single location, by a system of communal property redistribution introduced by Joseph Smith in 1831. This "Law of Consecration and Stewardship....was intended to be a major instrument in reorganizing the social and economic patterns of life among his followers. Moreover, it was to provide a model upon which all human society would be organized when the Savior returned to the Latter-Day Zion."[79] That "Latter-Day Zion," located in Jackson County, Missouri, was the area where early Mormon settlement focused, until relations with non-Mormon neighbors worsened considerably, forcing Mormons to relocate, first to Illinois and eventually to the Great Basin.

The combination of physical relocation and social reorganization, as well as the sheer tenacity with which Mormons pursued such experiments, was what set apart their attempts to create cooperative communities in the West. As historian Leonard Arrington observed, "There is something awesome in the sheer spectacle of Brigham Young attempting to organize a regional economy of more than 80,000 inhabitants into a communal commonwealth. The sheer scale of the undertaking imposed problems of magnitude that makes it hardly comparable to the small self-selected communes characteristic of nineteenth century American communitarianism."[80] Before the exodus of the Saints west, Mormons made several attempts to gather in a specific location and build the city of Zion according to Smith's egalitarian principles. These met with mixed success, but in spite of setbacks, Mormon leaders and the Saints (as church members referred to themselves) continued to attempt to build their city of God based on the principles enumerated by Smith.

Following the Mormons' expulsion from Nauvoo, Young began coordinating the Herculean task of evacuating roughly twenty thousand men, women, and children west across the Mississippi River, though North America's central plains, and over the Rocky Mountains. Displaced families were settled in camps strewn along the Mississippi River for the winter of 1846 and 1847. The first party of Mormons reached the Salt Lake Valley on July 24, 1847. Young decided to stop there and commence building Zion at the foot of the western Rockies, a location with an ample supply of timber and water and far enough away from settlements on the Pacific Coast to guarantee their isolation. The relocation of the Mormon populations west continued for several years, as missionaries convinced new converts in Britain and elsewhere to leave their homes and join in the gathering.

Mormon settlements along the Wasatch Front expanded dramatically between 1856 and 1880, aided by external events (the discovery of gold in California and Utah's vast mineral wealth) that were often viewed with caution and suspicion by the Saints. Westward migration proved a tremendous boon to the struggling Utah economy, beginning in the gold rush years and continuing as Americans moved westward to settle throughout the West. Mormon settlers along the Wasatch Front resented the presence of Gentiles in their midst. Brigham Young angered federal authorities by entering into extralegal treaty relationships with Great Basin Indians.

By 1858 the Mormons under Young were considered to be in open rebellion against the US government. Federal troops sent in 1858 to quell the "Mormon rebellion," although hated by most Saints, also provided a market for goods that Mormon communities produced. In addition, these same troops discovered Utah's potential mineral wealth, an industry that brought in the majority of the territory's non-Mormon settlers and drove its economy until well into the twentieth century. The arrival of federal troops in 1857, and the subsequent exploitation of Utah's mineral wealth, carried the region's economy through the Civil War years, and the completion of the transcontinental railroad in 1869 connected the territory with markets and communities to the east and west in unprecedented ways.[81]

This massive expansion of Mormon settlements inevitably brought Mormons into conflict with the indigenous peoples of the Great Basin. The Saints, like many later progressive reformers, felt that they were uniquely benevolent in their treatment of native peoples in the West and initially wished not to exterminate or remove them, but rather to, in their minds, civilize and uplift them from a degraded state. Such benevolent impulses stemmed from the unique Mormon belief that held indigenous peoples of the Americas to be literal descendants of the Jews, led by God to a new land. This notion, supported by sacred religious texts, shaped Mormon attitudes toward native peoples in uniquely contradictory ways. These attitudes and subsequent actions were not always as benevolent as many Mormons made out; Mormon settlers often clashed violently with Indians in the Great Basin. Early relations with Indians soured quickly, and Mormons were supported in their campaigns against Utah's native people by state militias and US Army surveying parties. Mormons also found themselves at the nexus of a regional captive trade network that encompassed much of the Southwest and connected Spanish and Mexican settlements in the South with American settlements and Indians in the northern Great Basin. Mormon revulsion against the thriving trade in Indian and Mexican captives prompted territorial laws preventing slavery, which angered Utes especially and prompted violent conflict between Indians and Mormon settlers. In addition, Mormon policies on land use and their agreements and relations with various bands of Indians in the Great Basin often brought them into further conflict with the federal government, which reserved to itself the right to negotiate all relationships between native peoples and American settlers.[82] Mormons also continued, throughout the nineteenth and twentieth centuries, to send missionaries to the Shoshone, Utes, Paiutes, and Gosiutes throughout the Great Basin, with limited success. Eventually Mormon relations with native peoples in the region mirrored those in the rest of America, as miners and developers eager to exploit the mineral reserves under reservation lands came into conflict with the Indians there.

Ironically, indigenous people were not the only ones who felt besieged in the Great Basin. Mormon settlers had to deal with the ever-increasing numbers of non-Mormon settlers in the region, attracted by Utah's newly discovered mineral wealth. The Mormon settlers sent south from the Utah Valley along the Wasatch Front were charged with creating communities based on sustainable communal agriculture and only rarely if ever took advantage of the mineral resources of the lands they settled. It was the federal agents sent to answer Brigham Young's defiance of federal authority who first glimpsed the region's mineral potential. Soldiers at Fort Douglas in Salt Lake City were the first to notice outcroppings of gold, copper, and silver in canyons along the Wasatch Range. Their early discoveries set off a mining boom in Utah that expanded exponentially after 1869 and flooded the territory with non-Mormon miners and settlers, setting off a pitched political battle over the peculiarity and "un-American" activities of the Mormons. Polygamy was of course the primary target, with the Mormon's communalism and clannishness a close second. In addition to American Gentiles, the expansion of mining and railroad construction and their attendant industrial development brought large numbers of Chinese laborers to the region in the nineteenth century. Utah's development and the increase in outside capital and non-Mormon settlers proved either a blessing or a curse for the region's inhabitants, depending on one's perspective. For indigenous peoples, conquest and colonialism brought death, disease, alienation from land and resources, and ultimately full displacement. For Mormons, increased settlement brought the Janus-faced influence of Gentiles in the form of economic development but decreased political autonomy and an end to polygamy and communitarian ventures.[83]

Mormons, Miners, Soldiers, and Everyone Else

Like hundreds of other men, George Q. Cannon arrived in California in December 1849. Unlike most of his contemporaries, Cannon spurned the search for gold and viewed mining with derision. Writing some twenty years later about his experiences, his scorn for chasing gold was scarcely diminished. "There was no place I would not rather have gone to at that time than California," Cannon reminisced. "I thought it a very poor business for men to be running over the country for gold. There is no honorable occupation that I would rather not follow than hunting and digging for gold."[84] Cannon's distaste for the work of mining was born of a peculiar agrarian sensibility that Mormonism produced in the West. His words could have been, and very nearly mirrored, those of the church's president and prophet, Brigham Young. Although it was ironic that Young himself had sent Cannon with a small group to the California goldfields, it was a sensible move. Young was concerned that Saints would be lured away to the California goldfields, but he also realized the potential value such limitless wealth could have for Salt Lake City's depressed economy. In the end, it was better to send a few truly faithful to reap the benefits of California mining than to lose the whole flock to the golden West, carts, teams, pans, and pickaxes in tow.[85] Cannon's entourage was one of the last in a long and important line of official Mormon expeditions to California between 1845 and 1849. California was originally on Brigham Young's short list of potential settlement sites for his community of Saints. Mormon settlers and soldiers played an important role in the American conquest of Spanish California, despite Young's eventual decision not to focus his settlement efforts there.

If the Mormons had struck out west to practice their peculiar form of millenarian communalism in peace and quiet, they were soon disappointed. The overland traffic through Salt Lake City to the California goldfield grew from a trickle to a stream to an absolute deluge. That it was a band of Mormons themselves who were responsible for this initially unwelcome flood of "Gentiles" only deepens the irony of the events. Young arranged for a group of Mormons under the leadership of Samuel Brannan to head to California from New York by sea in 1846 and create a Mormon colony there.[86] The *Brooklyn*, a passenger ship carrying a group of Mormons, arrived in the sleepy village of Yerba Buena in July 1846, the same month that the nation they were rushing to escape raised its flag over San Francisco Bay. The arrival of some two hundred American residents, which nearly doubled the population of Yerba Buena in a single day, alarmed the Mexicans, who were rushing to stave off American forces south of San Francisco. After many tense nights the Mormon settlers eventually formed their own village, New Hope, on the Stanislaus River. They had come prepared to settle. Blacksmiths, carpenters, farmers, dairymen, millers, and Brannan's printing press were all part of the cooperative Mormon enterprise at New Hope. They began to prepare the way for the expected influx of fellow Saints from the east, according to Brannan's understanding of Brigham Young's orders.[87] They never came. Thinking his companions lost, Brannan traveled east with a small party to find Young and guide them to California. He found them in Wyoming and entered the Salt Lake Valley with Young in 1847. Despite Brannan's urgings to continue west, Young was resolute in remaining in the valley and publicly declared the search for a site for the new Zion over, ordering his Saints to begin the work of settlement. His words to Brannan were unambiguous: "We have no business in San Francisco. The Gentiles will be there pretty soon."[88]

Brannan returned to the New Hope settlement and the *Brooklyn* colonists chastened by Young, but still in firm ecclesiastical control of the growing community.[89] He soon met with yet another party of Mormons in California, not settlers but soldiers, the remnants of the "Mormon Battalion" drafted by the US Army at Council Bluffs to march over the Santa Fe Trail south and west to meet the Mexican forces in southern California. The battalion was formed out of economic necessity rather than nationalist fervor, and the advance pay given these volunteers helped to finance the removal of their families and friends west under Young's leadership. For Young's part, the battalion was a way to demonstrate the church's symbolic loyalty to the United States (in spite of Mormon grievances) and raise much-needed cash to outfit the movement west.[90] The battalion saw no combat, arriving in California after hostilities ended, and the men were released from duty on July 16, 1847, at the Pueblo de Los Angeles.[91] They collected their pay and headed north in two parties. The Hancock party marched through California's central valley to Sutter's Fort, and the Hunt party followed the coast to San Francisco. At Sutter's Fort the men of Hancock's party met with a disgruntled Samuel Brannan on his way back to California from Salt Lake City, a day ahead of his traveling companion, John Brown. Brown arrived with a letter for the battalion members from Brigham Young, instructing those without families to head east to the Salt Lake Valley and the others to remain where they were until spring. One hundred men set out east, and fifty returned to the fort. Part of Hunt's group at San Francisco headed to Sutter's Fort as well.

Brannan, by this time the publisher of the newspaper *The California Star*, had broken off his relationship with the church and was pursuing his interests apart from the growing community of Saints in California. The *Star* was published on the press Brannan had brought from New York on the *Brooklyn*, and he employed ten men, ex-battalion members, to carry copies of it to the East Coast.[92] The American community remained small, and most were Mormons spread between Sutter's Fort and San Francisco. News from California reached the East on a Mormon press via Mormon express riders. John Sutter noted that he employed "about 80" discharged Mormon Battalion soldiers at his fort (his early Hawaiian companions, including his common-law Hawaiian wife, had by this time apparently left), performing a variety of both skilled and unskilled labor. Six of these men, sent to work on Sutter's new sawmill under the direction of John Marshall, were present when Marshall noticed gold-colored flakes in the mill's tail racings. The journals of Henry Bigler and Azariah Smith, two ex-soldiers from the Mormon Battalion, confirmed the date of the discovery of gold as January 24, 1848.[93] By that summer Sutter was unable to keep his laborers employed in any effort at the fort. According to Sutter, his Mormon workers "behaved decently" and "were sorry for the difficulties in which I found myself." Although "some of them remained to finish their jobs," nearly all abandoned the quest for gold and journeyed east to Salt Lake City.[94]

Brannan's *California Star* riders carried the news east. Quotes from the *Star* were cobbled together and made front-page headlines in New York, St. Louis, Baltimore, New Orleans, and Philadelphia.[95] Salt Lake City residents, for obvious reasons, received the news much earlier. Following President James K. Polk's announcement of the discovery to Congress in December 1848, California was inundated with an incredibly cosmopolitan and overwhelmingly male population of fortune seekers, many of them upper- and middle-class Americans and others who could afford to outfit a proper mining expedition.[96] Salt Lake City became a natural way station and supply point for those miners traveling overland from the East. "The effect of the Gold Rush upon the Mormon economy of 1849 and succeeding years is clear and unmistakable," wrote Leonard Arrington. The "Argonauts" provided Mormons in the Great Basin "with a convenient circulating medium ... and the wherewithal to launch giant immigration, colonization, and other programs essential to the growth and development of their projected Kingdom." The discovery of gold in California created Mormon Utah. The influx of overland travelers to California transformed the struggling Mormon settlements into successful towns and cities.[97] Mormons were instructed pointedly to stay in the Great Basin valleys, under the threat of literal damnation by their prophet. "If you Elders of Israel want to go to the gold mines," Brigham Young stated pointedly, "go and be damned." The majority of Saints heeded his counsel.[98]

Thus staving off a mass exodus, Young did of course remember the Mormon community already in California. He sent two men to California to collect tithing from the Saints there, to "minister to the Saints there," and to "establish a gathering place."[99] It was one of these men who would eventually command George Q. Cannon and nine other companions to leave California and preach as missionaries in Hawai'i. Henry Bigler accompanied Cannon as a missionary to both the goldfields and Hawai'i. The gathering place Young envisioned in California never materialized. The party of men he sent back, however, led by Charles C. Rich and Amasa Lyman, collected nearly $60,000 in tithing from Saints in California. In addition, Bigler and Cannon, among others, panned for gold in the American River, though with limited success.[100]

Brigham Young was successful in preventing a mass exodus from the Great Basin to the California foothills, but managed through selective "callings" to maintain connections between Mormons in California and Utah. In addition, the despised Gentiles passing through Salt Lake City en route to California saved his project of building the Kingdom of Zion. But if American gold seekers created modern Utah, it was a far more international body of miners that characterized early gold mining in California.

The decision to send several of the missionaries from the California goldfields to Hawai'i must be seen as an eminently practical one. In 1850 the men in the mining camps of the Sierra Nevada foothills and riverbanks, as well as the growing towns, were hardly receptive to a religious message that advocated, among other things, agrarian communalism, a literal gathering of faithful followers in a struggling set of small communities strung along the slopes of the Wasatch, and such cultural oddities as polygamy. These things were very nearly the polar opposite of what most of those in California had come there to find. Hawai'i was comparatively close, close enough for some miners, to avoid the exorbitant prices charged for even the most basic services in the mining camps, to send their clothes to be laundered in Honolulu.[101] These same high prices made it difficult for the men to support themselves as missionaries.[102] Passage on ships sailing back and forth from San Francisco to Honolulu was relatively easy to obtain, and a few of the men had previous experience there. They knew there was a settled population of *Haole* that held the promise of potential converts. Honolulu was at least as developed as San Francisco for a port town, had access to the same goods and services, and enjoyed the rule of a stable government friendly to foreigners. Under Rich's direction ten men, including George Cannon and Henry Bigler, were directed to travel to Hawai'i and focus their efforts on preaching there. In Rich's opinion, Bigler recorded, "it would cost us no more to spend the winter there than it would here, for we could make nothing in the mines in the winter season.... [W]e could live as cheaply there as perform the mission at the same time."[103] They obtained passage on the *Imaum of Muscat*, sailed for Honolulu in mid-November, and arrived about a month later, on December 12, 1850.[104]

Throughout the nineteenth century, increased trade and foreign activity created a new Pacific world characterized by connections between Oceania and countries along the east and west of the Pacific Rim. The Pacific maritime trade connected emerging markets with suppliers of goods throughout the region. Hawai'i emerged as a central stopping point for ships engaged in trading. Because of the increased presence of foreign ships, it also became an important market for lumber and other materials to outfit vessels for long voyages. The development of the port towns of Honolulu and Lahaina and the increasingly opulent living of the highest ranking *ali'i* also created a demand for overseas goods, both manufactured items and raw materials. The growth of the American whaling industry added to the already significant number of foreign vessels in the Pacific. As the nineteenth century progressed, British and American firms, backed by their respective governments, emerged as the leaders in Pacific maritime enterprises, with some competition in the fur industry from Russian traders.

In addition to the increased traffic in goods across the Pacific, international economic activity also provided increased mobility for Pacific Islanders as laborers in foreign ventures, as crew aboard foreign ships, and as settlers and sojourners outside their home islands. Native Hawaiians especially took advantage of the passing British and American vessels; the demand for Hawaiian seamen and laborers brought them in proportionately large numbers to the Pacific Northwest and California. While population loss in the islands caused by the introduction of foreign diseases may have contributed to this, it can also be seen as a continuation of the centuries-old tradition of Oceanian voyaging in a new context. Native Hawaiians acted to maximize the benefits of this increased foreign presence as they continued to expand the borders of their "sea of islands."

The same processes that brought Hawaiian voyagers to western North America brought *Haole* settlers and sojourners west to Hawai'i as sailors and missionaries. Mormon missionaries were included in this group and arrived on the heels of their experience as the advance guard of American settlers in the intermountain West and California. The discovery of gold in California increased traffic between that state and the Kingdom of Hawai'i after 1849. Mormons, who played central roles in both the American conquest and the early colonization of California, followed this increased traffic west. Thus it was a combination of global processes and local events that brought Hawaiians east and Mormons west and set the stage for a particular and peculiar religious settlement of Native Hawaiians and Pacific Islanders in the American West in the late nineteenth and early twentieth centuries. But first the Church of Jesus Christ of Latter-day Saints had to gain a foothold in Hawaii and establish itself in the fluid social, cultural, and political world there.

CHAPTER 2

The Hawaiian Mission

Lāna'i, Lā'ie, and the Gathering

Hawaiian voyagers who traveled east in the late eighteenth and early nineteenth centuries forged new paths and extended the boundaries of Oceania for a later generation of travelers. Ironically, the combination of rapid depopulation and the willingness of young Hawaiian men to work abroad led the Hawaiian government to pass laws regulating the emigration of its citizens.[1] As a result, emigration decreased considerably, while immigration of *Haole* into Hawai'i slowly increased.[2] Changes in land tenure in Hawai'i led to new responses by Hawaiians trying to hold and work communal land under a new legal system that replaced traditional Hawaiian patterns of land use and social organization with Western-influenced policies. The changes Hawai'i experienced under a new government transformed the monarchy into a liberal Western democracy, introduced and administered by *Haole* missionaries and their children. Native Hawaiians who converted to Mormonism after the arrival of the Mormon missionaries in 1850 adopted, to varying degrees, the teachings of the Church of Jesus Christ of Latter-day Saints in relation to these political, economic, and social changes. These same converts also used Mormon religious metaphors as a means to maintain familiar models of social and economic organization and to resist the changes that threatened their position in Hawaiian society, the result of increasing alienation from the land and the growth of plantation agriculture. Native Hawaiian Mormons reinterpreted the doctrines of the Church of Jesus Christ of Latter-day Saints in the context of their own cultural experiences and appropriated these doctrines in ways that differed from the understanding of the *Haole* missionaries. Far from rejecting the doctrines of the church, Native Hawaiians strategically appropriated certain Mormon religious doctrines in ways that helped them make sense of their changing historical circumstances.

Historian Laurie Maffly-Kipp argues that Pacific Islanders who converted to Mormonism in the nineteenth century "brought to their embrace of the faith particular ways of seeing the world based on indigenous customs, beliefs, and political needs in the face of an increasingly bewildering colonial situation. Theirs was a faith shaped not only by a context of Protestant persecution and intolerance...but also by the complexities of imperialism and missionary competition in an emerging global arena of the Pacific world." In addition, she argues that many of the Pacific Islander converts "were not necessarily led to the Church by the promise of a gathering nor by the sanctity of temple rituals...nor even by the many elements of the Mormon lifestyle that came to be so associated with the Church in the Great Basin."[3] Native Hawaiian converts to Mormonism in nineteenth-century Hawai'i certainly experienced a period of Protestant persecution as well as an almost constantly shifting political and economic landscape that culminated in Hawaiians' loss of their nation during the period of the church's "consolidation of power."[4] Yet for many Hawaiian converts, like so many converts in Europe and the eastern United States, the promise of a literal gathering to Zion continued to shape their understanding and experiences of their new faith. Mormon missionaries in the Pacific Islands, from Tahiti and Tubuai to Hawai'i and Samoa, advocated that converts work toward the ultimate goal of gathering in Utah with their fellow Saints, and the experiences of many of these early Saints for several decades were seen as preparation for this ultimate act of faith and devotion. As early as 1851 Pacific Islanders, although only a small number, began to travel to the western United States to participate in this gathering. The doctrinal concept of the gathering was rarely far from Pacific Islander Saints' minds or experiences in the nineteenth century.

This chapter focuses on three events in the history of the Church of Jesus Christ of Latter-day Saints Hawaiian mission between 1850 and 1885 that highlight the efforts of Native Hawaiian Mormons to make sense of their newfound faith in the rapidly changing social, economic, and political landscape of nineteenth-century Hawai'i. First was the initial gathering of Mormon converts in Hawai'i at the Palawai Basin on the island of Lāna'i. The second event was the establishment of the mission plantation in Lā'ie on O'ahu and the subsequent "'Awa Rebellion." Third was the growth of the Kahana Hui and its religious ties to both Lā'ie and eventually Iosepa in Utah. All of these events were based on the obligation of nineteenth-century Mormons to align their spiritual and temporal lives by removing themselves from the Gentile world and establishing cooperative communities in preparation for a millennium that loomed large in the minds of believing Mormons. Before looking at these events in detail, we must consider the social, economic, and political changes that characterized Hawaiian politics in the mid-nineteenth century, for it was in this dramatically shifting world that Native Hawaiian Mormons came to experience their new faith.

CHANGES IN THE HAWAIIAN POLITICAL SYSTEM, 1820–1887: ECONOMY, POLITICS, AND SOCIETY IN PRE-*HAOLE* HAWAI'I

In the half century between 1835 and 1887 a veritable sea change in Hawaiian politics transformed a sovereign nation into an economically dominated vassal state controlled by an imperial power. The path from political independence to the eventual overthrow of the Hawaiian government in 1893 resulted from the greed of American businessmen bent on controlling Native Hawaiian land and labor for their own economic gain. The growing imperialist sentiment of the US government at the end of the nineteenth century provided military power to back the actions of its citizens abroad. The growth of the Church of Jesus Christ of Latter-day Saints in Hawai'i began in the midst of this period of radical transformation, and Mormons found themselves uniquely poised to take full advantage of this shift in economic and political power.

Many historians have compared pre-*Haole* Hawaiian political and socioeconomic organization with European feudalism. This serves several purposes. Characterizing pre-*Haole* Hawai'i as a "feudal" society recasts Hawaiian history in terms of a supposedly universal global economic progression from precapitalist to capitalist forms of economic production. Hawai'i is placed on an imposed historical timeline, one that presumably ends in the midst of a modern era characterized by the political realities of colonial occupation. The history of Hawai'i, and indeed the history of all colonial states, is seen not in its own terms, but as an addendum to the histories of more powerful colonial states. Such a model errs, however, by assuming the inevitability of current relationships of power and domination. Reclaiming Hawaiian history from a Native Hawaiian perspective allows historians to understand it on its own terms. Hawaiian politics and society were intimately bound up with Native Hawaiian cosmology and the relationship of *Kanaka Māʻoli*, or the Native Hawaiian people, to the physical and spiritual world around them.

Between 1800 and 1819 Hawai'i underwent a series of profound changes that set the stage for the political transformations of the remainder of the nineteenth century. The consolidation of power under a single ruler for all eight Hawaiian Islands began years before the first permanent European settlers arrived, but the introduction of Western weapons and military strategies accelerated the process. By the end of the first decade of the nineteenth century Kāmehameha, a brilliant military and diplomatic strategist, had united the entire Hawaiian archipelago under his rule by applying Western military technology with an impressive command of statecraft particular to the Hawaiian political and cultural environment. The hegemony of Kāmehameha over the united Hawaiian Islands ended the political divisions between individual islands and districts and inadvertently facilitated the rapid spread of the widespread economic, political, and social changes of subsequent years.[5]

Several key events after Kāmehameha's death in 1819 allowed the rise to power of Native Hawaiian political leaders heavily influenced by the increasing number of *Haole*, or white foreigners, residing permanently in the islands. The first of these was the breaking of the *'aikapu* by Kāmehameha's wife, Ka'ahumanu. The second was the arrival of American missionaries in 1820. The third event was the development of the sandalwood trade, which restructured labor relations between *ali'i* and *makā'ainana*, established a permanent population of foreign merchants, and introduced money and foreign manufactured goods into the Hawaiian economy. While Ka'ahumanu's actions proved fortuitous for *Haole* in the islands after 1819, foreigners manipulated the other two events to their ultimate advantage and set into motion the political changes of the mid- to late nineteenth century. Although never a truly unified political force, the islands' growing *Haole* population lobbied the ruling chiefs of Hawai'i to introduce important social, economic, and political changes in response to the increasing number of visiting foreign ships and the introduction of both money and foreign manufactured goods into the Hawaiian economy.

Put simply, the *'aikapu* (from *ai* meaning "food" or "to eat" and *kapu* meaning "restricted" or "forbidden") was a law that forbade men and women eating in one another's presence. On a far less superficial level, the origin of the *'aikapu* from the perspective of indigenous Hawaiian cosmology is rooted in the dualist structure of Eastern Oceanian myth and ritual. The *'aikapu* reminded Hawaiians of the sacred narratives that related the story of their origins as a people. *'Aikapu* represented an outward manifestation of an established historical social order, a daily reminder of the central primordial event that metaphorically prescribed the *pono*, or right and proper, relationship between the *ali'i* and the *makā'ainana*. Segregated eating was an outward symbol of the dualities that structured Native Hawaiian religious practice. Upon Kāmehameha's death, Ka'ahumanu, his first wife, successfully convinced his successor, Liholiho, to eat in her presence. An ambitious and intelligent *Ali'i Nui* (high chief), Ka'ahumanu began to consolidate her power even before her husband's death. Her decision to break the 'aikapu and eat freely with men posed a challenge to the authority of Liholiho and established her power and authority as an Ali'i Nui. As Native Hawaiian historian Lilikalā Kame'eleihiwa argues, the overturning of ritualized behavior believed to maintain pono in the context of increasing disease and depopulation, as well as the increasing alcoholism of the chiefs and their indebtedness to foreign merchants, created a structural void, which Christianity was poised to fill.[6] In addition, the presence of Haole who neither succumbed to epidemic diseases nor seemed to suffer any of the negative consequences of various transgressions of kapu shook the foundations of Native Hawaiian social organization.[7] It was in this environment of social and cultural upheaval that the first groups of missionaries from New England arrived in Hawai'i in 1820.

The brig Thaddeus, the vessel that bore the first Christian missionaries to Hawai'i, arrived at Kohala on the island of Hawai'i on March 30, 1820. The missionaries were accompanied by Thomas Hopu, who was sent ashore with a ship's officer "to make an inquiry of the inhabitants respecting the state of the islands." The missionaries saw the news they received from Hopu and the officer as nothing short of providential:

How our hearts were surprised, agitated, and encouraged beyond every expectation, to hear the report—"Kamehameha is dead—his son Liholiho is king—the tabus are abolished—the images are destroyed—the heiaus of idolatrous worship are burned, and the party that attempted to restore them by force of arms has recently been vanquished!" The hand of God! How visible in thus beginning to answer the prayer of his people, for the Hawaiian race![8]

The missionaries, sent by the American Board of Commissioners for Foreign Missions, were poised to fill the void in tangible spiritual authority left by the breaking of the 'aikapu. The conversion of Ka'ahumanu, Liholiho, and other powerful Ali'i Nui to Christianity established the missionaries as powerful figures in the kingdom, replacing the kahuna, or priests, associated with the rule of the kapu system.[9] The ascendance of the Christian missionaries established Hawai'i as a Christian kingdom, despite opposition from some Ali'i Nui, including the Mō'ī (most exalted chief or ruler, often interpreted as "king"), Kauikeaouli.[10]

The continuing influence of these early missionaries and their descendants in the social and political life of Hawai'i can hardly be overstated. Initially the missionaries restricted their efforts to shape the spiritual and religious life of the kingdom, but in subsequent years their influence in economic and political affairs increased, often at the behest of Native Hawaiian leaders seeking advice in dealings with Western governments, with which they had little experience. Most of the radical changes in land tenure, legal structure, and political organization that followed were based on the advice of these missionaries, who subscribed to a religious and political ideology that linked Christianity and liberal democratic government. The initial arrival of these Christian missionaries altered the course of Hawaiian history in ways that continue to shape the social, economic, and political life of Native Hawaiians today.

The third event that changed the Hawaiian political landscape was less an actual event than a process, one that worked in a way that made it inseparable from religious transformation. This was the growth of the sandalwood market and Hawai'i's integration into the Pacific maritime trade that connected Canton, Oceania, and the Pacific Northwest, described in chapter 1. Despite his taste for foreign manufactured goods, especially military ones such as firearms and ships, Kāmehemeha had managed his finances shrewdly and avoided indebtedness to foreign merchants and Pacific traders. His heirs and many of the ali'i from throughout the islands were far less prudent. Lavish spending on consumer goods was financed in large part by the harvesting of sandalwood, which was accomplished on a large scale by diverting the labor of the makā'ainana away from production of kalo and other traditional crops and sending them to cut sandalwood in the mountains. Fine fabrics, furniture, china, silverware, and other luxury items piled up (and in some cases rotted) in the ali'i's storehouses. When combined with a rapidly decreasing population due to foreign disease, the result was large tracts of formerly heavily cultivated land lying fallow. The ali'i's mounting debts prompted impatient Haole creditors to appeal to their own governments to force Hawaiian ali'i to pay up or risk the threat of military engagement. Forced to reconcile with creditors, many ali'i staved off collection until the land reforms of the Māhele allowed them to transfer their lands as a method of payment.[11]

Anthropologist Marshall Sahlins characterized this period of lavish spending by Native Hawaiian ali'i during the sandalwood era as "the political economy of grandeur." The demand by American merchants for Hawaiian sandalwood as a means to continue the China trade injected a surplus of manufactured luxury goods into the Hawaiian economy. This "structure of the conjuncture," as Sahlins calls it, was the moment at which a vast increase in foreign goods met with a ferocious battle between ali'i to legitimate their social position "in the new medium of commercial prowess."[12] This obsession with consumption as a means to acquire mana (a spiritual power that translated into political power and social status) in an environment of political and economic competition led to a situation wherein the necessity to consume far outpaced the ability to pay.

The culmination of social, economic, and political events in Hawai'i between 1819 and 1850 created an environment of rapid change in which traditional Native Hawaiian relationships of reciprocity between the chiefs and the people were severed to make way for an expanding market economy that individualized both risk and reward. As demonstrated in the previous chapter, many of the *makā'ainana* responded to their increasing alienation at the hands of chiefs and foreigners by leaving their homes altogether and seeking better lives elsewhere. With little conception of how or inclination to reorganize their lives to accommodate capitalist cycles of production and consumption, Native Hawaiians braced themselves for the equally radical changes of the latter half of the nineteenth century.

THE ARRIVAL OF THE MORMONS

One can assume that the Mormon missionaries who arrived in 1850 did not realize that they had just entered a nation described by one historian of the period as "in crisis."[13] Initially the ten men who arrived in Hawai'i from San Francisco planned to preach only to the *Haole* population of Honolulu. They could not speak Hawaiian and intended only to spend the winter before returning to continue the work they had begun in the California goldfields. Reminiscing about his first contact with Hawaiians aboard the arriving ship, Cannon noted: "I little thought at that time that I would ever learn their language, or become as familiar with their customs as I afterwards did."[14] After they disembarked the missionaries split up into groups of two and divided their work among five of the eight Hawaiian Islands. In most areas the Protestant (and mostly *Haole*) missionaries and government officials resisted efforts at Mormon proselytizing and rebuffed attempts by Mormon missionaries to gather publicly.[15] Philip B. Lewis, a missionary in Hawai'i in the early 1850s, recorded in his journal the second meeting he had with "Revd Mr Baldwin" in 1851, the tenor of which was indicative of the general relationship between representatives of different Christian sects in the islands:

> In the evening Bro Hammond and myself called on the Revd Mr Baldwin for the second time, he appeared very uneasy in our presence. We asked him if he would like to converse further on our doctrine, he said he did not really know as he had time, and said he should like to have a sign. If he should see a miracle performed he would have to believe as a matter of course....He said it was of no use to talk for we believe in revelation in the last days and that precluded everything else....[H]e said he did not wish to have any further conversation with us. And

that he considered us deluded &c...after I had borne my testimony and told him not to fight against it [he] replied that he felt it his duty to fight against it and should do so.[16]

Finding the Protestant clergy unreceptive to their message and the bawdy sailors hardly less so, the Mormons soon realized the folly of continuing to focus their efforts on the islands' foreigners and began to make efforts to learn to speak Hawaiian. Several of the missionaries were so discouraged by the cold reception that they abandoned their work and headed back to California and Utah. The remainder, George Cannon included, stayed and began to learn Hawaiian and preach to the Native Hawaiian population.[17]

Historian and political scientist Hōkūlani Kamakanikailialoha Aikau argues that there were two key reasons the Church of Jesus Christ of Latter-day Saints was able to consolidate power in Hawai'i in the nineteenth century. The first was the identification of Native Hawaiians as Lamanites (God's chosen people of Israel as identified in the Book of Mormon). The second was the economic and political changes in Hawai'i that allowed foreign ownership of Hawaiian land.[18] Aikau also notes the way that historians have failed to link the growth of the church in Hawai'i with "the political and social turmoil" in the mid- to late nineteenth century.[19] In this sense historians of the Church of Jesus Christ of Latter-day Saints in Hawai'i have failed to contextualize its growth and development within nineteenth-century Hawaiian history in terms that explain both the racializing shift toward pursuing Native Hawaiian converts and the attempts to gain access to Hawaiian lands. The Māhele of 1848–1854 privatized Hawaiian land, precipitating the widespread alienation of many Native Hawaiians from their 'aina hānau (lands of their birth), while at the same time allowing foreigners, including Mormons, to purchase land. Nevertheless many Native Hawaiian converts to Mormonism appropriated key tenets of church doctrine and practice to resist social, economic, and political changes in Hawai'i. Although the efforts to resist these alienating forces from within the church achieved mixed results, the fact that Hawaiian Saints resisted colonialism from within a colonial institution complicates our ideas of culture and cultural imperialism in nineteenth-century Hawai'i. Mormon missionaries in Hawai'i acted as agents of colonialism and as such reaped the benefits of the colonial political economy. But Native Hawaiian Saints were far from passive as they resisted imperial encroachments and negotiated the new political landscape as both Hawaiians and Mormons.

HAWAIIANS, PACIFIC ISLANDERS, AND THE "MORMON RACIAL DOCTRINE"

Throughout much of its history Mormonism has had a unique and problematic relationship with race. Mormon religious doctrine has long associated "dark skin with a curse from God," an idea that traces its origins to Mormon sacred texts, especially the Book of Mormon, as well as to racial ideas prevalent in early nineteenth-century America.[20] The Book of Mormon tells the story of several families led by God from Jerusalem in approximately 600 BC to the American continent, set apart by God as a "promised land" and described as "choice above all other lands." The purpose of this divinely inspired relocation was to "preserv[e] a righteous branch of the House of Israel" from the "wickedness" and "corruption" that had overtaken the Jews in the Holy Land. A schism immediately followed their arrival in the Americas, with one group remaining faithful followers of God (Nephites) and the other abandoning the faith they had brought with them from Jerusalem to their new home (Lamanites). As a punishment to the Lamanites, God "cursed them with a skin of blackness," marking them to prevent the two groups from intermarrying. The remainder of the Book of Mormon recounts a fratricidal war between the two groups that intensified generationally, with each group alternating between periods of "righteousness" and periods in which they ceased to follow the counsel of the many prophets who emerged among them and acted as political, spiritual, and military leaders. The focus of the Book of Mormon—indeed, its central event—is the visit of the resurrected Jesus Christ to the American continent following his crucifixion and death in Jerusalem. Jesus preached to the people, established the "true gospel," and ascended again to heaven, promising to return.[21] The Book of Mormon provides, for believing Mormons, another witness to the divinity of Jesus Christ, a companion to the Gospels of the New Testament. Jesus's visit was followed by two centuries of peace before the Nephites and Lamanites returned to warfare, this time with both sides descending into "an awful scene of wickedness" that ended with the extinction of the Nephite people. North American Indians are believed by Mormons to be the descendants of the (dark-skinned) Lamanites who remained.[22]

The association of dark skin with a curse from God was not a unique or innovative religious concept; it had a long history in Western representations of non-Western people in the context of colonial encounters. In both Europe and colonial America, a similar racial ideology functioned as a justification for the Atlantic slave trade. European settlers in America struggled to explain the existence of the region's indigenous inhabitants within the almost universally accepted biblical creation narrative. These explanations ranged from Native Americans descending from one of the lost tribes of Israel to the land bridge migration theory.[23] Although Mormon theology followed this line of thinking closely, the Book of Mormon was unique in that it offered a narrative history for this explanation. Many Mormons past and present subscribed to a version of the "curse of Ham" theory regarding people of African ancestry, but the Book of Mormon offered a detailed account of the alleged Semitic origins of American Indians, previously only surmised by some Europeans baffled by the existence of a formerly unknown (to them) race of people. The Book of Mormon also offered a not-so-subtle justification for American colonialism and even genocide against the indigenous Americans, as a judgment meted out by God for their own genocide against the continent's former white inhabitants. The Book of Mormon prescribes a set of behavioral characteristics to Lamanites' darkness: they became "an idle people, full of mischief and subtlety."[24] Consistent with early nineteenth-century racial discourse in America, "darkness" was a category laden with an abundance of negative connotations.[25]

Placing indigenous Americans in the context of this religious narrative created a special responsibility in the minds of white Mormons to educate the Indians they encountered about their true genealogy, which would allow them to return to a rightful knowledge of their privileged place among God's children. Joseph Smith stressed the importance of missionary work among the modern-day Lamanites, a tradition that was continued by Brigham Young following the Saints' relocation to the Great Basin. Because Young's colonization efforts after the Saints' trek west invariably focused on the few well-watered and fertile valleys along the Wasatch Front, Mormon settlers found themselves fighting the indigenous peoples of the region as often as they were preaching to them.[26] Irrespective of these often violent conflicts and the understandable fear many white Mormon colonists harbored of Indian attacks, white Mormons still considered it their sacred duty to pursue peaceful relations with Indian communities and to convert them to Mormonism. At the same time the characterization of Lamanites in the Book of Mormon offered a comforting justification for racist policies and actions against Indians by white Mormons throughout the nineteenth and twentieth centuries, in spite of many simultaneous efforts aimed at their conversion.[27] Above all, white Mormons considered their mission to the Indians, and indeed to all remnants of the Book of Mormon Lamanites, a civilizing one, aimed at their conversion and uplift, with a special goal of teaching them the "arts of civilization."[28] The Mormons' civilization.

The tension between Mormons' sense of spiritual and temporal obligation to Native Americans and the reality of two culturally distinct peoples occupying the same physical space produced an uneasy period of strained relations between Mormons and Indians after the Mormon trek west. Mormon leaders, especially Brigham Young, spoke often of the responsibilities of the Saints in Utah to the "Lamanites." The attitude of white Mormons in the West toward Native Americans is best described as benevolent paternalism, characterized by the exhortation of church leaders to treat Indians with compassion instead of violence.[29] For the most part, however, relations between indigenous Americans and Mormons in the Great Basin "vacillated unpredictably between generosity so open-handed it imposed on white settlers a 'most oppressive burden'...and extermination campaigns that sometimes failed to discriminate between hostile and friendly."[30] This tension lasted well into the twentieth century, when mineral discoveries on designated reservation land in the Uintah Valley created another battleground for white settlers, Ute Indians, and other bands who had been removed to the reservation.

The extension of the label "Lamanite" to Pacific Islanders did not begin with Joseph Smith or Brigham Young, but has its genesis in the history of Latter-day Saint missions in the Pacific. It was later accepted by a wider group of church authorities and linked to missionary work throughout the Pacific, which until after 1950 was concentrated in Samoa, Tonga, Tahiti, Hawai'i, and New Zealand, almost exclusively among Polynesian peoples.[31] In early records of addresses and official statements concerning foreign missions, the Pacific Islands were not singled out as a region specifically important because its inhabitants were Lamanites. Some of the earliest references to Pacific Islanders as descendants of the Lamanites came from Cannon. Discouraged at the lack of success among the *Haole* population of Hawai'i, and with several of his companions ready to abandon the Hawaiian mission, Cannon and his four remaining companions directed their attention toward Native Hawaiians. Cannon felt he had received a revelation from God that Native Hawaiians were indeed Lamanites; as such it was his duty to stay and try to convert them. Referring to a Book of Mormon passage, Cannon wrote that:

> If the sons of Mosiah could relinquish their high estate, and go forth among the degraded Lamanites to labor as they did, should not I labor with patience and devoted zeal for the salvation of these poor red men, heirs of the same promise?...The soul of a Sandwich Islander or a Lamanite is as precious in the sight of the Lord as the soul of a white man, whether born in America or Europe. Jesus died for one as much as the other, and to the men of red skins the Lord's promises are great and precious. Those who administer the ordinances of salvation to them will have fully as great joy over them in the day of the Lord Jesus as if they had been more enlightened.[32]

Cannon equated the past, present, and future of Native Hawaiians and Native Americans in overtly religious terms. This was a doctrinal shift that would shape the course of the Hawaiian mission as well as Mormonism in Hawai'i and the Pacific. Ultimately it justified a continued church presence in Hawai'i and established the key rationale for acquiring land and establishing a gathering place in the islands.[33] The changes in land tenure that began to take effect just a few short years prior to the arrival of the first Mormon missionaries created an opportunity for Mormons to make their goal of gathering Hawaiian converts to Zion a reality.

THE MĀHELE

Historian Jonathan Kamakawiwo'ole Osorio has provided the clearest picture of the political devolution of Hawai'i in the nineteenth century from a sovereign nation led by a monarch to a vassal state effectively run by foreign business interests. In his view the event known as the Māhele (1848 to 1854) was "the single most critical dismemberment of Hawaiian society."[34] The Māhele (literally a "division" or a "sharing") was a set of laws passed between 1848 and 1854 that allowed for the private ownership of land by both *makā'ainana* and *Haole*. If constitutionality paved the way for a set of laws that respected individual rights and universal equality, the Māhele put that doctrine into practice regarding the private ownership of Hawai'i's lands.

In theory the division of Hawai'i's lands among the government, the crown, the chiefs, and the people would allow all to compete on an equal footing in a capitalist system of individual gain and reward. In practice the Māhele cleared the way for massive dispossession of Native Hawaiians from their lands in the years that followed.[35] The Māhele was almost experimental in nature: it was created cautiously, one piece of legislation at a time, over a nearly ten-year period, and resulted in a massive shift in the lives and fortunes of the *makā'ainana*. The impact of the Māhele, once completed, was rapid. The impetus for such widespread change in the land tenure laws was the influence of the *Haole*, who had infiltrated the Hawaiian government and thought that the shift to a capitalist market economy was inevitable and should happen sooner rather than later. These men hoped to continue along a course that would sever all interdependency between the *ali'i* and the *makā'ainana*. Another factor that motivated the architects of the Māhele was the continuing decrease in the population of Hawaiians from outbreaks of epidemic diseases and decreased fertility. A diminished population left much of Hawai'i's land uncultivated, and at the time the rapid decline looked irreversible.[36] This was undoubtedly an important factor in the *ali'i*'s capitulation to *Haole* pressure for land tenure reform.

According to Osorio, "The Māhele was a foreign solution to the problem of managing lands increasingly emptied of people."[37]

A basic understanding of traditional Native Hawaiian land tenure is necessary to understand the impact of the Māhele on the *makā'ainana*, which comprised the majority of the Native Hawaiian population. In pre-Māhele Hawai'i, the Western concept of private land ownership did not exist; all land was owned by *ke akua*, the gods. *Ali'i*, however, exercised almost total control of all lands by virtue of their rank and status as literal descendants of *ke akua*. Lands were divided into increasingly smaller parcels: each island had six *mokus*, a major land division, and each *moku* was divided into *ahupua'a*, pie-shaped wedges of land that came to rough tips at the top of the mountain and widened as they neared their base at the seashore. Within each *ahupua'a* were still smaller land divisions, and *makā'ainana* were granted use of a house plot and a farm plot, but still retained access to communal fishing and gathering areas within the *ahupua'a* boundaries. In return for use of these resources, *makā'ainana* contributed a portion of their bounty or labor to local *ali'i*, who acted as agents of island chiefs. *Ali'i* could also call upon the labor of *makā'ainana* for public projects such as roads, paths, the maintenance of fishponds, and the like. The authors of Māhele laws were tasked with creating a system by which the *makā'ainana* retained individual access to the lands they had traditionally worked, while still retaining the rights of the *ali'i* to control large tracts of "public" land under their control.

The Māhele began with the establishment of an Organic Act that created a Board of Commissioners to Quiet Land Titles in 1845. Rising conflict between *Haole* and Native Hawaiians over land in the previous years had become common as *ali'i* allowed foreigners the use of portions of their lands to pay off debts. Foreigners came into conflict with *makā'ainana* living and cultivating the land more and more frequently, often over issues of water allocation and use rights. After the commission was created in 1845, lands began to be sold in small parcels in select regions of the islands, although not totally in fee simple (foreigners could only sell the lands to subjects of the kingdom, and only foreigners who were full-time residents could own the land at all). Immediately following this development, *makā'ainana* protested the ability of *Haole*, even those who were residents and citizens of the kingdom, to own land. Petitions from the *makā'ainana* reveal their acute awareness of their impending dispossession, although ultimately they deferred to their representatives (many of whom were *ali'i*) or decried the idea of representation at all. "There is no use electing a representative," wrote the people of one district, "because the lands are being sold."[38]

Despite the persistent protests of the *makā'ainana*, roughly a year later the *Haole*-dominated commission extended more liberal ownership rights to foreigners, and eventually the ultimate goal of the Māhele began to be fully realized: a division of Hawaiian lands among the Mō'ī, the konohiki (local agents of the ali'i, some of whom were foreign residents with dual citizenship), and the makā'ainana, in which fee-simple ownership was the rule. Under the Kuleana Act of 1850, makā'ainana could claim lands that they presently lived on and cultivated. Although the ownership of the land that they successfully claimed was indeed theirs, the makā'ainana were bereft of the traditional protection of the ali'i and were instead thrown into a capitalist system of ownership utterly foreign to Native Hawaiian concepts of land tenure. The traditional ability of the ali'i to direct the labor of the makā'ainana was replaced by a system of taxation, a burden to those who had little in the way of liquid assets. The new system severed these traditional rights and removed access to critical resources. Makā'ainana struggled to produce goods for sale without full access to the resources of their ahupua'a. In the end, of the approximately 4.2 million acres in the kingdom, the 80,000 remaining makā'ainana owned about 28,000 acres. The 251 konohiki and Ali'i Nui received about half a million acres.[39] By 1851 the seeds of the ultimate dispossession of Native Hawaiians from their lands had been sown.

THE HAWAIIAN MISSION—LĀNA'I, LĀ'IE, AND THE GATHERING

In 1851 George Q. Cannon and other missionaries were learning to speak Hawaiian and focusing their efforts on gaining converts from the Native Hawaiian community. This was made possible to a large extent by the patronage of several prominent Native Hawaiians who converted to Mormonism on the island of Maui. Jonatana Napela and Kaleohano were two prominent early converts to Mormonism who joined the Haole missionaries as they traveled and preached on Maui and the Big Island. Kaleohano was baptized first, traveled with several Elders to the Big Island to preach, and helped the missionaries win converts among Native Hawaiians. He also helped train newly arrived missionaries in the language. Napela was descended from high-ranking Maui chiefs[40] and like Kaleohano was a graduate of Lahainaluna, an academy set up for the children of chiefly families by the Protestant missionaries in the 1820s. From their days at Lahainaluna, Kaleohano and Napela were literate in Hawaiian and probably some English, were Christian, and had experience dealing with Haole. Napela was a direct descendant of Ka'ahumanu, the first and favorite wife of Kāmehemeha I. He was a circuit court judge in the Wailuku district of Maui, a respected civic leader, and a prominent member of a local Calvinist congregation. Napela also grew and sold potatoes on his land for sale at the markets in Lahaina. We can reasonably assume that Napela's land had recently been granted to him during the Māhele and that he was an acting *konohiki* over it.[41] In Western terms, civic titles, church membership, and land served as proof of Napela's position as a prominent member of Hawaiian society. In Hawaiian terms, Napela's community actions and service were symbols of his inherent *mana*, or spiritual power, itself a result of his high birth. To the *Haole*, Napela's civic accomplishments spoke to his virtue. To Hawaiians, Napela's accomplishments served to both increase and testify to his *mana*.[42] From either perspective, Napela was a powerful and influential ally to the Mormons in their struggle to gain a foothold in Hawai'i. When he first met Cannon, Napela was thirty-nine years old. His decision to become a Mormon effectively ended his tenure as a judge, but he retained his land and devoted his time to translating the Book of Mormon into Hawaiian and teaching the *Haole* missionaries the Hawaiian language.[43]

Mormonism gained many converts as a result of the work of both Hawaiian and *Haole* missionaries throughout the islands. Although they continued to face opposition from Protestant clergy and government officials,[44] their influence in the islands was growing. There were elements of Mormon doctrine that many Native Hawaiians found attractive. One such doctrine was the church-condoned practice of polygamy, taught by Cannon and others. At a mission conference in April 1853 Cannon addressed an audience of nearly one thousand on "the revalation on Celestial marage and explain the same having prepard and translated it into the native language it tuck well with them this agreeing with thare former practises before the whites came among them."[45] Another tenet of Mormonism readily accepted, and more often the subject of religious sermons, was the concept of the gathering. The gathering of all Mormon converts and members to Zion was a central aspect of the religious sermons of the *Haole* Mormon missionaries and a prospect that they dwelled on frequently among themselves. Although the ultimate goal for all of the converts gained in Hawai'i was to gather with the rest of the Saints in the Great Basin,[46] the continuing decline in Hawai'i's population caused the legislature to pass increasingly restrictive emigration laws between 1842 and 1887. In addition, many of the Native Hawaiian converts came from the *makā'ainana* and had little material wealth that they could liquidate to pay for an expensive voyage.[47] As a result, Brigham Young counseled the missionaries in Hawai'i directly on this subject from the time of their arrival, encouraging them to "find a temporary gathering place, and the way would eventually be opened for Hawaiians to gather to Zion on the mainland."[48] As the number of converts in Hawai'i grew, the missionaries felt a more pressing need to find a suitable location for this "temporary gathering place." In 1854 that place was found.

The changes in land tenure following the Māhele made it possible for Mormon missionaries to acquire Hawaiian land on which to gather the Native Hawaiian Saints in preparation for their eventual journey to Zion. The decision to find this temporary gathering place for the Native Hawaiian Saints fell on both Cannon and Napela, who eagerly supported and aided in the project.[49] But how did Mormon efforts to gather Native Hawaiian Saints look in relation to this recent upheaval in the traditional Hawaiian concept of land tenure? It is reasonable to assume that Native Hawaiians converts received the Mormon commandment to gather in the context of the Māhele and made their decisions to gather or not to gather based not only on the depth of their individual religious commitment but by calculating the costs and rewards of such a relocation. It also seems reasonable that the *makā'ainana* who were not granted title to lands under the 1850 Kuleana Act were more likely to gather with the rest of the Saints than were those who had received title to their lands.

The first gathering of Saints in Hawai'i may be viewed in retrospect as a failure. It was eventually abandoned and resulted in many early converts leaving the church or experiencing severe and lasting discouragement. In the beginning, nowhere near all of the converts to Mormonism, whether Native Hawaiian or *Haole*, actually heeded the call of the missionaries to gather. But for those who did, the power and meaning of the metaphor of the gathering was strained under an intense amount of pressure from events in Hawai'i and the church in Utah. The failure of this first community was a major setback for the church in Hawai'i and left a lasting impression on Native Hawaiian Saints. In the end, however, many of those who gathered at the Palawai Basin on the island of Lāna'i continued to support the notion of the gathering.[50]

The Iosepa colony at the Palawai Basin on Lāna'i was organized by the *Haole* missionaries in a manner much like the other colonizing endeavors that Brigham Young undertook between 1848 and 1856. Initially the goal for Native Hawaiian Saints was to gather at the Great Basin with the other Saints. Much of the energy of the missionaries was focused on this goal once the decision to gather the Hawaiian Saints at a single location had been made. To accomplish this, several of the missionaries, under the direction of the mission president, Phillip B. Lewis, weighed the decision of purchasing a ship to transport the Hawaiian Saints to a gathering place that several church leaders were attempting to establish in San Bernardino, California. The Native Hawaiian Saints were to be settled nearby.[51] Brigham

Young explained the rationale for the settlement of Native Hawaiians in California in a letter to another Mormon Elder:

> I advised [the missionaries] to appoint a delegation at their earliest convenience, instructed them to proceed and examine the count[r]y from the Mojave to Iron County, consult with the Presidents of Cedar City and Harmony, and the Indians in the region named, located some site or sites for the Islanders where they can be located among a peaceable and industrious portion of the remnants of Jacob [Indians] their brethren, and enjoy a climate as similar to their own as we can at present furnish, and be aloof from the contaminations of the white settlements of California, and within reach of the proper supervision and counsel.[52]

Lying at the far southern end of the Great Basin, the San Bernardino settlement was part of what Brigham Young envisioned as the State of Deseret, with borders extending from the northern Great Basin south with access to a seaport on the Pacific Ocean in California.[53] Young and the other missionaries were explicit about their reasons for settling Native Hawaiian Saints there as opposed to the northern Great Basin around the Great Salt Lake. A letter from Young to Amasa Lyman, a Mormon settler at San Bernardino, listed the choice of a potential location and his reasoning behind it, the most important being the proximity the Native Hawaiian Saints would have to "a mild spirited, industrious portion of the remnant of Jacob, their *blood* brethren, who are welcoming our missionaries with warm hearts and open arms."[54] The notion of Native Hawaiians as literal kin of Native Americans and of Semitic ancestry was endorsed wholly by the Mormon prophet.

By all indications a large number of Native Hawaiian Mormons willing to gather to Zion awaited eagerly the procurement of a means of transportation east across the sea. Although those willing to emigrate by no means represented all Native Hawaiian converts, there were enough for the missionaries to vigorously move forward in their efforts to buy a vessel. The settlement plans for the mainland were eventually abandoned on account of money: "[S]uch is their poverty at present that it would be impossible to emigrate them to America."[55] With little access to cash or assets that could be liquidated to pay for their journey, the prospect of gathering Native Hawaiian Saints at a location in California was abandoned. Initially a small number of converts from Hawai'i and the Pacific Islands (primarily Tahitian and Native Hawaiian second wives to Mormon missionaries) were gathered at San Bernardino. This group (numbering fewer than ten) abandoned the church and the settlement one by one, disillusioned with either Mormonism, racism, the bleakness of the desert landscape, or a combination of all three.[56]

When faced with the failure of this initial plan, the decision to remove themselves to a central gathering place for Saints in the Hawaiian Islands remained the only viable option. Once again the shift in land tenure laws after the Māhele opened up several options for the Saints, and they eventually chose Lāna'i out of many locations available to them through the representative of Kekau'ōnohi, an *Ali'i Nui* who had been granted large parcels on several islands during the Māhele.[57]

Once Palawai had been evaluated as a settlement site and terms for lease of the land and settlement were agreed upon, the work of creating a Mormon cooperative community began. Jonatana Napela tried to bring his considerable influence to bear on the procurement of the land at Palawai in a letter to Kamehameha III. The parcel of land in question was a portion of government land, designated as such during the Māhele. Eventually the land was granted to the Mormons by a Maui chief. Napela's letter to Kamehameha III hinted at how he conceived of the purpose of gathering: "The reasons of this leaving and abandoning our former places are these: Destruction is going to visit this Government, which destruction has been foretold by prophets...the second reasons for leaving....That our religion may go to Lānai...and the people will be taught there the deep things of God's kingdom, and where a person can live holy or not."[58]

Napela had accepted many of nineteenth-century Mormonism's millenarian tenets and conceptualized the gathering at least partially in these terms. Others did not. Many Native Hawaiian Mormons chose not to gather at Lāna'i, a fact that concerned and perplexed many of the *Haole* missionaries, and perhaps Napela as well. In a letter to Brigham Young, Silas Smith commented that the reasons many Native Hawaiian converts chose not to gather at Lāna'i included "the love for the places of their births; that they had sooner sacrifice their right to the kingdom of God than to leave their homes and gather with the Saints."[59] Native Hawaiian Saints were far from unanimous about the decision to gather at Lāna'i. It is hardly surprising that many of the *makā'ainana*, perhaps having recently received title to their own parcels of land, would not willingly abandon them at the behest of yet more *Haole*.

The community at Palawai, dubbed "Iosepa" in honor of Joseph Smith, lasted from 1854 until 1863 and can de divided into roughly two phases. The first was from 1854 to 1858, during which the settlement saw modest growth as Native Hawaiian Saints began to gather in small numbers in the Palawai Basin and plant crops both for their own use and for sale to the vessels in port at Honolulu and Lahaina. The second phase, from 1858 to

1863, was dominated by Walter Murray Gibson, whose later work in King David Kalakaua's administration in the 1880s made him a major figure in nineteenth-century Hawaiian history. Once settled in the Palawai Basin, the Saints began to focus their efforts on planting cash crops for sale to wintering ships in Honolulu and Lahaina harbors. Seeds for these crops came from other Mormon settlements in the West and included grapes, corn, melons, and potatoes. The harvests were modestly successful, but several factors put a damper on the early economic outlook of the community. An outbreak of worms plagued the early harvests, and the market for their goods was subject to fluctuating demand from whaling and trading vessels, which were in turn tied to global markets for Pacific products. Transportation of the crops to the markets proved a serious hurdle as well. This fledgling Mormon community operated in an environment in which Hawai'i's position in the Pacific maritime economy circumscribed the range of their decision making and their ultimate success.[60] In light of these failures, mission leaders as early as 1857 decided to begin searching for a new gathering place in the islands.

The event that ultimately ended the Palawai settlement and temporarily ended the Hawaiian mission took place thousands of miles to the east. In 1857 the US government ordered federal troops to Salt Lake City to quell what was seen at the time as a Mormon insurrection, the "Utah War." Once the Utah War had broken out, all of those engaged in foreign missions were called to return to the Salt Lake Valley. The Hawaiian Mission was officially closed in 1858, and the all *Haole* missionaries prepared to return to Utah. The Native Hawaiian Saints at Palawai were left in an ambiguous position: Iosepa was already on the brink of collapse and was about to be abandoned by the missionaries. Now the search for a new gathering place on the islands was halted, and the Native Hawaiian Saints in Iosepa were left in a sort of limbo, having to maintain and pay rent on land with scarce fresh water under trying economic circumstances. Between 1858 and 1861 Iosepa was left under the direction of two presidents, Kailihune and Solomona Pi'ipi'ilani, who continued church services and conferences and sent missionaries to other islands to try to win more converts.[61]

It was at this moment that Walter Murray Gibson arrived on the scene. Prior to his arrival in Hawai'i, Gibson was headed west, speaking wherever he could about the benefits of American colonization in Malaysia. Following a well-received lecture he gave on the subject in Salt Lake City, Gibson was baptized as a member of the Church of Jesus Christ of Latter-day Saints, and in 1861 Brigham Young sent him as a "roving missionary" west across the Pacific. Gibson stopped in Palawai and remained there. With a keen eye toward fulfilling his own personal ambitions, Gibson declared himself the leader of the church in the Pacific and took control of Iosepa, ushering in his own activities and methods of leadership and organization. It was obvious to the Native Hawaiian Saints that Gibson's methods differed radically from those of the previous Mormon missionaries, and they reported to Salt Lake City on his behavior. A party from Salt Lake City was sent to investigate the allegations, Gibson was excommunicated, and the same committee set about finding a more suitable gathering place for the dwindling number of faithful Native Hawaiian Saints.[62]

In the final analysis the Lāna'i cooperative Mormon community experiment had failed. In this respect it was like many of the other Mormon colonies established throughout the West, including San Bernardino, which was also abandoned at the time of the Utah War. But the decision was made to give up on Iosepa even before the *Haole* elders were called back to Utah. Although ultimately abandoned due to pressures on the church in Utah, the settlement faced other key challenges that would have ended the experiment anyway, including a less than stellar market for the goods they produced. Records from Iosepa indicate other issues, including a profound disconnect between Native Hawaiian Saints and *Haole* missionaries regarding the structure of such a cooperative community under the metaphor of the gathering.[63]

Although it is impossible to know for sure the assumptions with which the Native Hawaiian Saints approached Iosepa, they were undoubtedly different from those of their *Haole* counterparts. For the white missionaries, both the gathering place they chose and the way it operated revolved around models of Mormon communalism that exploited capitalist markets even as they sought to distance themselves from them. In this sense Mormon communalism was a strategic way of manipulating capitalism while circumventing what were perceived as its more corrosive aspects. At the heart of the model, the cooperative religious community produced goods not for subsistence but as commodities for the market, a model that differed significantly from Mormon settlements in Utah. In Iosepa Native Hawaiian Saints worked diligently when it came to tending their own plots of land, but seemed less than enthusiastic about working to produce goods for sale rather than for direct consumption in a communal setting.[64] For the Hawaiian Saints who came to Lāna'i, the gathering seemed to provide an opportunity to practice a familiar sort of communal subsistence organized under religious principles. They were willing (and perhaps needed) to leave the land that they worked and become *kama'aina* (literally "children of the land") in a new place. This would require them to create a new attachment to a specific place, while not abandoning more intelligible models of production and exchange. Such models were in fact a method by which attachment to a new place could be forged. In the aftermath of the Māhele, this strategy might have offered an effective way to cope with the onset of a new and impersonal capitalist system that tied them to processes beyond their control. The church and the gathering metaphor that it espoused offered an "alternative space to capitalism" and provided the trappings of a communal system that seemed more familiar and intelligible.[65]

As far as the missionaries were concerned, those who did not gather at Lānaʻi were less faithful than the others, unable to allow their commitment to Mormonism to trump their commitment to their own lands. Those who chose to gather, however, still experienced the volatility of capitalist markets, and although traditional Hawaiian methods of production and distribution of goods and resources were hardly free from fluctuations between scarcity and abundance, the Mormon communitarian model offered little better in the way of production and was based on foreign concepts of labor and reward. The Native Hawaiian Saints at Iosepa hoped to replicate something resembling the pre-Māhele model of community production. The missionaries' goal, however, was to change the labor patterns of Native Hawaiian converts to reflect Mormon notions of "civilization" and "industry."[66] The failure of Iosepa at Palawai proved a major blow for the struggling Mormons in Hawaiʻi. In the aftermath of Iosepa's collapse on Lānaʻi, the church searched for a new place to gather the Native Hawaiian Saints until they could emigrate to Zion.

The Move to Lāʻie

Seeing the mission on its last legs and the waning commitment of the converts who remained, a committee from Utah was sent by the First Presidency of the Church to choose a new gathering place and acquire land to resettle the Saints. This time church leaders acquired, nearly in its entirety, a large ahupuaʻa on northeastern Oʻahu. In January 1865 the missionaries purchased the approximately six-thousand-acre tract for $14,000 from Thomas Dougherty, a Scottish sea captain who had acquired the land from an aliʻi named Charles Kanaina. After the Gibson debacle on Lānaʻi, Oʻahu was deemed a far better location, closer to the capital in Honolulu. Adding to the importance of this shift was that the underlying economic model that was supposed to sustain Iosepa on Lānaʻi had now changed. The American whaling industry was severely curtailed by the adoption of kerosene as a fuel, and the island's economy in the years following the US Civil War moved toward the production of a crop that would dominate Hawaiʻi's and Lā'ie's future—sugar.[67] This shift in agricultural production between Lāna'i and Lā'ie, from diversified food crops to large-scale, single-crop production, would transform the gathering of the Native Hawaiian Saints and further complicate the relationship of the church to the larger landscape of Hawaiian politics and society. Lā'ie would remain the church's central project in the Pacific for more than a century, but not without serious strains to the metaphor of the gathering as it competed both in Hawai'i and Utah with the growing demands of increasingly powerful national interests and the capitalist modes of production that sustained them. Most important, Lā'ie was not an empty land. Separate from but nestled within it were many *kuleana* parcels, land granted to *makā'ainana* tenants in prior years as a result of the 1850 Kuleana Act. Although some of these residents were already members of the church, the result of Mormon missionary work in Lā'ie prior to 1850,[68] many were not, and difficulties with the new landowners continued to arise well into the twentieth century. (They still do.) The expansion of the Lā'ie Sugar Plantation in the late nineteenth and first half of the twentieth centuries would make these issues even more acute.[69]

From the beginning Lā'ie faced many of the same challenges Iosepa had in the Palawai Basin. Windswept, dry, and vulnerable to drought, only the northernmost portion of the *ahupua'a* was suitable for large-scale agriculture, watered by a set of springs famous since ancient times.[70] Lā'ie was one *ahupua'a* divided into two distinct parts. Lā'ie molo'o, the southern portion, was dry, barren, and treeless east of the foothills. Lā'ie wai, the northernmost portion, was watered by springs and a series of perennial streams that had formed the valley that snaked into the northern Ko'olau mountains. It was fertile and productive land for growing *kalo*, the traditional staple crop in Hawai'i. It was in this portion that the vast majority of the *kuleanas* were (and are) located. The name Lā'ie wai (*wai* is a general Hawaiian term referring to water) indicates the nature of the landscape in the northern portion of the *ahupua'a*. The central problem for the church in Lā'ie was the same as it had been on Lāna'i: the land had to somehow provide "enough financial viability to provide sustenance and work for the many Hawaiian converts they hoped would gather in Lāie."[71] For the mission to produce successful and reliable harvests, it would need a plentiful water supply. The shift to large-scale sugar production would only exacerbate the problem.

The change to sugar production in Lā'ie proved a labor-intensive affair. The cultivation and harvesting of sugar cane on the scale required for commercial production demands a large and dedicated workforce. Up until the early twentieth century in Lā'ie, that labor force was made up of Native Hawaiians, a situation found almost nowhere else in the islands. The comparatively large numbers of Hawaiians who continued to work on the

Lāʻie Sugar Plantation at a time when Native Hawaiian labor was generally replaced by imported Asian labor in Hawaiʻi was due to their desire "to maintain their connection to the ʻāina (land) in the face of encroaching commercial agriculture." This was accomplished through the use of the metaphor of the gathering—a concept that although understood differently by the Native Hawaiian Saints and the *Haole* missionaries, functioned intelligibly for the community and its mostly Native Hawaiian workforce into the early twentieth century. In the end the diminished importance of the gathering for the church both in Lāʻie and in Utah strained the metaphor that had maintained a shared sense of purpose between two different cultures and transformed the plantation into a place that more closely resembled the other plantations in Hawaiʻi with which it competed.[72] The beginnings of this strained metaphor are evident early on in Lāʻie's history and shaped several key events that in turn set the stage for a larger migration of Hawaiians to Utah under a peculiar set of circumstances.

From Whaling to Sugar

Sugar production dominated Hawaiʻi's economy from 1860 until the 1950s, but the beginnings of sugar production for sale to commercial markets began nearly two decades earlier. The transition to sugar as the dominant cash crop and staple of the Hawaiian economy was neither smooth nor immediate. It proceeded in a fashion one historian has accurately described as both "makeshift" and reflective of a "period of political and economic transformation."[73] Indeed, commercial agriculture was certainly nothing new to Hawaiʻi prior to the shift to sugar. The main business of supplying provisions to American whaling ships, augmented by the sale of produce, especially potatoes, to California, was central to the Hawaiian economy, along with the grog shops, brothels, and merchant houses that lined Honolulu's and Lahaina's streets. Potatoes from Jonathan Napela's large fields, described by Ephraim Green in 1852, most likely ended up in the cargo hold of an American ship, bound for either the North Pacific Japanese fishing grounds or San Francisco. But it would take the radical reforms of the Māhele to allow for the large-scale production of Hawaiʻi's most notable crop. The shift from whaling to sugar, then, was less a shift to commercial agriculture than in the type and scale of the products grown.[74]

Several developments in the global economy, along with the subsequent changes in the Hawaiian political landscape discussed previously, coalesced to produce the meteoric rise of sugar in Hawaiʻi. The history of the Church of Jesus Christ of Latter-day Saints's Hawaiian Mission was intimately tied to these shifts. The Māhele opened up lands for sale to foreigners, who converted them to sugar production and experimented with processing, refinement, and labor organization, with varying success. After 1851 the productive valleys and plains of California, ploughed and planted by waves of American settlers, provided the produce for the growing economy of the Far West, ending the market for Hawaiian export crops there. American whaling ships continued to visit Hawai'i in large numbers until the early 1860s, when the shift to kerosene as a fuel oil reduced the demand for whale oil globally. Finally, the American Civil War effectively ended sugar production in the South and created a giant demand for sugar, prodding *Haole* in Hawai'i with access to capital to consolidate land, labor, production, and management strategies to compete with the Caribbean and other sugar-producing areas.[75] The fact that none of these events happened simultaneously guaranteed a slow and bumpy transition.

In 1865, when the purchase of Lā'ie by the church was finalized and Hawaiian Saints from Lāna'i and other areas of the islands began to settle there, the plantation moved quickly from diversified crop production to full-scale sugar production in a "modified" plantation model. The downturn in production of food crops for sale and the growing demand for sugar in the United States, coupled with a more general shift to sugar production in Hawai'i, made it a seemingly logical choice for the missionaries. Had they anticipated the lack of compatibility between the collective religious model implied in the gathering metaphor and a plantation model of production, they might have reconsidered their decision. The challenge before the missionaries, who were tasked with managing the plantation and its labor force, was to achieve a balance in Lā'ie among a plantation, a mission, and a gathering place. From the perspective of the missionaries, however, this was less a conscious balance to be maintained than a taken-for-granted situation. The model of the mission rested on organizational principles developed in Jackson County, Missouri, and Nauvoo, Illinois, and adapted to the Great Basin environment. The key difference in the mind of the missionaries was the purpose of the settlement. Instead of being a community of equals, the missionaries envisioned themselves tasked with uplifting the Lamanites in the islands.

Between 1865 and 1874 the church plantation at Lā'ie worked toward realizing its managers' goals to become a profitable sugar production and refining facility with the capacity to supply the growing Utah market with its product. To this end the plantation managers, who served in a dual capacity as the presidency of the Hawaiian mission for the church, enjoyed a good measure of support from the Native Hawaiian Saints gathered in Lā'ie. Numerous letters written to Utah from various plantation managers during this period, many of which were reprinted in the *Deseret News*, a Salt Lake City–based and Mormon-owned publication, attest to this fact. Due to the long period of time between the establishment of the plantation and its ability to realize profits, both *Haole* missionaries and Native Hawaiian Saints cultivated various crops both to sell and to feed themselves. Native Hawaiians worked in a variety of roles—planting, harvesting, and refining sugar in the newly constructed mill and tending their own *lo'i*, or *kalo* patches, to provide food for themselves and their families. In addition, both *Haole* missionaries and Native Hawaiian Saints built homes, storage facilities, and buildings for religious worship, as well as maintaining their own residences. Missionary responsibilities were also shared; a period of time working on the plantation when the demand for labor was high would generally give way to a stint as a missionary on another island or another region on O'ahu, only to return again to labor on the plantation for another season. Although the majority of Native Hawaiian converts did not gather at Lā'ie, the expectation was that all would eventually gather in preparation for the time when they could relocate either as a collective body or in small groups to participate in the larger gathering in the Great Basin.[76]

The goal of establishing Lā'ie as a plantation based on sugar production was articulated early, with a keen eye toward a political climate in Hawai'i that pointed to success. In October 1867 plantation manager George Nebeker, who had also financed the purchase of the plantation on behalf of the church, made clear his ultimate vision for Lā'ie:

> Our improvements have been mostly in houses and fencing.... [W]e have recently put in a crop of sugar cane.... My opinion is, that this land could be made to produce sugar, with the necessary machinery, that would go far to supply the increasing demands in Utah. It is expected that the Reciprocity Treaty, now being negotiated with the United States government... will make this the most feasible point to obtain our supply of sugar for Utah.[77]

Nebeker's statement is revealing in several ways. First, Mormon missionaries, at least in this case, consciously sought to benefit not only from the availability of fee-simple land to noncitizens following the Māhele, but also from political changes that fostered the growth of a larger plantation economy in Hawai'i. Unlike many American planters, however, Nebeker's vision reveals the equally self-conscious connection between the plantation and the Mormon empire, still actively pursued by Brigham Young in the Great Basin and distinct from what Mormons viewed as the unwelcome presence of the United States in the Mormon Zion. Reporting in Mormon news outlets in the Great Basin like the *Deseret News* continued to reveal the ways that Mormons distinguished their presence in Hawai'i from that of other Christian groups, despite obviously similar connections between the plantation as a producer of raw materials for a religious, not a secular, state. By the end of 1868 missionaries at Lā'ie began assembling the machinery of the sugar mill, and by the middle of 1869 they were producing samples that they then introduced to the Utah market.

The effort to establish a profitable plantation made slow but steady progress between 1866 and 1874. The first object of the missionaries was to persuade the unconvinced of the purpose of Lā'ie and its benefits, both spiritual and temporal. "It was suspected," wrote George Nebeker in 1866, "that the native brethren would gather to Lā'ie for the purpose of improving their condition by laboring under the direction of the servants of God and receive a just renumeration for their labors."[78] The "improvement of their condition," a goal that implied a current condition both spiritually and temporally unsound from the missionaries' perspective, meant turning their hands at least partially to nonsubsistence labor and their hearts toward a less ambiguous manifestation of acceptable Mormon religious mores. For the Native Hawaiian Saints who chose to gather in Lā'ie, it would not be long before the focus of a large portion of their labor was expected to be sugar production and the emerging plantation economy. This delicate balance proved nearly impossible to achieve in the context of two fundamentally different approaches to the gathering metaphor—that of the *Haole* missionaries and that of the Hawaiian Saints.[79]

The *'Awa* Rebellion

The most obvious rupture in that model, one that missionary Harvey Cluff later called "the most serious affair that has transpired in the Hawaiian mission save that of Walter Gibson," occurred in 1874. The event that has come to be known as the "*'Awa* Rebellion" is remembered far less often and is accorded far less importance than the Gibson affair at Lāna'i. That this is the case can perhaps be attributed to the fact that it did not coincide with the closing of the Hawaiian mission or abandonment of the gathering project underway at Lā'ie, as was the case at the Palawai Basin. What the "*'Awa* Rebellion" resulted in, however, was a decisive split in the community of Native Hawaiian Saints at Lā'ie and the establishment of an alternate gathering place for those Saints organized under a separate and distinctively Native Hawaiian communitarian model that responded directly to both the Māhele and its aftermath.

'Awa was almost certainly brought to the islands by the first people who discovered and settled the Hawaiian archipelago. It is a tuber that is ground into a fine powder, mixed with water, and drunk in ceremonial or social settings throughout Oceania. Its effects are mildly intoxicating, and it produces a calming, almost lethargic sensation when consumed in large amounts. 'Awa was also used medicinally to cure a variety of ailments. In 1850 it was illegal to drink 'awa in Hawai'i, its consumption no doubt being lumped in with alcoholism as an affront to the move toward temperance. 'Awa was grown on the Lā'ie plantation both as a cash crop and for community consumption, a practice that was rarely mentioned by Haole missionaries prior to the 'Awa Rebellion.

A new mission president, Frederick A. H. Mitchell, arrived and took leadership of both the mission and plantation in June 1873. Mitchell's actions throughout his life revealed "a zealous and dogmatic nature."[80] In addition to his lack of experience in Hawai'i, Mitchell's abrasive personality provoked confrontations with Mormon and Gentile alike throughout his life. Upon his arrival in Lā'ie, his unfortunate tendency toward imprudent behavior continued unabated. Mitchell was concerned about the use of 'awa, as well as its cultivation on the plantation as a cash crop.

Shortly after his arrival at Lā'ie plantation, Mitchell ordered the entire 'awa crop destroyed, announcing his decision at a leisurely community gathering and invoking "the ancient custom of the konohiki (head man of an ahupua'a) when proclaiming the law of the land."[81] Both Mitchell's decision and his method of communicating it to Lā'ie residents caused widespread anger. The current 'awa crop was worth "several thousand dollars," a considerable sum for the still cash-strapped residents of Lā'ie, who in the mid-1870s were responsible for payment of a variety of taxes in cash only. As the acting konohiki and plantation owner, Mitchell enjoyed exemption from these taxes, a fact that many of the Lā'ie makā'ainana may have known.[82] The destruction of the 'awa with no notice was certainly viewed as unreasonable by both the Native Hawaiian Saints and the Haole missionaries.[83] The Native Hawaiian Saints' anger at what they no doubt considered arbitrary and unfair treatment provoked a response that was intelligible from their perspective: they prepared to leave the ahupua'a of Lā'ie and relocate in the nearby ahupua'a of Kahana, some ten miles to the south. This decision had a precedent in Hawaiian culture as a response to a konohiki or ali'i who was cruel or reticent in performing his duties as defined in the reciprocal relationship between the ali'i and the makā'ainana. In retaliation for this defiance of his ecclesiastical authority, however, Mitchell moved to "disfellowship" the group from the church. Undeterred, the 'awa "rebels" pooled their resources and purchased the ahupua'a of Kahana.[84]

The Kahana Hui was part of a larger Hui movement throughout the islands. The word *hui* can be used as a noun to mean "group" or "club," and when used as a verb means to "gather" or to "band together." The Hui movement was an attempt by *makā'ainana* to resist alienation from their *kuleana* lands, awarded at the time of the Māhele, by encroaching (mostly *Haole*) speculators using recent changes to Hawaiian law to acquire Hawaiian lands. The Hui movement responded to this disenfranchisement using "legal arrangements that were uniquely Hawaiian" and "sprang up spontaneously from the people." The Hui movement is important because it represents a proactive counter by Native Hawaiians to encroaching Western land-tenure systems using Western legal means. Embedded within the Hui solution was a conscious return to pre-Māhele forms of social and economic organization that emphasized cooperation and community decision making.[85] The Hui system established *luna*, a designation akin to a manager or a supervisor, who shared power with Hui members, each of whom purchased a portion of land within a specific *ahupua'a* both to cultivate and as a home lot. The designation of these land parcels guaranteed, as in pre-Māhele times, that the occupant would have access to the all of the resources of the *ahupua'a*, from the sea to the upland areas, in addition to a home lot and a set number of *lo'i* to cultivate. The *luna* acted as an arbiter of disputes should they arise and as the spokesperson and manager of the Hui's total holdings. Far from wielding arbitrary power, the *luna* was required to act in the interests of the collective. Failure to do so could and in the case of the Kahana Hui did result in the dismissal of a designated *luna*. In all of these roles, relationships between the *luna* and the individual parcel holders reflected the relationship between *ali'i* and *makā'ainana* prior to the advent of Western land-tenure systems. As mentioned previously, although the Māhele granted some *makā'ainana* parcels of land in fee simple, it often severed their access to resources from the upland areas and the ocean, resources on which their continued subsistence depended. In addition, it cut off their reciprocal relationship with the *ali'i*.[86] The Kahana Hui operated in a decidedly pre-Māhele manner, restoring access to all of the resources of the *ahupa'a* as well as re-creating in a new setting the relationship between the "new *ali'i*" and the *makā'ainana*. In at least two respects, however, the Kahana Hui was unique: the composition of its membership and the religious nature of its original organization.[87]

The Kahana Hui was composed of both old-time residents and *kuleana* awardees of Kahana as well as residents of Lā'ie from other areas of the islands who were part of the group disaffected by Mitchell's heavy-handed leadership. Some of these Kahana residents had originally gathered at Lā'ie and were now returning to the place of their birth in Kahana. The Kahana

Hui's decision to purchase the entire *ahupua'a* of Kahana rather than simply purchase selected *kuleana* parcels indicated that the control of all Kahana according to the precepts of Hawaiian social organization was a priority. This purchase was facilitated in part by the fact that one of the early Kahana Hui members, Miriam Kekuku, was married to the *Pāke* (Chinese) Ahmee, who had purchased the *ahupua'a* several years earlier.[88] Although the Kahana Hui did not prohibit non-Mormons from becoming members, the vast majority of its members were indeed Mormons, and some of the Hawaiians not originally from Kahana were allowed into the Hui based on their church membership.

This heavily Mormon component of the Kahana Hui is a point worth considering. It is not surprising that the Hui's original members were Mormons; the Hui was made up of a large number of the disfellowshipped members from Lā'ie.[89] But the fact that the Kahana Hui favored Mormon members and continued to prioritize their full fellowship in the Mormon Church suggests that the move to Kahana was not a rejection of their religious faith but a conscious effort to create a social and economic model that the *Haole* plantation managers and mission presidents in Lā'ie could not. The organization of the Kahana Hui as a collective body according to traditional Hawaiian concepts of reciprocal obligation between *ali'i* and *makā'ainana* was an attempt by a group of Hawaiian Saints to succeed in executing the principle of the gathering where they felt Lā'ie had failed. The Kahana Saints retained strong ties with Lā'ie, enjoyed good relationships with later *Haole* mission leaders and plantation managers, and formed a core component of the Hawaiian Saints who migrated to Utah in 1889. They did not, however, rejoin the Saints in Lā'ie even after Mitchell's departure. The Kahana Saints constructed the first Mormon chapel on O'ahu in 1879 (which still stands today), and many sold their Hui shares at Kahana to pay for the journey to Utah. The Kahana Hui organized the landscape based on the *ahupua'a* system, and this commitment to Native Hawaiian cultural practices remedied some of the failures of the gathering principle both on Lāna'i and in Lā'ie.

Gathering to Zion

Like the Iosepa community on Lāna'i, Lā'ie was not originally seen as an alternative to Utah as a gathering place. Rather, it was viewed as a temporary place for the Hawaiian Saints to prepare to gather to Zion in Utah. This preparation, as mentioned previously, was a conscious attempt on the part of Mormon missionaries and church leaders to alter Native Hawaiian notions of collective social organization to match Mormon models.

Like the Palawai Basin on Lāna'i, Lā'ie was a landscape perceived by Hawaiians and *Haole* in two very different ways. Native Hawaiian Saints viewed the *ahupua'a* of Lā'ie in Hawaiian terms. Its resources were distributed from the mountainous uplands and extended beyond the beach and onto the reefs and into the waters farther offshore. Subsistence for any household was accomplished through access to all of these resources. *Haole* missionaries perceived the landscape differently. Lā'ie was a desirable location not because the *ahupua'a* could be purchased whole, which retained access to all of its resources, but because of its large plain and relatively stable access to water. Its resources, from this perspective, were distributed and diverse, but in very different ways. George Nebeker described Lā'ie in 1866, assessing its potential according to the agrarian sensibilities honed in the Great Basin: "We have some three miles of coast...there are 500 acres of good, arable land lying near the sea beach, the remainder is grazing and timber land."[90] The beach, as well as the reefs that lay beyond it, were not factored in by Nebeker as a resource. It was essentially unproductive space, despite the vast resources that could be gleaned from it. The difference between Native Hawaiian and *Haole* conceptions of Lā'ie was remedied by the Kahana Hui with their purchase of the *ahupua'a* of Kahana.

Perceiving landscapes is part of the work of culture, and it is a key determinant of how social relationships function politically, economically, and in the case of the Mormons, ecclesiastically. Religious beliefs and the unique circumstances Mormons found at the foot of the Rocky Mountains in Utah shaped Mormon ideas of how religious communities ought to function practically.[91] This language of sacred space, embodied in the encompassing metaphor of the gathering, shaped Mormon perceptions of Hawaiian landscapes. Replicating Great Basin agrarian organization in Lā'ie and organizing the labor of the Hawaiian Saints accordingly was one way the missionaries hoped to prepare them for the ultimate purpose of gathering them in Utah. Although the missionaries experienced challenges in this project, many of the Native Hawaiian Saints were indeed eager to gather in Utah, and many traveled there between 1874 and 1889. Once there, Native Hawaiian Saints would be forced to negotiate a new landscape, one that was also conceptualized in competing ways by both Mormons and non-Mormons. Native Hawaiian Mormons also internalized the gathering concept, but fit this pliable metaphor into models that provided a viable remedy to the massive changes in the Hawaiian political economy that dispossessed Hawaiians of their lands and livelihoods, forcing them onto plantations. The adoption of the gathering concept by Hawaiian Saints tempered "some of the more onerous aspects of plantation life" in Lā'ie,[92] but ruptures in the tenuous balance of this shared metaphor produced reactions by Hawaiians that skillfully balanced new political realities with traditional Hawaiian strategies of community organization.[93]

Beginning with the publication of Greg Dening's *Islands and Beaches* in 1980, historians of Oceania have come to accept the existence of culturally specific metaphors, "products of consciousness" that organize the worldviews of individuals and communities. A metaphor functions as an "instrument of daily understanding within a closed system." While these metaphors are hardly static and are subject to constant reevaluation by both individuals and communities based on new situations and experiences, they often retain their importance as models for understanding, even in the face of challenges to their utility posed by radical shifts in social, economic, and political circumstances. When people meet in the shifting landscapes of history, the metaphors they bring with them meet as well. The metaphor of "the gathering," a concept central to nineteenth-century Mormon theology, became the main terrain on which Native Hawaiian converts to Mormonism and Mormon *Haole* missionaries attempted to organize their relationships. Ultimately this concept affected the ways both Native Hawaiian and *Haole* Mormons in Hawai'i and eventually Utah perceived the landscapes they shared and the ways they organized their unique communities. The landscapes of their own histories gave further meaning to these encounters. For Native Hawaiian Saints, the radical changes in political organization and land tenure between 1820 and 1855 informed their understanding of the gathering doctrine in ways that were unintelligible to the missionaries. Native Hawaiians saw the gathering as a means to adapt traditional models to new realities. The Mormon concept of gathering relied on perceiving space in very specific ways. While both Native Hawaiian converts and *Haole* missionaries in Hawai'i agreed on the concept of the gathering in principle, when it came time to put that principle into practice in Lāna'i and Lā'ie, the differences in perceptions of landscapes within the same metaphor became apparent.

CHAPTER 3

Early Native Hawaiian Migration to the Salt Lake Valley

Beginning around 1874, roughly the time when the Kahana Hui was formed, small groups of Native Hawaiian Mormons began visiting and settling in the Salt Lake Valley. Most accompanied *Haole* missionaries returning to Utah. Restrictions on emigration from Hawai'i that had been put in place to fight rapid depopulation, combined with lack of financial means to pay for the journey, prevented a larger emigration of Hawaiian Saints to Utah between 1865 and 1889. In 1887 emigration laws were relaxed somewhat with the ratification of the "Bayonet Constitution," and Native Hawaiian emigration to Salt Lake City increased almost immediately.

Native Hawaiians who migrated to Utah in the late nineteenth century left a place in transition and turmoil. They had devised specific strategies to negotiate Hawai'i's shift to a plantation economy. Their destination in Utah proved equally tumultuous. Communities throughout the American West in the late nineteenth century grew quickly and haphazardly. Westward expansion proceeded in an irregular fashion, following boom-and-bust economic cycles as the finite resources of various regions were extracted and shipped to distant cities in the East and beyond. Richard White used the metaphor of a stream to describe the nature of westward migration in the nineteenth century:

> In the nineteenth century the stream of people that flowed from east to west was a river compared to the smaller migrations from Mexico north and across the Pacific from east to west. But this migration was not analogous to a wall of water advancing and flooding all the land as it goes. Even when it is a flood, a stream does not evenly cover the surrounding countryside. A stream in

flood...overflows its banks and covers the low-lying ground first. Our meta-phorical low-lying ground in the West was, however, often in fact high and mountainous. The migratory stream in the 1840's inundated agricultural lands along the Pacific Coast in Oregon and California and along the Wasatch Front in Utah, but it also covered the mountains of California during the Gold Rush of 1849. Afterwards, mineral rushes, like flash floods in the mountains, distrib-uted mining camps through the mountains of Idaho, Montana, Colorado, Utah, Nevada, Arizona, New Mexico, and South Dakota between 1850 and 1890.[1]

The nature of these settlements and of the economic forces that shaped them meant that most western settlers worked for wages or made a living serving large and growing populations of wage laborers.[2] The territory of Utah boasted an added level of complexity. Religious antagonism between the Mormon settlers and the expanding population of non-Mormon set-tlers grew as both groups increased in number. Despite the dependence of Utah's economy on trade with settlers migrating west and on the influx of mining-related capital, Mormons resented the presence of "Gentiles" in Utah and did little to maintain amicable relations with their new neigh-bors. Non-Mormons were equally contemptuous of the Mormons, whose behavior seemed incongruous with the attitudes of mainstream eastern Protestant beliefs. Nineteenth-century Mormons valued cooperation over competition; resented the United States for past injustices; demonstrated ultimate allegiance to their ecclesiastical leaders (notably Brigham Young); and most disturbingly for non-Mormons, practiced polygamy. This pecu-liar and antagonistic relationship between Mormons and non-Mormons in Utah laid the foundation for the development of a unique "Mormon culture region," separate and distinct from the rest of the American West economically, socially, and politically. Mormons strove to maintain their dominance over the region's economic and social life by translating their numerical superiority into electoral victory. As non-Mormons vigorously resisted their efforts, this ideological struggle came to define the region's unique culture.[3] According to White, Mormons were the sole group in the American West that attempted to "alter basic family, economic, and gov-ernmental structures prevailing in the East."[4] That they would run afoul of later generations of migrants to the Utah territory seems inevitable.

The Native Hawaiians entered this maelstrom in a precarious position: as Mormons, they sided with their coreligionists in the pitched battles over political, economic, and cultural hegemony in the Great Basin. But they also experienced discrimination at the hands of white Mormons in the region, whose attitudes toward people they considered racially infe-rior mirrored those of most settlers in the American West. For the vast majority of white settlers, African Americans, Mexican Americans, Native Americans, and Asian American and Eastern European immigrants in the early twentieth century occupied a lower rung on the social ladder. Race and class remained largely inseparable categories in the American West throughout the nineteenth and twentieth centuries. Native Hawaiian settlers came to occupy a similar position in the West's social and economic hierarchies.[5]

Hawaiian settlers in the Great Basin were forced to negotiate the shifting economic, political, and social landscapes of the American West. They experienced it as both Native Hawaiians and Mormons, and this hybrid identity undoubtedly shaped their reactions to and interactions with the people and places of a very foreign landscape. Beginning with three stories, this chapter traces early Native Hawaiian immigration into the Great Basin, explores popular representations of Pacific Islanders in Utah and the West, and examines the pressures that mounted and eventually forced the expulsion of the Hawaiian Saints from Salt Lake City and the consequent formation of the Iosepa colony in Skull Valley in 1889.

"THE FIRST OF THAT RACE WHO HAS VISITED THIS COUNTRY"

By 1869 Jonatana Napela had already been a member of the Church of Jesus Christ of Latter-day Saints for eighteen years. His work as a Hawaiian language teacher, assisting George Q. Cannon in translating the Book of Mormon into Hawaiian, and as a missionary for the church throughout the islands gained him the friendship and admiration of dozens of *Haole* missionaries and church officials. His chiefly rank made him a person of authority who commanded a high degree of respect among Native Hawaiian Saints as well. Napela was a graduate of Lahainaluna Seminary, a district court judge in Wailuku from 1848 to 1851, and a merchant who sold the produce grown on his land to foreign ships in Lahaina and Honolulu. The first Mormon chapel built in Hawai'i, in Pulehu, Maui, was on land donated to the church by Napela. He had a long-standing desire to see Salt Lake City firsthand, but restrictions on emigration for Hawaiian subjects prevented him from making this journey. In the spring of 1869, however, his opportunity to visit Utah finally came. On June 22 of that year Napela left Honolulu with George Nebeker on the *D.C. Murray*, bound for San Francisco. They carried with them a substantial amount of the sweet products of Lā'ie plantation, samples of sugar and molasses bound for the Utah market. Arriving in San Francisco after a three-week journey, Napela and Nebeker continued on to Salt Lake City by train. Napela spent nearly six months in Utah, observing the territory and the people who lived there.

During his stay Napela attended the temple, a significant religious experience not available to church members in Hawai'i, where he was also "baptized as a proxy for King Kamehameha I." He had a portrait taken by Salt Lake City photographer Charles R. Savage and met with the prophet and president of the church, Brigham Young. Napela's observations of Utah's people, country, and customs survive in a letter he wrote to Young nearly eighteen months after their meeting. The letter included Napela's report on his journey to Lotu Kapua'iwa, Kāmehameha V, immediately after his return to the islands in November 1869. Napela's opinion of Utah and its people was favorable, and his admiration of Young as both a religious and political leader comes across as genuine even though the reader is Young himself. Although this also probably explains the lack of any negative observations about Utah on Napela's part, he was clearly impressed by what he saw. His conversation with the king, according to the letter, dwelled on matters both spiritual and worldly. Napela explained to the king the significance of the temple garment, which all Mormons who have entered the temple are required to wear, and conveyed to the king what he perceived as the spiritual nature of Young's impressive power in the region. Napela returned to Lāʻie after his journey, presumably conveying his favorable impressions of the land that had sent the "white men from the Rocky Mountains" whose religion so many had elected to follow. All this stoked many others' desire to gather permanently to Zion.[6]

"HE LABORED AS A CARPENTER ON THE TEMPLE BLOCK"

Like Jonatana Napela, John W. Kauleinamoku made the journey to Salt Lake City in the late nineteenth century. After completing a mission to the South Kii district in Kona, Kauleinamoku apparently found a way around the law that prohibited any "native subject of the King...to emigrate to California or any other foreign country." In January 1875 he accompanied Frederick Mitchell east, relocating to Utah permanently. Described as an "intelligent native and fluent speaker," Kauleinamoku was popular among Salt Lake City Mormons. He addressed the assembled Saints at the semiannual conference in April 1875, and his remarks in Hawaiian became the subject of a satirical "translation" in the *Salt Lake Tribune*'s coverage of the event by the paper's non-Mormon editors seeking to malign the Mormon practice of polygamy. In the late spring of 1876 a party of six Hawaiians traveled to Salt Lake City with the returning missionary Alma L. Smith. Accompanying this group was a woman named Likibeka, who journeyed to Utah "for the purpose of uniting in marriage with Kauleinamoku." Kauleinamoku and his new wife were included in an 1884 Salt Lake City directory, in which he was described as being employed as a "stone-cutter."

Around 1887 Kauleinamoku was called on a mission to New Zealand. He returned to find work as carpenter building the Salt Lake City temple. At some point during this period he purchased a lot and built a home in the Warm Springs district in Salt Lake City, an inexpensive, working-class neighborhood of Scandinavian migrants and Native American families on the outskirts of the city. By the time he returned from his mission in 1889, the community of Native Hawaiian Saints living in Salt Lake had grown considerably, as had the tensions between Mormons and non-Mormons over political control in the years leading up to statehood. Several other Native Hawaiian families joined Kauleinamoku in the Warm Springs district and found themselves underemployed and generally ostracized by white Utahns. Tensions between the growing Native Hawaiian community and white residents of Salt Lake City erupted in 1888 with a single diagnosed case of leprosy in a Native Hawaiian resident. Kauleinamoku was chosen to represent the community on a committee tasked with finding a place to relocate the Hawaiians outside of the city. When the Rich ranch in Skull Valley was selected, Kauleinamoku and his family left their home and moved to the new community, which they named Iosepa. He remained a community leader and confidant of Joseph F. Smith, who was ordained prophet of the Mormon Church in 1892, and they remained in close correspondence up to the time of Kauleinamoku's death. Sometime in the 1890s Kauleinamoku contracted leprosy, and he died in Iosepa on July 21, 1899.[7]

"HE ACQUIRED A HOME AND MADE A MODEST LIVING"

Solomona Piʻipiʻilani lived an incredible life that spanned nearly the entire nineteenth century. He was born sometime around 1800, well before Kāmehameha I consolidated his rule over the entire Hawaiian archipelago. He was a young man, probably in his early twenties, when the ʻaikapu was broken and the first Calvinist missionaries arrived. One of the earliest Native Hawaiian converts to Mormonism, Piʻipiʻilani joined the gathering at Iosepa in Lānaʻi in 1854, then went on to Lāʻie in 1865. Although there is no evidence that he left Lāʻie with the Kahana Hui, his reaction to Frederick Mitchell's ban on ʻawa growing and consumption was to steal some of his own confiscated crop back. After his wife died in 1879, he emigrated to Utah with his granddaughter. He left Salt Lake City when the decision was made to relocate the Native Hawaiian Saints to Iosepa; he died there at the age of ninety-one in 1892. Although we know far less about the details of Piʻipiʻilani's life, we know he experienced three-quarters of a century of transformation in his homeland of Hawai'i and a good deal more in his adopted home in the American West. Indeed, the century in which he lived was one of radical transformation globally. Despite his modest circumstances, his was no common life.[8]

Whatever the differences may have been between Native Hawaiian Mormons who gathered in the Salt Lake Valley in the late nineteenth century and their European and American coreligionists, they shared a religious ideology that interpreted the landscape around them in deeply spiritual terms. This was no temporary gathering place, no way station for Saints in the preparatory stages of building the Kingdom of God on Earth. This was Zion, and the battle there between the servants of God and those who served Mammon was in full swing throughout the last four decades of the nineteenth century. Regardless of their ethnic, national, or personal backgrounds, faithful Latter-day Saints were expected to demonstrate total obeisance to the church in spiritual and temporal affairs, and the division between the two was a fuzzy one. The full frontal assault of "Gentile" forces in the valleys along the Wasatch Front posed a constant and unending threat to Mormon solidarity and success in pursuing their communitarian vision and their quest for a theocratic empire, a literal Kingdom of God that would someday spread beyond the mountains and encompass the entire earth. The antagonistic and often hostile relations between the US government and the Mormons, led through most of this period by Brigham Young, was the clash of two empires with mutually exclusive plans for the same piece of real estate in the American West.[9]

Mormons in the West interpreted everything—the surrounding landscapes, their removal west, and the region's indigenous inhabitants—in overtly religious terms that drew from both the Bible and the Book of Mormon. Fancying themselves both literally and figuratively the children of Israel in the "latter days," the Mormons remade the trek west as a modern-day exodus led by a prophet to the Lord's promised land, a region which, despite the pressures that they faced from "Gentiles," the Lord had given to them to rightfully possess and make use of as they saw fit. Native Hawaiian Saints who immigrated into the valley had internalized this perspective and the religious narratives that sustained it, at least in some sense. As for converts elsewhere, the doctrinal imperative of the gathering at work in the nineteenth century created a strong pull eastward for many Native Hawaiian converts.

EARLY HAWAIIAN MIGRATION TO THE SALT LAKE VALLEY

At a semiannual conference of the Hawaiian Mission of the Church of Jesus Christ of Latter-day Saints in Honolulu in 1869, Elder William W. Cluff ended his address on the publishing of the Book of Mormon in Hawaiian with the following words: "I am soon going to return home, and hope that when we meet again it will be in Zion."[10] In the years of uncertainty after the excommunication of Walter Murray Gibson and before the church's gathering project in Lāʻie established itself financially, there was every reason to wish for the accomplishment of the original goal of the Native Hawaiian Saints to gather in the Great Basin. Following Napela's 1869 visit, many Native Hawaiian Mormons were eager to gather to Zion, the center of the Kingdom of God in the "Mauna Pohaku" (Rocky Mountains).[11] However, the legal and financial challenges of moving the Native Hawaiian Saints remained, and until such time as they could afford the trip, Lāʻie would serve as the temporary gathering place in Hawaiʻi. San Bernardino, the original location chosen to gather the Saints from all regions of Oceania, was abandoned in 1857, about the same time that Iosepa in the Palawai Basin was. The desire of many members to emigrate did not abate, and *Haole* missionaries from Utah continued to encourage Native Hawaiian Saints to emigrate to Zion.

A *Deseret News* reprint of a letter from Harvey H. Cluff, the president of the Hawaiian Mission, revealed the multilayered reasons that the *Haole* missionaries, at least, thought it advisable to relocate Native Hawaiian Saints to Utah: "The Hawaiian race sank so deeply and rapidly into sin and vice introduced by foreigners, that we find it a task of great magnitude to persuade them [this people] to abandon those evils and take a course to perpetuate the race."[12] Like many *Haole* observers in the late nineteenth century, Cluff reasoned that the blame for the continuing depopulation of the islands rested with Native Hawaiians, a result of their giving in to foreign vices. The way to "perpetuate the race," in Cluff's mind, was to relocate Native Hawaiian Saints to Utah. Accomplishing this would accomplish both their temporal and spiritual salvation. Acknowledging the legal challenges to relocating, Cluff wrote: "Should the scheme now being agitated, to annex these islands to the United States, be carried into effect, then there will be an opening to emigrate some of our native members to a congenial part of Utah." The early annexationist movement in Hawaiʻi found temporary allies in the Mormon missionaries, not for any love of the US government, which was seen as a repressive entity in Utah, but because it would presumably remove the legal restrictions that prevented gathering Native Hawaiian Saints to Zion. Meanwhile, Native Hawaiians were forced to deal with the increasingly acrimonious political climate of the 1880s at home.

The 1880s were a tumultuous decade for the Hawaiian monarchy, led by King David Kalākaua. The decade ended with the king being forced to sign a constitution that stripped him of nearly all his power. King Kalākaua's subtle and not so subtle moves to legitimize his rule and win the support of his Native Hawaiian subjects, especially his resurrection of the *hula* and other forms of Native Hawaiian cultural expressions, which had long been banned by the missionaries, outraged the *Haole* business community. Kalākaua and representatives of the Hawaiian National Party managed to attract the majority of Native Hawaiian voters in the elections of 1884 and 1886, an outcome that signaled to the *Haole* business elite that "the Native electorate had finally been corrupted beyond all redemption." Although there were many Native Hawaiian voters who rejected Kalākaua's lavish and expensive displays on the grounds of moral and fiscal responsibility, voting against him meant supporting a *Haole* elite that both thought them inferior and sought greater political control at their expense.[13] The effects of the Bayonet Constitution of 1887, as it came to be called, extended far beyond merely limiting the powers of the monarch. The new constitution "significantly altered the meaning of citizenship and nationhood in the kingdom" and redefined suffrage requirements, disenfranchising huge numbers of Native Hawaiians and transferring political power to a nonciti-zen *Haole* elite.[14]

Kalākaua remained an important visitor to Lāʻie and was welcomed there on several occasions with an appropriate degree of pomp and ceremony. Kalākaua's 1882 visit to Lāʻie was recorded in the journal of mission presi-dent Harvey H. Cluff, who described it in detail and transcribed portions of the king's address. Cluff was clearly impressed with Kalākaua, referring to him even in his personal journal as "His Majesty." After a royal welcome for the monarch that included a decorated gate, welcoming banner, and double file procession, Kalākaua addressed his subjects from the veranda of the mission home. Cluff's description of the king supports the notion of a monarch who worked to demonstrate his affinity with and concern for his Native Hawaiian subjects. Following the introductions and a tour of the *ahupuaʻa*, Cluff recorded Kalākaua's address to the crowd and the reactions of the Native Hawaiian Saints of Lāʻie to his speech.

The King warmly shook with all of us, which greeting was feelingly returned. . . . [He] was dressed in plain suit of blue flannel pants and red overshirt-the uniform of his retinue-and could not have been recognized as a King by strangers. . . . [H]e is easy in his manner, sociable, and is certainly the finest specimen of a native that I have had the pleasure of seeing since my sojourn on these islands. . . . Our great chief, Kamehameha left a memorial which marks his reign, and it claims that the old men and women slept in safety on the highways. Kamehameha II left another memorial which marked his reign, he abolished the kapus so that all can eat together. Kamehameha III also left his memorial and said-"The good are my people." These are the three eras in modern Hawaiian history. Now what shall I do to mark my reign, what shall be done to signalize it? This is my grand desire-to witness an increase in the population of these Islands. But I cannot do this alone, you must assist me. I see before me the plants which we must nourish in order to increase the population. You parents must take care of your sons and daughters that they may become good citizens. Teach them to become industrious, and to work that they may have good homes. I have observed that where they are industrious as here, they are numerous as here and healthy (Mr. Mitchell told His Majesty that the births in this colony numbered thirty within six months.) I am gratified to hear this statement and hope it will continue.

Cluff noted that "when the King started out in the aisle...the people took a general stampede, seizing His hand and Kissing it with the greatest affection.... [T]he interest which the present King has taken in his subjects has already won for him laurels in the estimation of his people and also in the estimation of foreigners."[15] Kalākaua made several return visits to Lāʻie, on one occasion laying the cornerstone for the I Hemolele chapel at its dedication in 1883. This close relationship with the community of Lāʻie, as indicated in the journals of *Haole* missionaries serving at the time, suggests that a strong majority of the Native Hawaiian Saints supported Kalākaua throughout the difficult 1880s. However, rather than acquiescing to the king's request to remain in the islands and contribute to the growth of the Native Hawaiian population, many Native Hawaiian Mormons continued to pursue their goal of gathering in Zion with their fellow Saints.

The method devised to circumvent Hawaiʻi's emigration laws was for small groups of Native Hawaiians to obtain special permission from the government to migrate with missionaries returning to Utah. This was undoubtedly made easier by Kalākaua's 1875 trip, during which he stopped in Utah en route to Washington, D.C. The first group of Hawaiians to emigrate to the Great Basin were "three juvenile Sandwich Islanders," who came to Utah in 1873 with William King, a returning Elder who had been on a mission to Hawaiʻi with his family for three years.[16] J. W. Kauleinamoku was the next to emigrate, in 1875. In July 1876 Elder Alma L. Smith arrived in Utah with "five natives of the Islands," all with "written permission of His Majesty, King Kalākaua, to leave the islands and locate to Utah."[17] The party that Smith arrived with actually included six Hawaiians: a family of three, two young girls, and a woman named Likibeka, betrothed to John Kauleinamoku.

There were no arrivals announced between 1876 and 1878, but *Haole* missionaries continued to lobby the Kingdom of Hawaiʻi's Minister of Foreign Affairs to grant permission to move small groups of Native Hawaiians to

Utah. A Mormon Elder named Henry P. Richards managed, with some difficulty, to obtain permission for "five natives to emigrate from the Islands" to Utah. As the *Deseret News* noted, the blessing of the Kingdom of Hawai'i "was not granted without some hesitation, as the government is opposed to the emigration of its subjects."[18]After 1879 the slow but steady trickle of Native Hawaiians east to Utah continued. When Richards returned to Utah in 1879, four emigrants came with him. In the summer of 1882 eight Native Hawaiians left for Utah with returning missionaries.[19] In 1884 Edward Partridge, the mission president in Hawaii, made mention of several missionaries returning to Utah from New Zealand who were accompanied by "some emigrating Kiwi Saints," the first two Maori known to have moved to the Salt Lake Valley.[20] The small community in the Warm Springs district slowly began to grow.

In 1885 a small group of "tourists" from Hawai'i stopped in Utah on their way home from the "Eastern and Southern States" on a trip representing Hawai'i at the New Orleans Exposition. These travelers, the Hon. Samuel Parker (a Native Hawaiian judge from the Big Island) and his wife (herself a Mormon, the daughter of Jonathan Napela), "took occasion to hunt up their country people who are residing in this city, finding some of them at work on the Temple Block, and also calling on some of them at their homes." During a visit at their hotel with several former missionaries to Hawai'i, the Parkers expressed "agreeable surprise at finding them so well situated, and so contented." Equally surprising, perhaps, was the sentiment expressed by many of the Native Hawaiian Saints that they wished to stay in Utah and not "return to the islands, if the means were furnished them to do so." These reports, although from an unquestionably biased source, indicate that the conditions of the Native Hawaiian settlers in Salt Lake City were generally favorable. Employment on the construction of the Salt Lake Temple seemed readily available, and several of the settlers, including the Kauleinamoku and Mahoe families, had purchased small lots in the Warm Springs district and built homes.

Between 1884 and 1889 the number of Native Hawaiians emigrating to Utah rose sharply. The largest increase in migrants to Utah was after 1887, when King Kalākaua was forced to sign the Bayonet Constitution, which nullified previous law restricting the international travel of Native Hawaiian subjects. The 1887 Constitution, written and promulgated by a small cadre of American businessmen, was signed by David Kalākaua under the threat of physical violence. Article 1 of the Bayonet Constitution stated: "God hath endowed all men with certain inalienable rights, among which are life, liberty, and the right of acquiring, possessing, and protecting property, and of pursuing and obtaining safety and happiness." Based on this article and another that nullified any previous legislation deemed unconstitutional by the 1887 Constitution's standards, former restrictions on emigration were removed. Ultimately the increased emigration of Native Hawaiians, who were Kalākaua's primary constituency, hurt the king politically. This legislation had several effects on Native Hawaiian Saints beyond easing the restrictions on their ability to emigrate permanently. The Bayonet Constitution also established strict property and literacy requirements for suffrage, a situation that conceivably would have disenfranchised many Native Hawaiian Saints. Although it is not clear what effect this provision might have had on potential emigrants, it appears that the signing of the Bayonet Constitution was the spark that ignited the flood of emigrants from Hawai'i to Utah between 1888 and 1895. In the spring of 1888 Elder Jacob F. Gates left Hawai'i for Utah with eight Native Hawaiians, and the *Deseret News* quoted Gates as saying that "many others are quietly getting their little possessions in shape for disposal, hoping soon to follow."[21] Less than one month later six more Native Hawaiian Saints, "Kahananui and his wife Elena—their sons Liloa and James, with their wives Helalea, and Jennie Kili" left for Utah with departing missionaries. "The spirit of the gathering," wrote Elder Millard F. Eakle to the *Deseret Evening News*, "is strong with the Hawaiian Saints. Many are striving hard to prepare for emigrating, and 'Mauna Pohaku,' Rocky Mountains, is a favorite theme with them. Some thirty native Saints will sail with returning Elders to take up their abode in the valley of the mountains."[22] Four days later the same newspaper reported that "16 Hawaiian Saints emigrating to Utah, namely: Joseph and Miliama Kekuku and their four children; Napiha and Moehau and their five children; Lima and Ane and their child." The remainder of the Native Hawaiians bound for Salt Lake in this group were temporarily way-laid but departed the following day.[23] In 1889 no fewer than fifty Hawaiians traveled to Utah with departing *Haole* missionaries. The rapid growth of the community soon caught the attention of the city's white population.

Race relations throughout territorial Utah mirrored those in the remainder of the American West. The cosmopolitan nature of the West, which brought together former Mexican citizens, Chinese and Japanese contract laborers, freed or fleeing African American slaves, and eastern European immigrants, among others, forced white settlers of northern European ancestry to reevaluate the racial categorizations that had served them so well in the East. As Patricia Nelson Limerick noted, "The diversity of the West put a strain on the simpler varieties of racism. In another setting, categories dividing humanity into superior white and inferior black were comparatively easy to steer by. The West, however, raised questions for which racists had no set answers."[24] Western racism and nativism developed differently in response to the presence of Chinese, Japanese, Native Americans, Mexicans, and Eastern Europeans in different places, but the general response was essentially the same: white vigilantism and violence against anyone deemed not to be white, followed by legal codification of new racial definitions and hierarchies. Utah was no exception to this process. White settlers, both Mormon and non-Mormon, exhibited extreme, and often violent, antipathy toward those they considered of inferior stock.

The experience of Utah's Chinese population is instructive in this regard. Chinese laborers first arrived in the territory as workers for the Central Pacific Railroad. After the completion of the transcontinental line at Promontory Point near present-day Ogden in 1869, many Chinese stayed to work for the railroad, living in converted boxcars, which often housed as many as eighteen men. After a twelve-hour railroad shift, the men would drink, gamble, soothe their bodies in hot baths, play music on the *lo* (gong) and *nu'kin* (two-string fiddle), and write letters home to their loved ones. They joined an already cosmopolitan band of Utah residents. In April 1870 the *Utah Reporter*, a newspaper published in the town of Corinne, reported that its population consisted of "some five hundred Indians, two or three hundred Chinese, and quite a number of citizens of African descent," in addition to its white population.[25] Many Chinese were literate, and although most were railroad employees, many worked as grocers and storekeepers and ran laundries or other family-owned businesses. The area known as Chinatown developed in Ogden due to its proximity to the railroad. Ogden had 33 Chinese citizens in 1880 and 106 in 1890, and the town had five Chinese-owned laundries. After 1900 the Chinese population was centered in Salt Lake City, mainly as a result of the slowdown in labor on the railroad lines and increased union activity, which fostered white nativism. In 1890 there were 271 Chinese in Salt Lake City, which developed a Chinese section of its own. The presence of Chinese workers in the mining industry is also evident from the large numbers of Chinese in mining towns like Park City. As more and more white workers settled in Utah, violence against the already established Chinese community increased in the first few years of the twentieth century, spurred on by the nativist rhetoric of labor organizations such as the Western Federation of Miners. "Shall the widows famish while the heathen Chinese feast?" asked white labor leaders in 1903. "All members of organized labor are in duty bound to patronize only white labor, and such establishments as employ only white labor.... The unorganized laborers of the camp who patronize the Oriental competitors of our race...are a greater menace...than an equal number of 'scabs.'"[26] A nineteenth-century Utah handbill read:

Patronize Home Industry

By Spending Your Money With Your Own Race, or Braid Your Hair and Move to
Hong Kong.[27]

Immigrants to Utah from Japan, Greece, Italy, Spain, and Pacific Island
nations experienced similar discrimination to varying degrees throughout
the twentieth century.[28]

The history of race relations in nineteenth-century Utah, however, is often
obscured by the history of a white community divided along religious lines.
The struggle between Mormons and non-Mormons did not so much replace
the discrimination, inequality, and violence so common throughout the
West as it has usurped it in the historical imagination. White Mormons and
non-Mormons alike, for all of their differences, certainly agreed on a hierarchical view of humanity based on the nebulous idea of race. For Mormons,
ideas about race were overtly religious, informed by supposedly universal and
authoritative doctrines and tempered only rhetorically with benevolent over-
tones. Despite white Mormons' occasional willingness to overlook racial difference for the greater good of maintaining political control over the region, Salt
Lake City remained divided into ethnic enclaves that crossed religious lines.

The discourse of race in Utah was often caught up in the
Mormon-versus-non-Mormon dynamic, but rarely were accepted racial
hierarchies seriously called into question by either group. Non-Mormons
regularly accused Mormons of being overly friendly with Native Americans
and providing direct monetary support for "inassimilable" groups of
migrants through Brigham Young's Perpetual Emigration Fund, but these
complaints were largely meant to provide evidence of Mormon treachery
to federal officials. White Mormon laborers despised and feared the influx
of Asian contract labor as much as their white non-Mormon neighbors did,
and both groups ultimately acted in concert to remove Native American
communities from their homelands to make way for increasing white settlement and mining. The situation of the Native Hawaiian Saints in Utah
provides ample evidence of this paradox. Faithful and steadfast Mormons,
Native Hawaiians sacrificed to make the journey to the Great Basin and fulfill their religious duty to gather to Zion, often leaving behind possessions
and family and enduring great hardship. Instead of being welcomed by
their brothers and sisters in the church, they found themselves placed near
the bottom of a racial hierarchy in the West that severely circumscribed
their social and economic choices. As demonstrated by the rhetoric surrounding Chinese residents, race and labor were inextricably linked in the
West, where white settlers often adapted their racism to a new and often
far more cosmopolitan context.[29]

Native Hawaiian Saints who settled in Salt Lake City suffered under the racial discourses at work as the United States met foreign peoples in the context of immigration and imperial expansion in the late nineteenth and early twentieth centuries. Newspaper articles in the West that reported news from the Sandwich Islands shaped white Utahns' conceptions of Native Hawaiians as savage, barbarous, and unclean. Evolutionist pseudo-science created racial hierarchies in which Native Hawaiians were given a fixed position. Newspaper accounts in Utah of missionary adventures in Hawai'i often followed the formula of the travelogue, as missionaries with their own religious ideas about race flirted with the popular perception that "present-day savages represented living fossils of Stone Age mentalities and lifeways." These writings were a regional version of what was a nation-wide discourse "repeated in an endless and self-sustaining loop of observation and theory."[30] While Utah's sons traveled simultaneously back through space and time to engage the Other on a civilizing mission abroad, Utah residents also encountered "foreigners" at home. Such encounters created a discourse of Self and Other that blended rhetorically with Mormons' own peculiar ideas about race, religion, and history.

Representations of Pacific Islanders in the Nineteenth-Century West

Settlers throughout the American West might have considered themselves knowledgeable about Native Hawaiians, whether through newspaper accounts of happenings in the Pacific Islands or through the occasional opportunities they had to work with and live among the "Kanakas." As Native Hawaiian Mormons made their way east from Honolulu to San Francisco aboard passenger and other vessels, they would certainly have met with other Native Hawaiians working as seamen.[31] The reception many of them encountered in San Francisco, a city and region of the nation certainly no stranger to Native Hawaiian full- and part-time residents, was indicative of the reception they faced as they traveled farther east to Salt Lake City.

The construction of racial difference in the United States from the colonial era forward rested on discursive constructions of Self and Other. Whether encountering Native American communities in the process of colonial settlement and westward expansion, justifying slavery in the British colonies and antebellum United States, or encountering either foreign peoples abroad or immigrant groups at home, white Americans drew on a familiar set of descriptions that created normative whiteness. Most whites in the West, however, knew what little they did about Native Hawaiians from the plethora of newspapers that printed various accounts of Hawaiian politics, social life, and customs, as well as sensational events from throughout the Pacific. Although the news from Honolulu covered items of general interest in addition to politics, the elements of sensationalism common to stories about the "South Seas" were present in stories on Hawai'i as well. In addition, Western reporters rarely differentiated among various types of Pacific Islanders, using the general term "Kanakas" and adding to the perception of Oceanic peoples as an undifferentiated group with little distinction made between customs and behaviors of very different peoples. For the white citizens of the Salt Lake Valley, both Mormon and non-Mormon, the sensational and steady stream of news about "Kanakas" fed on negative racial stereotypes that shaped the relations between Native Hawaiians and other Pacific Islanders in Utah and their white neighbors.

A common genre of writing about Hawai'i and Native Hawaiians in the Salt Lake Valley and the West was periodic reports from missionaries in Hawai'i, which related the progress of missionary work in the islands and the perceived strangeness of those they had traveled so far to convert. In April 1860 the Deseret News included a short piece on the "pleasant reunion" of former missionaries to Hawai'i, who had gathered to sing, dance, and converse with one another "in Kanaka, which, of course, was not as interesting to those who were unlearned, as to those who were well-versed in that peculiar language." Also present to "serenade" the missionaries during their festivities were a "party of friends," whose attendance was taken as a show of support for "those who were so long from home in one of the most undesirable missions that the Elders of Israel have had to perform." Although it is unclear whether the Elders who actually served on missions in Hawai'i shared their companions' opinion of their missions, the perception of the Hawaiian mission as undesirable is telling. First, the designation of Hawai'i as an "undesirable" mission serves to heighten the sense of sacrifice on the part of the missionaries, an important part of the Mormon belief in the necessity of individual sacrifice in working to "build God's Kingdom." Second, regardless of the missionaries' conceptions of their time spent in the Hawaiian mission (which might well have been favorable), the article's purpose is to highlight the difference between Zion, home of the "pure in heart," and the rest of world, dark and mired in sin, in this particular case represented fully by the "peculiar" Pacific Islands.[32]

By far the most common news coverage of Hawai'i in Utah and western newspapers concerned leprosy. Hansen's disease, commonly known as leprosy, has a long historical association in the Western world with uncleanliness and sin. As one scholar of leprosy in Hawai'i noted, "While some societies would regard leprosy as a disease like any other, the stigmatizing of leprosy was largely a cultural construct of the West."[33] Leprosy was seen as the physical manifestation of a spiritual or moral affliction, evidence of God's punishment of the victim, and often associated with sexual sin. The development of germ theories of disease in the latter part of the nineteenth century produced various explanations for the origins and spread of leprosy. In the context of colonialism and imperialism leprosy became associated with descriptions of colonized peoples as "poor, unsanitary, uncivilized, and unclean." The spread of leprosy in Hawai'i was explained in a colonial context that constructed Native Hawaiians in highly sexualized terms that played on categories of civilized versus uncivilized, clean versus unclean, and moral versus immoral. The social construction of leprosy and disease in general used the same language of racial and cultural superiority underlying *Haole* assertions that Native Hawaiians were naturally morally inferior and unfit for self-government, which developed into a justification for American imperialism in Hawai'i as early as the late 1860s.[34] Newspaper articles in the American West, including the Great Basin, included many sensational stories of leprosy in Hawai'i that drew on these racial constructions.

Between 1862 and 1920 nearly three hundred articles appeared in Utah newspapers that referenced leprosy in precisely these terms. The connotation of "leprosy" as uncleanliness and filth and of "leper" as a category or person worthy to be shunned was often juxtaposed with news items about the spread of leprosy in the Hawaiian Islands, as well as the peculiar characteristics of Native Hawaiians that supposedly facilitated the spread of the disease. Leading up to the establishment of the Iosepa colony in 1889, the news coverage of leprosy in Salt Lake City newspapers rose dramatically. For Mormon audiences, the primary readership of the *Deseret Evening News*, the leprosy "epidemic" in Hawaii might have been seen as the fulfillment of prophecy; in many ways this justified its inclusion in the Mormon newspaper in addition to the more obviously sensational appeal. The Book of Mormon spoke specifically of the "wrath of God" that would afflict the Lamanites in the last days, a condition that would necessarily bring suffering and affliction in the form of both disease and domination by European and American "Gentiles."[35] Leprosy was a fitting affliction replete with biblical precedent as a preferred form of God's punishment for sinners and unbelievers. In addition, nineteenth-century constructions of racial difference intelligible to Mormons and non-Mormons alike resonated with white readers in the Salt Lake Valley and beyond. Although early references to leprosy generally associated the spread of the disease throughout the western United States and even Hawai'i with Chinese immigration, the focus soon shifted to the perceived conditions that facilitated its spread in Hawai'i.

Prior to the 1880s news coverage in Utah of leprosy in Hawai'i occurred regularly enough to create an association between Native Hawaiians and the disease in ways that profoundly affected the lives of Native Hawaiian settlers in the Salt Lake Valley at the end of the nineteenth century.

In the October 21, 1868, edition of the *Deseret Evening News*, a short item announced: "Arrived the steamer *Idaho,* from Honolulu, with advices to October 5th. Leprosy prevails to a considerable extent among the different islands."[36] Although it is not known for certain when and how Hansen's disease was first introduced to Hawai'i, its presence there possibly dates back to as early as 1835. It was not until 1863, however, that the disease was mentioned by an official with King Kāmehameha V's board of health. The name by which the malady was known in Hawai'i, *ma'i pāke*, or "Chinese sickness," associates it primarily with Chinese immigrants.[37] Although board of health officials after 1863 devised several strategies for dealing with the disease, Native Hawaiian reactions to those afflicted with leprosy were vastly different from those of the *Haole* in the islands. Most Native Hawaiians showed little aversion to close physical contact with leprosy patients, and many viewed the disease and the official reaction to it (which included segregation and quarantine with varying degrees of severity) as a device used by the *Haole* to disrupt Hawaiian social and familial relationships. The easy familiarity Native Hawaiians had with Hansen's disease patients was often pointed to by *Haole* observers as the main reason for the disease's rapid spread in the islands, in addition to the usual blame placed on the moral and hygienic failings attributed to Native Hawaiians. Even those Native Hawaiians who did not oppose solutions that involved segregation and quarantine disliked what were perceived to be draconian government policies toward Hansen's patients.[38] Whites in the United States and Hawaii viewed Native Hawaiian attitudes toward leprosy patients with shock and derision.

The association between Hansen's disease and Native Hawaiians in the Great Basin represented a sort of morbid fascination, replete with detailed accounts of the unintelligible reactions of Native Hawaiians to the pestilence in their midst. Hansen's disease in the West became associated with the large numbers of Chinese laborers coming into the region. A February 1869 newspaper article in the *Deseret Evening News* commenting on a bill protecting "Chinese from mob violence" at the hands of white citizens assessed any such measure as follows:

> Witness the deplorable condition of our sister State of California. Her rivers and hills once teemed with glittering wealth, and gave profitable employment to thousands of industrious men; but a mistaken policy permitted the Chinese

to enter and usurp the place of nobler men....The white men were forced to flee from contact with such a degraded race, and the mines were, in a great measure, abandoned to the Pagan; and today, in the shadow of the Cross, the idol of paganism is nestled in fancied security.

Seriously gentlemen, you cannot be so dead to the best interests of the state as to attempt to fasten by law such a scourge upon our people. We have fled from the leprosy; do not, I pray you, bring it again into our presence.[39]

Another Utah newspaper, reprinting an excerpt from the *San Francisco Chronicle* in 1873, wrote that "David J. Lee, M.D., writes to the Chronicle that the terrible disease, leprosy, actually exists in San Francisco, and that there is a possibility of its spreading and becoming permanent in that city. The disease was brought to the coast by the Chinese and is communicated by the class the visit the Chinese quarter of that city."[40] In February 1870 the *Deseret Evening News* reported: "A writer in the S.F. *Tribune* says that three-quarters of the cigars smoked in San Francisco, are manufactured by Chinese, and that three fourths of these Chinese cigar manufacturers suffer from the itch and leprosy, and have their hands covered with open sores. The most innocent man is, by smoking those cigars, always exposed to a fearful and loathsome disease, which he can, even by a kiss, communicate to his wife and children."[41] The warning in this passage was especially poignant for Mormon readers, urged by their religious beliefs to avoid tobacco. By obeying God's commandment to refrain from smoking tobacco, the prudent Mormon would indeed avoid the plague of leprosy, not incidentally spread by the Chinese, long maligned as purveyors of vice. These excerpts reveal the underlying fears of Hansen's disease, as well as the social construction of the disease and its associations with both race and class issues that were boiling over throughout the West. The association of Hansen's disease with the already dangerous influx of Chinese is seen through the eyes of white citizens in the West as both a just punishment for tolerating the presence of a "pagan" race and an added danger of Chinese immigration. The religious connotations of Hansen's disease as a punishment from God fit neatly into the racial and class tensions created by the increasing presence of Chinese workers throughout the West.

The debate over the importation of foreign (especially Chinese) labor was mirrored in Hawai'i and widely reported with great interest throughout the American West and the Salt Lake Valley. A letter to the editor in the *Hawaiian Gazette* reprinted in the *Deseret Evening News* echoed from a different perspective *Haole* concern in the islands about what they saw as the threat of Chinese labor. The anonymous writer was specifically concerned with the effects of introducing foreign labor into "Hawai'i nei" given the "increasingly horrible...state of disease and rottenness" in "Hawaiian social life." The moral failings of the Hawaiian nation, the writer argued, made evident by the high percentage of couples "openly living in adultery," created a dangerous condition in which to introduce what they regarded as an equally licentious class of foreign laborers. "Now it is to this corrupt state of social life that we owe the terrific spread of leprosy, and the general prevalence of venereal diseases of every type, within the last few years."[42] In this case it is the Hawaiian nation itself that is portrayed as at risk from the disreputable moral state it had sunk into, which had brought upon it the plague of leprosy and venereal disease, bound to spiral even further downward with the introduction of a mostly male population of foreign laborers. For Mormon readers in Salt Lake Valley, the purpose of reprinting such a letter was clear: the moral degradation of society received its just rewards, in modern times as in biblical, and in many cases the method of God's punishment was the same.

The "scourge" of leprosy in Hawai'i and elsewhere was gruesomely detailed for Salt Lake Valley readers. An 1873 newspaper article entitled "Hawaiian Lepers" included the following passage:

> A brief description will suffice to show the terrible nature of the destructive plague. The patient is attacked with irregular liver red spots in the face, and at a late period the ears and nose are similarly attacked. In many instances the whole body is more or less covered with them or with a somewhat scaly eruption. Slight itching is sometimes felt, but not always. These spots are slightly elevated, shining, and after a time become darker.... [T]he face now becomes much disfigured, the skin rough, full of wrinkles and fissures, similar to the skin of an elephant.... The joints are thus attacked and destroyed in succession by the slow progress of this terrible disease which renders those who are affected with it objects of horror until the grave conceals them.[43]

Another *Deseret Evening News* article in 1888 stated that "there is no more horrible disease known to humanity than leprosy" and included a similarly gruesome account of the disease's more advanced symptoms.[44] One article detailed the painful separation of Native Hawaiians from their loved ones as leprosy patients were taken their homes and families, "never to return." The author gave a conciliatory nod to the "painful sundering of ties of love and friendship," but concluded that part of the reason for the disease's rapid spread was that "[i]t is impossible for the authorities to ferret out all the cases of leprosy existing, the victims being concealed or secreted by relatives or friends, that they may not be doomed to perpetual banishment, as the strict sanitary regulations require." Although recognizing that "the finer feelings of human nature exist in the hearts of these poor Kanakas as sensitively as in the superior race," the article plays on the apparent irrationality of Native Hawaiians in allowing their loved ones to be sequestered from them due to the "terrible" nature of a disfiguring disease. All of these judgments are passed, of course, with the reassurance that "leprosy confined itself almost exclusively among the native population. I have heard of but one case on these islands where a white person was attacked by it." Also reinforced in this article are the stark differences that were perceived to exist between whites, "the superior race," and "Kanakas," in this case an appeal to rationality versus an understandably "emotional" response to a situation with no obvious alternative. The final fate of a "leper" was inevitable: to be "[c]ast out from among the habitations of men."[45] The connotation of Hansen's disease as an affliction that rendered one "unclean" would have resonated with an audience who viewed Native Hawaiians as a fallen and degenerate race, already cursed by God and now suffering his continued wrath for their historical fall from favor.

In addition to references to Native Hawaiians and Hansen's disease, popular representations of Native Hawaiians in the West also drew on general stereotypes about Pacific Islanders that emphasized cultural practices, both real and imagined, which for white readers provided evidence of the Pacific Islanders' "savagery" and "lack of civilization." Typical of many articles in valley periodicals was an 1860 story that appeared in the *Valley Tan*, "Infanticide in the Hawaiian Islands," in which the author stated:

> [I]t is a common thing for Kanaka mothers (the word "Kanaka" in the Hawaiian tongue means only a man, but in its English sense it means anything native to the Sandwich Islands) to kill their children and adds that it is not to be wondered at, since the example is given by the Royal family. He asserts that Dr. Rooke, physician to the King, told him that all legitimate children born to Kamehameha I and the present Queen Dowager, were strangled soon after birth by some female member of the royal family.... He adds: "The old Pagan faith did not teach the Kanakas the least aversion for infanticide, and though they are now disguised as Christians, they have not become a bit more scrupulous in regard to murdering new-born infants."[46]

Despite the lack of any corroborating evidence for such fanciful imaginings, the myth of infanticide and cannibalism in Hawai'i remained a popular subject of sensational newspaper accounts in communities along the Wasatch Front. An 1869 *Deseret News* article reprinted a story about cannibalism by a gang of "Kanaks," referring not to Native

Hawaiians but to New Caledonians (ni-Vanuatu) and relating in gory detail the methods by which such atrocities were ceremonially perpetrated. Beginning with the sentence, "If any of us look forward to being eaten by cannibals, he may wish to be informed how he is likely to be cooked,"[47] one has to wonder how many readers were able to discriminate between the ni-Vanuatu "Kanaks" who were the subject of the article and the Native Hawaiian "Kanakas" so often the subject of valley news items. Given the propensity of valley newspapers to reproduce uncritically the most exoticized accounts of Pacific Islander behavior with little regard for cultural heterogeneity, it is likely that few readers were capable of making the distinction.

Throughout the late 1870s and the 1880s many regional newspapers frequently reprinted articles specifically about the Hawaiian monarchy. Nearly all of these articles perpetuated an image of David Kalākaua as a hapless, bumbling figure and portrayed the perceived backwardness of Native Hawaiians as due to their allegiance to monarchical forms of government. Such representations mirrored the lampoons of the king's *Haole* detractors in Honolulu, which were common in Hawaiian periodicals and US political cartoons of the time. In 1881 the *Deseret News* reported an alleged plan by Kalākaua and his advisers to "enter into an arrangement by which Chinese Merchants line of steamers were to land 1,000,000 Chinamen on the islands, on which a capitation tax was to be levied. They were then to be made citizens and the kingdom turned over to the Chinese empire for this consideration. The scheme was balked by the actions of foreign residents and officials. Chagrined at the issue and his resulting unpopularity, the king went off on a tour of the world."[48]

Equally popular in Utah newspapers were descriptions of Native Hawaiians emphasizing their perceived need for the "civilizing" influence of Mormon missionaries. Summarizing a letter from missionary Enoch Farr in 1885, the *Ogden Standard Examiner* related the following:

> Elder Farr is proud to state that he can eat "poi" (a mess of pottage of which we have given an account in Elder Hyde's letter from the islands) and fish first-rate, but the Kanaka language comes slowly, being quite a queer vernacular. But Enoch says he'll wrestle with it till he has conquered it, even should he have to live with and among the aborigines with no white people around. One complaint our friend has about the natives is their deficiency in the matter of cleanliness, of which he gives some ludicrous illustrations....As far as the natives conduct towards the Elder is concerned Bro. Farr reports favorably. He says the natives are a nicer race of people than he had any idea of. They are a strong, hearty, and robust set, the women being among the most finely developed females he

ever saw, although their features may be somewhat coarse and common bearing traces of their original savagery.[49]

In a similar dispatch from the "Sandwich Islands" mission four years earlier, the return of two Mormon Elders was the subject of an article that reported on the condition of the mission and the success of conversion efforts there: "Missionary work among the natives is uphill business. There is no difficulty converting them, but to keep them in the strict line of moral rectitude is no easy, but, in many instances, [an] impossible task."[50] The *Deseret Evening News* regularly printed items relating news from the Hawaiian Mission, which spoke to an audience hungry for the exotic. The coverage of Elder Jacob F. Gates's return from a three-year mission in "the Sandwich Islands" (he was accompanied home by a party of Native Hawaiians migrating to Utah) occasioned the same unflattering reflection on the progress of missionary work in Hawai'i.

Between the heavily racialized descriptions of Native Hawaiians throughout the West and the increasing association of Native Hawaiians with Hansen's disease, the growth of the Pacific Islander Mormon community in Salt Lake City between 1870 and 1889 did not go unnoticed. However, the number of Native Hawaiians and Pacific Islanders in the city remained under one hundred, and those individuals lived in close quarters in a neighborhood on the outskirts of the city generally reserved for nonwhites. This growing community was hardly competitive with skilled white labor, and it was small enough not to threaten to disrupt the wages of unskilled labor. Yet in 1889 they were all but forcibly removed from the Salt Lake City community. Why? The answer lies partly in the prevailing notions among whites in the American West about "Kanakas" constructed in the local news press and other popular outlets, partly in prevailing racial sentiments, and partly in the unique struggle in the Salt Lake Valley between Mormons and non-Mormons for political and economic dominance in the region. In addition, the specter of Hansen's disease haunted the community. This was the source of public outcry against Native Hawaiian immigration both before and after the removal of Pacific Islander migrants to Skull Valley in 1889. An 1883 article in the *Salt Lake Tribune* entitled "The Spotted Boy-Kanaka Immigration" made explicit concerns about Native Hawaiian immigration. In a tirade against the growing numbers of Native Hawaiian immigrants that was sparked by the alleged diagnosis of a recently arrived youth with Hansen's disease, the columnist argued:

> We are not discussing this matter because these people who come here, come as Mormon converts. If they were Methodists or Baptists of Catholics or Free

Thinkers we should have the same objection.... There is no possible reason why the United States should suffer the danger of having an incurable and most loathsome disease planted in the heart of the Republic, through bringing these people here. Moreover it is frightfully cruel to the people themselves. They have been all their lives accustomed to a climate of perpetual summer, half their food heretofore has been tropical fruits. They have never been accustomed to hard labor. To live here at all they will have to bear the rigors of this climate, they will have to eat food to which they have never been accustomed, and they will have to work unceasingly. Their own country is so much in need of laborers, that thousands of Chinese are sent there annually. So the bringing of these wretched creatures is an outrage all around.... If the Mormon authorities have a particle of either humanity or common sense they will stop this Kanaka immigration at once.[51]

In their open call to stop Native Hawaiian immigration, the *Tribune* editors revealed some of the key perceptions of whites about Pacific Islanders in the Salt Lake Valley. The widespread knowledge throughout the American West of leprosy in Hawai'i played on fears of the "wretched" native as a bearer of filth and disease to an imagined virgin population in the Salt Lake Valley. Native Hawaiians were portrayed as at once incapable of work, based on a false idea of tropical primitive affluence, and in demand as plantation labor at home. The evocation of the specter of Chinese labor would have been well received by white Utahns a year after the passage of the 1882 Exclusion Act. Most telling, however, is the *Tribune*'s disavowal of religious-based motivation for its opposition to Native Hawaiian immigration, couching its claims in an appeal to shared racial sensibilities among whites regardless of faith.

For Native Hawaiian and Pacific Islander Saints, such a dynamic created a difficult situation: though clearly committed Latter-day Saints, they were marked by the inescapable stigma of racial difference. This unique situation continually placed them in an ambiguous position in relation to white Mormons in the Salt Lake Valley. In the years leading up to the contentious 1889 election in Salt Lake City, a debate over Native Hawaiian eligibility for US citizenship revealed the contours of race and religion at work in the Great Basin.

By 1885 non-Mormons in Utah were bombarding Mormons with challenges to their political, economic, and cultural hegemony throughout the region. The "Mormon culture region," an area defined by geographer Donald Meinig in an influential 1965 article, extended from southeastern Idaho to northern Mexico and from eastern Oregon to western Colorado. Mormon cultural mores, including community organization, settlement patterns, and economic exchange, dominated the Great Basin region in varying degrees from a core area in the Salt Lake Valley.[52] From the earliest Mormon settlements in 1847 through the next four decades of both Mormon and non-Mormon settlement in the region, the groups viewed each other with suspicion at best and often with outright hostility. Mormons continued to pursue separatist, community-based projects that emphasized total independence from non-Mormons. These met with varying degrees of success, but they remained a goal for prophet and president Brigham Young and his successors. Beginning in 1869 the completion of the transcontinental railroad at Promontory Point near Ogden, Utah (an event that the majority of Mormons looked upon favorably) opened up the territory to settlement by non-Mormons and to fuller integration into the larger global economy. Settlers from the eastern United States viewed the Mormon practice of polygamy with revulsion; the rhetoric of northern reformers before and after the Civil War ranked polygamy alongside slavery as one of the "twin relics of barbarism." Settlers also resented the general policy of Mormons of preferential commerce within their own ranks, a practice that appeared to run counter to American notions of democratic participation in economic activity and an open market for goods and services. The high percentage of Mormons who occupied law enforcement and local government offices throughout the territory; the application of Mormon moral codes with respect to prostitution, gambling, and alcohol; and the tendency of Mormons to take their political cues from ecclesiastical leaders led the non-Mormon population of Utah to view the Mormons as essentially antidemocratic and therefore un-American in actions and character.[53]

The two most destructive pieces of federal legislation for the Church of Jesus Christ of Latter-day Saints in the nineteenth century were the Edmunds Act of 1882, which outlawed polygamy and made cohabitation with plural wives a crime, and the Edmunds-Tucker Act of 1887, which extended the 1882 legislation in several ways. The Edmunds-Tucker Act increased the risk of prosecution for Mormon leaders who remained in polygamous marriages, dissolved the corporation of the Mormon Church by outlawing any financial holdings of the church over $50,000, and required that voters renounce polygamy in word and deed. In addition, it abolished women's suffrage in the territory, a right originally granted to women in Utah in 1870. These two pieces of legislation transformed the church's response to non-Mormon political pressure from confrontation to accommodation and changed the face of Mormonism forever.[54]

As Mormons with strong ties to high-ranking church leaders, Native Hawaiians in Utah were swept up in the tensions between Mormons and non-Mormons, which included, among other things, commands from church leaders against conducting business with Gentiles, which were designed to create a wide distinction between Mormons and non-Mormons in the region. However, they soon realized that Mormonism was far from the most meaningful marker of difference in the territory. In the months leading up to the critical county elections of 1889, in which the Mormon People's Party faced serious challenges from the Liberal Party (which had anti-Mormonism as one of its key positions), Mormon leaders strongly encouraged members who were not US citizens to acquire citizenship in order to vote in local elections. Several Native Hawaiian Saints in Salt Lake City, determined to support the church's position of dominance in the political affairs of the territory, sought to become naturalized citizens in their new home. Their efforts did not go unnoticed.

NATIVE HAWAIIAN SAINTS AND THE CITIZENSHIP CONTROVERSY

Several US historians have traced the links between notions of citizenship from America's colonial period through the twentieth century. The American West in particular has emerged as a region in which questions of citizenship increasingly revolved around race. Ian Haney-Lopez's 1996 book *White by Law: The Legal Constructions of Race* details the history of legal attempts in the United States to define citizenship on racially exclusionary grounds. According to Haney-Lopez, "The racial composition of U.S citizenship reflects in part the accident of world migration patterns. More than this, however, it reflects the conscious design of US immigration and naturalization laws."[55] The response of Utah's Supreme Court to the Native Hawaiian Saints' request for citizenship occurred at the intersection of nationwide efforts to define citizenship on the basis of race as well as regional concerns in the Salt Lake Valley over the religious status of the applicants.

In June 1889 the Supreme Court of the Territory of Utah decided a case in response to the application of "Kanaka Nian to be admitted to citizenship" in the United States. Kanaka Nian, who was identified later in the *Deseret News* as G. W. Kamakaniau, apparently represented "four natives of the Sandwich Islands [who] appeared before Judge Sanders as applicants for naturalization."[56] This case is identified by Haney-Lopez as one of fifty-two "prerequisite cases," or cases in which race became a prerequisite for US citizenship.[57] This relatively small set of prerequisite cases established a strong legal foundation for defining racial qualifications for citizenship and helped create the racial systems and ideologies that in many instances remain in place today. Decided on the basis of both legal precedent and the scientific racism of the late nineteenth and early twentieth centuries, each case laid another brick in a legal foundation that effectively denied full personhood and citizenship to those individuals defined by the courts as "nonwhite." *In re Kanaka Nian* established through legal precedent the fact that Native Hawaiians were not white and thus not entitled to US citizenship, a ruling that remained in force even after Hawai'i was annexed to the United States in 1898.

The decision against Kamakaniau was based in part on a kind of means test for citizenship combined with a racial component that exhibited all the hallmarks of late nineteenth-century eugenics. Despite passionate arguments by his Mormon attorney, Le Grande Young, Kamakaniau's application was denied on the grounds that "a native of the Sandwich Islands, belonging to the Hawaiian race, is a Polynesian, belonging to the Malay races, and as such is not eligible for citizenship." Although he had lived in the United States for six years, Kamakaniau was deemed ineligible for citizenship based on his inability to identify the president of the United States and on the federal Chinese Exclusion Act, passed seven years earlier.[58] In his decision Judge C. J. Zane concluded that Kamakaniau "in appearance was of Malayan or Mongolian complexion, a shade lighter than average for his race." Zane cited several "professors" on the general classification of races, concluding that "[t]he highest authorities, therefore, classify Hawaiians among the Malay tribes." He further reasoned that "[i]n mentioning the Chinese as excluded it is claimed that Congress intended to exclude all other races.... We are of the opinion that the law authorizes the naturalization of aliens of the Caucasian or white races and of African races only, and all other races, among which are the Hawaiians, are excluded."[59] In a sympathetic piece covering the decision, the *Deseret News* provided additional information buttressing the arguments of Kamakaniau's attorney, who not only asserted that Hawaiians did "not belong to the Chinese race," but challenged the ruling based on the fact that Judges Zane and Hunter had both previously admitted Hawaiians as citizens.[60] The court, however, concluded that in those instances it had been "too lax in the admission of citizens."[61] In all likelihood the impending election prompted the change in the court's attitude about citizenship requests. Several days before the *Salt Lake Tribune* also covered the decision, claiming: "It is well known that Church leaders are exciting themselves to have all alien Mormons who have lived in the United States during the past five years naturalized to register for the August election, and during the last week some pretty tough specimens of humanity have been run through the mill. The climax, however, was reached yesterday afternoon, when a herd of Sandwich Islanders appeared in court and stated their desire to become citizens."[62] The Native Hawaiian applicants' desire to support the political dominance of the Mormon Church in the region brought to the surface the more disturbing issue of race.

Coverage of the case in Salt Lake City's competing newspapers softened the overt racism of Judge Zane's decision by recontextualizing it in the struggle between Mormons and non-Mormons for political power throughout the Wasatch Front. What the *Salt Lake Tribune* deemed the "tough specimens of humanity" represented by various nationalities of "alien Mormons" up to that point were most likely Cornish or Welsh, along with some Germans and Scandinavian immigrants. All of these groups, however, represented a more readily acceptable northern European stock that, though perhaps considered coarse in manners or habits, certainly did not exhibit the phenotypic markers of racial difference that marked the Native Hawaiian settlers. The perspective of the Mormon community, if that is indeed what the editors at the *Deseret News* represented, was that they were more than willing to overlook racial differences (so evident to many Mormons where the Chinese were concerned) to include their Native Hawaiian coreligionists. In any case the religious divide in the Salt Lake Valley and throughout the Mormon culture region extended to definitions of race when it suited the purposes of both Mormon and Gentile. For Native Hawaiians, however, such concessions on the part of Mormons must have done little to remedy the profoundly ambiguous situation in which they now found themselves.

Figure 1.
Lā'ie, early 1880s, looking up Po'oha'ili trail. LDS missionary families pose with sugar and taro fields in the background. Used by permission. Brigham Young University Hawai'i Archives. All rights reserved.

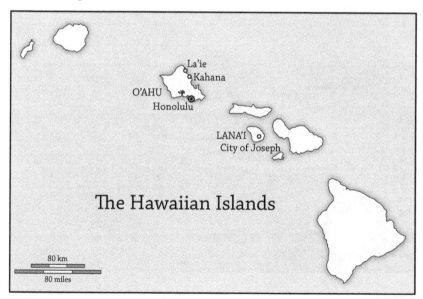

Figure 2.
Map of the Hawaiian Islands.

Figure 3.
I Hemolele, the Church of Jesus Christ of Latter-day Saint's chapel in Lā'ie, photographed here at the chapel's dedication in 1883. Used by permission. Brigham Young University Hawai'i Archives. All rights reserved.

Figure 4.
The Church of Jesus Christ of Latter-day Saints mission complex in Lā'ie, photographed in the mid-1890s. Used by permission. Brigham Young University Hawai'i Archives. All rights reserved.

Figure 5.
L.D.S. missionaries and sugar cane workers in Lāʻie, late nineteenth century. Used by permission. Brigham Young University Hawaiʻi Archives. All rights reserved.

Figure 6.
Grave of J. W. Kauleinamoku, Iosepa cemetery, Skull Valley, Utah.

Figure 7.
Jonathan Napela, one of the earliest converts to the Church of Jesus Christ of Latter-day Saints, photographed in Salt Lake City, Utah, in 1869. Used by permission. Church of Jesus Christ of Latter-day Saints Historical Department. All rights reserved.

Figure 8.
Solomon Pi'ipi'ilani, photographed in Salt Lake City, Utah, circa 1890. Used by permission.

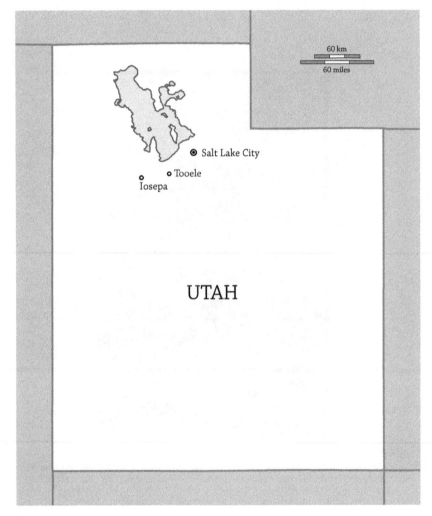

60 km

60 miles

⊙ Salt Lake City

○ Tooele

○
Iosepa

UTAH

Figure 9.
Map of Utah.

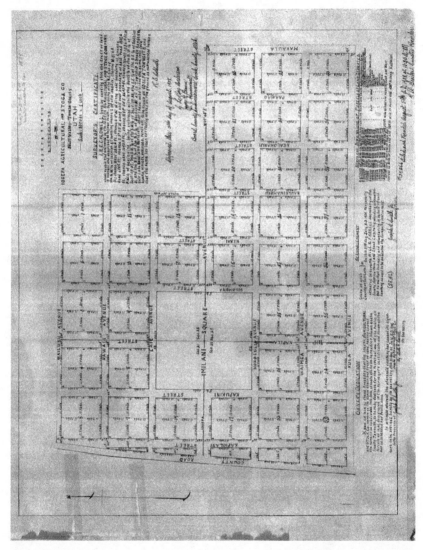

Figure 10.
Street map of Iosepa, Skull Valley, Utah. Used by permission. Tooele County Courthouse.

Figure 11.
The Iosepa Troubadors, circa 1905. The performing group composed of Native Hawaiian residents of Iosepa traveled through northern Utah and played at the homes of prominent LDS leaders like Benjamin Cluff, former missionary to Hawai'i and president of the Brigham Young Academy. Used by permission. Utah State Historical Society. All rights reserved.

Figure 12.
Ranch workers at the Iosepa Agricultural and Stock Corporation pose atop a horse-drawn wagon at Timpie Station. Used by permission. Utah State Historical Society. All rights reserved.

Figure 13.
Portrait of unidentified mother and daughter from Iosepa, circa 1910. Used by permission.
Brigham Young University Hawai'i Archives.

Figure 14.
Iosepa residents, Pioneer Day celebration, August 28, 1913. Used by permission. Utah
State Historical Society.

Figure 15.
Portrait of two unidentified young Native Hawaiian women in Salt Lake City, no date available. Used by permission. Utah State Historical Society. All rights reserved.

Figure 16.
Unidentified men posing in front of an Iosepa Ranch home, circa 1910. Used by permission. Utah State Historical Society. All rights reserved.

Figure 17.
Pouring cement sidewalks in town, circa 1910. Used by permission. Utah State Historical Society. All rights reserved.

Figure 18.
Portrait of Harvey Harris Cluff, president of the Hawaiian Mission of the Church of Jesus Christ of Latter-day Saints from 1879 to 1882 and manager of the Iosepa Agricultural and Stock Corporation from its founding in 1889. Used by permission. Brigham Young University Hawai'i Archives. All rights reserved.

Figure 19.
Dedication of the Hawai'i Temple of the Church of Jesus Christ of Latter-day Saints, Thanksgiving Day, 1919. Upon Joseph F. Smith's announcement that a temple would be built in Hawai'i, nearly all of the residents of Iosepa abandoned their homes in Skull Valley and returned to the islands. Many settled along what became known as Iosepa Street. Used by permission. Brigham Young University Hawai'i Archives. All rights reserved.

Figure 20.
Home of the John Broad family, Iosepa, Skull Valley, Utah, circa 1910. Used by permission. Utah State Historical Society. All rights reserved.

Figure 21.
The Iosepa memorial plaque and sculpture. The bust of a Hawaiian chief was sculpted by Jan Fisher and looks out over the cemetery across Skull Valley toward the Deep Creek mountain range. Used by permission. Brigham Young University Hawai'i Archives. All rights reserved.

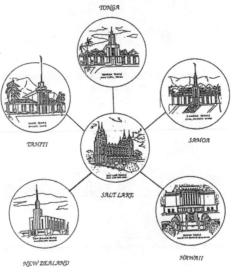

IOŚEPA POLYNESIAN FIRESIDE

August 27, 1989
7:00 pm
Assembly Hall
Temple Square
Salt Lake City, UT

Fruits of Spiritual Labor

Figure 22.
Cover art on a program for a fireside, part of the centennial celebration of the founding of Iosepa, 1989. The image depicts the five Church of Jesus Christ of Latter-day Saints temples in the Pacific surrounding the Salt Lake City Temple in the center. The Iosepa centennial celebrations emphasized a pan-Pacific identity based on the theme "Polynesian Pioneers." Used by permission. Brigham Young University Hawai'i Archives. All rights reserved.

Figure 23.
Cover of the Iosepa Centennial Celebration program, displaying the image of a Polynesian voyaging canoe. Used by permission. Brigham Young University Hawai'i Archives. All rights reserved.

Iosepa Historical Society · Laie Hawaii
and
Iosepa Historical Association · Salt Lake City, Utah
request your presence to attend our
Centennial Celebration (1889-1989)
Dedication of the Monument
Honoring our Polynesian Pioneers
at Iosepa Cemetary,
Skull Valley, Tooele, Utah
on the
28th of August 1989
at 9:00 a.m.

Luau and Entertainment
will follow after the Dedicatory Services
at the Grantsville Stake Center

IOSEPA, SKULL VALLEY, TOOELE, UTAH

Figure 24.
Interior pages of the Iosepa Centennial Celebration program, displaying the official logo of the event and its central theme, "Polynesian Pioneers." Used by permission. Brigham Young University Hawai'i Archives. All rights reserved.

CHAPTER 4

Iosepa

Creating a Native Hawaiian Community
in Skull Valley, Utah

The Native Hawaiian colony in Skull Valley was founded during a time of transition. Facing external pressures from both federal and territorial officials, the Church of Jesus Christ of Latter-day Saints was moving away from the colonization projects that had created Mormon communities throughout the Mormon culture region during the latter half of the nineteenth century.[1] This region was formed in large part by a colonization program designed to populate Brigham Young's proposed state of Deseret, which originally included the entire Great Basin extending south to San Bernardino, California, and the Pacific Ocean. When the US government limited Young's ambitious plans, early colonies on the fringes of his proposed state were reined in and concentrated in the most fertile valleys along the Wasatch Front. The political and economic realities the church faced in the latter part of the nineteenth century also hastened the end of new colonizing ventures. The few colonies established between 1880 and 1900 were concentrated outside the Mormon culture region proper, in Wyoming, Canada, and northern Mexico. Though most resembled the colonization model the church had pursued since early western settlement (a select group of families, called as missionaries, sent to create a cooperative community based on agricultural production or local industry), all were organized as joint stock companies, capitalized by selling shares to members or participants. The shift toward such modified colonization models was in response to the restrictions imposed by the 1887 Edmunds-Tucker Act.[2]

The scope and nature of colonization projects were not the only factors that changed for the church between 1890 and 1930. This transitional period of Mormonism saw sweeping changes in both sacred and secular matters. Indeed, if there was a pattern to these changes, it was a *separation* of the sacred and secular in the Mormon religious experience. Major changes included Wilford Woodruff's 1890 "manifesto," which revoked the church's sanction for polygamous marriages; the dissolution of the Mormon People's Party; the shift away from communal social and economic activity toward individualism; and the shift in emphasis away from the literal gathering of the Saints to Zion. These doctrines and practices, established over the previous half century in Utah, had created a distinct and cohesive group identity that now faced real crisis.[3]

Historian Thomas Alexander argues that between 1890 and 1930 Mormonism embarked on a necessary project of "world maintenance," the task of "legitimizing the changes that were taking place" in the Mormon world among its members.[4] The attitudes of church members about politics, marriage, cooperation versus individualism, and the relationship between church and state were shaped in a period of crisis and contention during what was seen by many Mormons as a struggle between the Kingdom of God and the Kingdom of Man. The changes in institutional focus necessary for the church's survival faced the strongest challenges from its own members. Ultimately, while some of these changes proved more difficult than others, the church's foundational doctrine of prophetic revelation provided a base upon which to build and create a a new set of strategies to cope with the changes of the twentieth century. New ideas about political affiliation and participation, marriage and family, the doctrine of the gathering, and communalism proved the most difficult traditions for Mormonism to abandon during this period of transition. These were replaced by emphases on other distinctive markers of Mormon group identity, namely adherence to a strict dietary code (the "Word of Wisdom," or abstinence from alcohol, tobacco, tea, and coffee) and building a comprehensive educational alternative to public schooling. These new markers of group distinction assumed a more prominent position in twentieth-century Mormonism, replacing older traditions that proved incompatible with American social norms.[5]

Alexander's work sheds light on the shifting social world of the Mormon culture region during the period of Iosepa's existence. Ultimately the communal ethos of nineteenth-century Mormonism that characterized Iosepa and its theological justification in the concept of the gathering eroded as the nineteenth century gave way to the twentieth, and the community felt it. In 1890 an ailing President Wilford Woodruff, just weeks before his declaration disavowing polygamy, visited Skull Valley on a short tour of church interests in the West and dedicated the land for the gathering of the Saints from the Hawaiian Islands and from all the "isles of the sea."[6] Ten years later, in 1900, the church distanced itself from any colonization projects, at least publicly, and President Lorenzo Snow "urged Church officials not to encourage members to emigrate to Utah." By 1907 church leaders were discouraging converts abroad from gathering to Zion, even though converts and members from Hawai'i, Samoa, Tahiti, and New Zealand continued to migrate in small numbers to Utah and to join the colony in Skull Valley.[7] Iosepa, born in the context of the gathering, ultimately grew less and less to resemble the changing face of Mormonism in the early twentieth century.

Iosepa was initially organized according to a model that blended the labor organization of the church's sugar plantation in Lā'ie and the "Mormon village" model of spatial and social organization.[8] Like many other plantation communities in Hawai'i, Lā'ie localized social life within a multiethnic plantation population. Lā'ie was primarily a Native Hawaiian community through the 1890s, when changes in the ethnic composition of the workforce shifted the demography of Lā'ie in ways that made it resemble neighboring plantations, with a large population of Chinese, Japanese, and after the turn of the century, Filipino workers.[9] Iosepa was organized around a hybrid economic model that combined the features of Mormon communal colonization projects with plantation social and labor organization, the latter borrowed from the church's ongoing experience running a Hawaiian sugar plantation. Laborers lived in housing provided by the company and relied on the community of laborers for most aspects of their social life.[10] Work was centered on farming and raising stock. The community was made up of a small village or town settlement with surrounding farms and ranch areas.[11] Before the advent of cash wages in Iosepa workers drew compensation against expenses owed to the company for housing, clothing, food, and other necessities of life that could not be produced within the household unit. Unlike in early sugar plantations in Hawai'i, Native Hawaiian labor in Lā'ie and Iosepa was not organized through contracts enforced by the power of the state. Instead, it was based on a collectively shared religious ideology that envisioned cooperative communities as a particular manifestation of righteous living.

Although the purpose of Iosepa was originally to provide means for Native Hawaiian Saints who settled in the Salt Lake Valley to rise above the status of "common laborers," the Iosepa Agricultural and Stock Company envisioned them as exactly that—laborers. Iosepa was a joint agricultural and stock company in which the lines between ecclesiastical and economic authority were intentionally blurred, with Native Hawaiians serving as laborers and white plantation managers and mission presidents managing the daily operations of the ranch, overseen by a board of directors comprised of principal shareholders. Although the more onerous aspects of plantation labor were absent from Iosepa, the colony nonetheless operated on principles that resembled those applied at the church's sugar plantation in Lā'ie. As in Lā'ie, in Iosepa Native Hawaiian language and cultural values dominated daily social life even in a radically different labor and physical environment.

The very public decision against granting citizenship to George Kamakaniau and the other Native Hawaiian applicants was hardly their first inkling of ill feelings on the part of their white neighbors, both Mormon and non-Mormon. Although the court's decision and subsequent media coverage occurred in June 1889, indications of serious problems faced by the Native Hawaiian community in Salt Lake City had been present for years. According to several reports, Native Hawaiian Saints "were not assimilated very well with other Latter-day Saints" and were often relegated to the most menial work and seasonal unemployment.[12] In addition, the death of a community member from Hansen's disease (leprosy) provoked an outcry among Salt Lake City residents. By the time Judge Zane handed down his verdict in *In re Kamaka Nian*, a committee led by former Hawaiian mission president Harvey Cluff, in response to rising public sentiment against the Native Hawaiian community's presence in the city, had been working feverishly for nearly a month to find a place to move them. On May 16, 1889, Cluff received a letter from Wilford Woodruff, the prophet and president of the church, calling him on yet another mission. Its purpose was to locate "land suitable for the colonization of the Hawaiians who have emigrated and may emigrate to Zion."[13] Cluff and the rest of the committee proposed the idea to the Native Hawaiian community that month:

> On this day the appointed committee met with the presidency in their office in Salt Lake City to whom the President outlined the scheme or policy of colonizing the Hawaiians. By request the committee visited the Hawaiians near the Warm Spring where they had settled down close together, and presented the plan as outlined by the Presidency. They willingly accepted the proposition and there and then appointed Elders J.W. Kauleinamoku, Kamakaniau, and Napeha a committee to act with the committee appointed by the Presidency to visit in several counties and report to the Presidency our findings with recommendations as to the most suitable place on which to place the colony.[14]

The committee evaluated four sites, but the eventual decision to purchase the ranch of Brother John T. Rich, located about seventy miles southwest of Salt Lake City in Skull Valley, rested with the First Presidency, the church's highest administrative and ecclesiastical-level body. Other potential sites included farms near Ogden, Provo, and Garfield, all much less remote than the Skull Valley site. The committee returned on June 14 to "report to the Presidency who decided by unanimous vote to purchase the John T. Rich ranch in Skull Valley." It is unclear to what extent, if any, the committee influenced the decision to colonize the Saints in the most remote and far-removed of the potential settlement sites.

Despite its isolation (and its ominous moniker), Skull Valley had several characteristics that made it desirable for settlement. It was noted for winters that were "milder than Salt Lake or Tooele valleys." More importantly, the ranch was one of the few portions of the valley with an adequate supply of fresh water for both drinking and irrigation. In his report to Woodruff, Cluff described the potential site:

> In Skull Valley, Tooele Co. we find the property of Brother J. Rich can be obtained, which consists of 1920 acres with twelve miles of good substantial pole w/ wire fence, 640 acres of the above is a school section, and in them the pasture enclosure, for the balance, 1280 acres he has the government title, the other lands there are 200 acres under cultivation, with very fine growing crops...and the exclusive right of small streams from the East Range of mountains, which streams are conveyed in one ditch, this being the only running stream within a radius of many miles.... In addition there are a number of large springs on the property, one of which forms a fish pond nearly a thousand feet long, and from all indications an abundant additional water supply can be obtained from flowing wells.[15]

The ranch was close to an ample supply of timber and to lumber mills, as well as material to make adobe bricks, a popular construction method in early Mormon settlements. It was purchased with farm machinery intact, including plows, a thresher, and some cattle and other livestock. However, it lacked suitable structures to house even a small number of families through the winter, a problem that would become far more serious as cold weather began to set in.

Although Skull Valley was for the most part dry, desolate, and barren, the Rich ranch, like nearly all lands claimed by whites in the Great Basin, was located in an area with a stable supply of water. Tiny and isolated, the ranch was a small oasis in the midst of a very large and truly hostile and foreboding desert, thirty miles distant from Grantsville, the nearest proper town, and fifteen miles north of the reservation of the Skull Valley band of the Gosiute Indians. Cluff noted this in his report to Woodruff, stating that "the property in Skull Valley being thirty miles distant from Grantsville the nearest settlement makes it somewhat isolated, so far as social and religious considerations are concerned."[16] In fact, isolation was the ranch's most obvious characteristic. It was not the climate or the lack of arable land that made Iosepa different from other Mormon communities, but its isolation. By 1890 the string of settlements along the Wasatch Range that extended from Cache Valley to Parowan and St. George in the south was established and well-populated. Early Mormon settlement patterns radiating out from Salt Lake City followed a distinctly north-south pattern, originally extending to San Bernardino with the ultimate goal of solidifying Mormon control over the gargantuan "State of Deseret," which was to reach the Pacific Ocean in the southwest and envelope most of present-day Nevada, southern Idaho, western Wyoming and Colorado, and northern Arizona. Formal settlements ventured slowly westward into the valleys of present-day Tooele County, the poor soil and lack of water proving formidable barriers to expanding Mormon settlements. Even though settlements established in the earliest years of Mormon expansion in the Great Basin extended much farther than the seventy miles that separated the Rich ranch from Salt Lake City, Skull Valley remained an isolated outpost.

Roughly three months passed between the initial decision to remove the Native Hawaiian Saints from Salt Lake City and their arrival in Skull Valley. By the time the committee had decided on the Rich ranch in Skull Valley as the site they would purchase, it was already June. There was little time to prepare the ranch for the arrival of the first fifty settlers. Nevertheless, nearly all of the Native Hawaiian community left the city to settle there. On August 28, 1889, named "Hawaiian Pioneer Day" by Cluff, forty-eight settlers left Salt Lake City with their possessions loaded onto wagons and made the journey west to Skull Valley. That afternoon Frederick Mitchell, with the help of his son, began to survey the town site, divide up home lots, and build homes. The settlers christened their new home "Iosepa," in honor of Joseph F. Smith. One of the first decisions the settlers made was to select a site for the cemetery. On September 15 Makaopiopio, the mother-in-law of J. W. Kauleinamoku, died, and she was buried in Skull Valley. Despite the sadness that this event must have occasioned, in church services the following Sunday, "the Brethren and Sisters expressed great satisfaction and gratitude to God for bringing them to this place."[17]

IOSEPA, 1889–1900: "FIRST WE ARE TRIED AND THEN WE ARE BLESSED"

The settlers at Iosepa faced significant challenges during the colony's first ten years. Settlers worked as ranch hands and were paid wages in company scrip, redeemable at a ranch store. Dissatisfaction with labor relations, unfamiliar work, and a radically different environment, combined with a series of unusually severe winters, made for a miserable start. National events offered no relief. A series of economic depressions in the 1890s crippled the livestock market and drove the ranch deep into debt. Many wished to return home, and several families abandoned the colony, returned to Salt Lake City, and petitioned the Hawaiian government to repatriate them. The climate took its toll as well. Pneumonia and influenza contributed to a high death rate that affected primarily the elderly and children. An outbreak of Hansen's disease and the accompanying outcry caused both public and private turmoil for the inhabitants. The completion of the Salt Lake Temple in 1894 reminded community members of their isolation: the city was an expensive three days' travel from Iosepa. In ten years the population in Iosepa grew by only about fifty people.

Obtaining the means to purchase the ranch reflected the difficulties that the Church of Jesus Christ of Latter-day Saints faced after the Edmunds-Tucker Act passed in 1887. The legislation enforced a section of the Morrill Act, first passed in 1862, which prohibited the church from owning any property valued above $50,000. To maintain church control over new colonization projects and cooperative industrial ventures, such undertakings were structured as joint stock corporations after 1887, with the church holding large shares of stock alongside private investors (usually prosperous Mormons.)[18] The Iosepa Agricultural and Stock Company was one of seven new joint stock ventures the church embarked on between 1885 and 1900.[19] The main participants in the company's incorporation were former missionaries to Hawai'i, including mission president Harvey H. Cluff and his brother William, Frederick Mitchell, Henry Richards, and several others. J. W. Kauleinamoku purchased a small number of shares as well. Most of these men also served on the committee that selected Iosepa as a colonization site for the Native Hawaiian Saints. Native Hawaiians who owned property in Salt Lake City, including Kauleinamoku, Peter Kealaka'ihonua, A. H. Kapukini, Solomona Pi'ipi'ilani, and the Maka'ula family,[20] agreed upon a fair price with John Rich and applied the sale of their property in the city to the ranch's purchase price, which was to be paid in several installments. Unlike many of the other joint stock ventures founded by the church during this era, almost no one outside of those immediately connected with the Iosepa Agricultural and Stock Company purchased shares. As stated in the Company's Articles of Incorporation, its purpose was "to carry on the business of agriculture, stockraising, merchandising and manufacturing, and the sale and purchase of real estate in the Territory of Utah."[21] The company was organized into a seven-member board of directors. Initially all of these men were non-Hawaiians who had purchased a substantial quantity of the corporation's shares. They exercised full authority over the colony's affairs. For all practical purposes, it was these men and those who replaced them who managed the agricultural, livestock raising, and speculative affairs of the ranch, with the Native Hawaiian residents serving as wage laborers.

The company purchased John T. Rich's ranch, both land and "improvements," for $35,000. The livestock on the property, which included 129 horses and 335 head of cattle, cost an additional $12,279. The land included 1,920 fenced acres, 200 of which were under cultivation. It also included several springs and a large pond. The several streams that ran from the Stansbury Mountains onto the property were diverted into a ditch. The property also included several "large springs."[22] Rich received a $5,000 down payment for the property, the balance to be paid in installments of $4,285.71 for seven years at 8 percent interest. Over the next three years sections of land were added to the original lands purchased. Several parcels were later obtained by company officials and subsequently sold back to the company. Two Native Hawaiian colonists, James Halemanu and John Mahoe, filed on 160-acre sections of land and sold them to the company in 1915 and 1916, respectively, probably as a means to pay for their return trip to Hawai'i or to recoup the expenses they had incurred building homes in Iosepa. In 1906 a portion of the company's land holdings was sold to railroad agents for the Western Pacific line for $25,000, the company's only profitable speculative venture until the liquidation of its holdings in 1917.[23] "Altogether, during the twenty-eight years of its existence, the company purchased 5,273.19 acres at an aggregate price of $58, 302.78." The sum of the sale to the railroad and the final sale of the company's property to the Deseret Livestock Company in 1917 for $150,000 means that in twenty-eight years, the Iosepa Agricultural and Stock Company made approximately $90,000 on property transactions in Skull Valley.[24] Iosepa remained incorporated under its original name, the Iosepa Agricultural and Stock Company, until its demise in 1917 and the subsequent sale of the ranch. Although the buying and selling of land in the valley ultimately proved profitable, speculative real estate ventures were never the primary goal for the company. Instead, agriculture and stock raising were intended to provide the majority of its revenue. To make money, the company grew and sold feed to stockmen on neighboring ranches, sold produce and staple crops, boarded livestock, and eventually purchased livestock to raise and resell.[25]

The company's organizational strategy and profit model was a blend of enterprises suited to the landscape of the West with a labor model based on the experience of the church in Hawai'i. Ecclesiastically, Iosepa was run as a mission (a branch or a ward was the typical model for the church's other colonizing and settlement ventures in the West).[26] This meant that as in Lāʻie, the ranch manager also served as the mission president. This person was expected to oversee both the temporal and spiritual lives of those who labored for the company and lived in the town. The mission president reported directly to the First Presidency of the Church, a status that potentially provided privileged access to the upper echelons of Mormon power and authority. However, residents were also expected to labor on the ranch not for cash wages, but for credit at the company store. This system, though unknown in any of the church's other colonizing ventures in the West, was common by the late 1880s and early 1890s for contract labor on sugar plantations in Hawaiʻi, and Lāʻie was no exception. During Iosepa's first decade, the two men the First Presidency of the Church called as both ranch managers and mission presidents (Harvey H. Cluff and William King) had also served in the same capacity in Hawaiʻi. The same patriarchal impulse that motivated church leaders in the Palawai Valley on Lānaʻi and in Lāʻie to "instruct and uplift" Native Hawaiian converts in the "arts of civilization"[27] motivated the organizational structure of Iosepa. By placing the ranch manager in a position of both managerial and ecclesiastical authority over the Native Hawaiian laborers on the plantation, the company was able to blur the lines between sacred and secular authority. This allowed the management to mobilize overtly religious language and metaphors to serve the labor needs of the ranch. This model proved in subsequent years to be the root of complex social tensions in Iosepa, much as it did in Lāʻie.[28]

Reports periodically published in the *Deseret News*, from Harvey Cluff and later from ranch manager and mission president Thomas Anson Waddoups, related the general condition of both the colony and company. A report from Cluff in the summer of 1892 stated:

> The colony is a prosperous condition. Our crops are abundant, there being four hundred acres under cultivation in hay and grain. We have now gathered our first crop of lucern, amounting to over three hundred tons, and we shall commence cutting grain in the early part of next week. Our crop of wheat, oats, and barley will reach about six thousand bushels. In addition to hay and grain, we have corn, vines, and roots, in twenty-five acres. We enclosed with cedar posts and wire fencing, last spring, 1600 acres, cleared off the sagebrush, and planted the land with grain, vegetables, and vines, the growing crops therein are excellent this season.[29]

In December 1894 another *Deseret News* article reported that "the crops raised this year include 1,850 bushels of wheat, 1,650 of oats, 3,200 of barley, 200 of corn, and 500 of potatoes, besides 650 tons of hay, 125 tons of squash and pumpkins, and a large amount of garden produce...The Hawaiians at Iosepa have on hand sufficient breadstuffs to last them between two and three years." The article continued: "The colony will also market this year 150 head of swine."[30] It seemed that the community had begun to prosper.

LABOR

Despite these accounts of abundance, the company failed to turn a profit between 1889 and 1900, and during many years it operated at a loss.[31] Also absent in these accounts of the colony and company's "condition" was the underlying tension over wages and working conditions. In these years especially, labor conditions on the ranch were the subject of no small amount of consternation on the part of the Native Hawaiian settlers. Disputes arose primarily over wages, which were not paid in cash until after the first decade of the twentieth century. This proved to be an unacceptable situation to many Native Hawaiians, who reckoned that they could be paid higher wages, in cash, for their work in either Salt Lake City or one of the nearby mining communities. Tactics used by workers in disputes over wages in Iosepa ranged from work avoidance and slowdowns to organized walkouts and at least two strikes. Letters from Native Hawaiian settlers to both church and government officials mentioned wages specifically as a point of contention. It was primarily disputes over labor that caused the greatest threat to the community's existence in its early years. Dissatisfaction over wages, coupled with racism toward Native Hawaiians, eventually prompted the Hawaiian government to intervene on behalf of its subjects based on reports of mistreatment at the hands of church members and officials. For a brief period these issues also created two Native Hawaiian communities in Utah: one in Iosepa and one in Salt Lake City, composed of Native Hawaiians who had either refused to go to Skull Valley in the first place or had abandoned Iosepa because of perceived mistreatment.

The majority of Native Hawaiian settlers at Iosepa worked for the company as laborers. A smaller number of men worked as skilled laborers (blacksmiths and carpenters). Women's labor in the colony was focused primarily on household and child care, although there are several mentions of Native Hawaiian women providing domestic service in the plantation manager's homes, as well as contributing expertise as midwives or healers. Work was plentiful: fencing in newly acquired land, plowing and sowing fields, harvesting the crops and delivering them to market, and caring for livestock required the labor of all able-bodied men at the colony. Maintaining good labor relations was essential to ranch operations and keeping all of the

colonists busy. All worked for a daily wage and were compensated, throughout the years the colony existed, in various ways, either through credit for
living expenses and items available at the company store or in scrip redeemable for goods and (occasionally) cash. Not until 1907 were the workers
paid cash wages. Many younger men (and some older men as well) left to
seek employment in the nearby mining communities and at various times
even tried their hands at prospecting in the nearby canyons.[32] Some chose
to leave Iosepa to find work in Salt Lake City, while several families apparently refused to leave Salt Lake to settle in Iosepa, for unknown reasons.
Many workers saw the Iosepa Agricultural and Stock Company less as a
source of full-time employment than as a standby opportunity for work in
the absence of steady employment in the mines or other ventures nearby,
especially since wages in Iosepa were comparatively low and not paid in
cash. Nevertheless, abandoning Iosepa seasonally for employment elsewhere was frowned upon by the company, and community members were
reprimanded by church leaders for doing so. "Some revert to sin, leaving
Iosepa in the night, because they have many debts there," wrote Joseph F.
Smith in 1890. "They go to Iosepa in the cold times (in the winter), the time
when some cannot work.... They live there until the winter is done, getting
food, and other various things...and when spring comes, they can work,
they flee...without paying their debts."[33]

An issue that Iosepa faced between 1889 and 1891 was some of the colonists complaining to the Hawaiian government about wages in Iosepa. They
also complained about the general treatment they experienced at the hands
of church members and officials. This issue surfaced even before the Native
Hawaiian community in Salt Lake City was removed to Skull Valley, but it
continued and in fact gained intensity after their relocation. As a result of
the large number of Native Hawaiians living and working abroad throughout the latter half of the nineteenth century, the Hawaiian government
selectively funded the repatriation of Native Hawaiian "distressed sailors."[34] On June 22, 1889, D. A. McKinley, consul general for the Hawaiian
government in San Francisco, received a message from William F. Kinney,
a Hawaiian official in Salt Lake City, regarding several families of Native
Hawaiians who wished to return to the islands. Kinney alerted the consul
general to the situation of Native Hawaiian families whose wishes to return
home were frustrated because they, in his words, "did not have the wherewithal." He described the complaints of the applicants for repatriation:

As far as I can learn the natives are very well heated by the...large class of
Mormons in the city here who like many of the descendents of the missionaries at the Islands are very busy laying up treasure where moth and rust does

corrupt, and don't look at our Kanaka brethren at all or if at all only as next door to the darkey to be treated accordingly. Some of the natives get steady work others do not. All have to work for the money as they never did at home. It is not a case of destitution but of homesickness. The Supreme Court of the State of Utah has just held that Native Hawaiians are not eligible for American citizenship and this will greatly depreciate their political value to the Mormons. . . . The Church is in deep water here—the US govt has confiscated their property. . . . [Their] financial power is on the wane and much they could and did do for natives before and would like to do for them again probably will be soon out of their power to accomplish.[35]

Kinney's explanation confirms the depth of concern on the part of church members about racism toward Natives Hawaiians from both Mormons and non-Mormons. The letter also acknowledges the church's precarious political position, a situation that the Native Hawaiian community felt acutely during their time in the city. Kinney's sense of urgency regarding the condition of the Native Hawaiian community in Salt Lake City was reflected in the volume of correspondence on the matter received by the consul general's office in San Francisco. Three days after his first letter, Kinney sent a follow-up to his original inquiry, stating that he wanted instruction in the matter as soon as possible.[36] After receiving no response, Kinney followed up with a brief telegram that stated: "Those natives who expressed a desire to return now tell me that they are getting the cold shoulder from the church and cannot get work. I think their condition is more urgent than my letter indicates."[37] The response from the consul general's office, sometime after August 16, was that the applicants' request was denied, on the grounds that repatriation funds were set aside for the aid of "distressed seamen." While several of the Native Hawaiian families sought assistance from their government to return home, the committee to select a suitable site for a new colony deliberated. On August 28, 1889, forty-eight members of the community left their homes in Salt Lake City and moved their belongings to the Rich ranch in Skull Valley.

Acclimating to the environment in Skull Valley proved a daunting task for the Native Hawaiian settlers and was made all the more difficult by several unusually cold winters and the reality of sickness throughout the colony. Cold and sickness kept many from work. The onset of cold weather "drove nearly all of the Hawaiians indoors and the more they hovered around the fires with closed doors and windows, the more difficult it was to get them out to work."[38] "One great drawback with the natives," wrote Cluff, "in standing our mountain winter weather [is that] when indoors they close every door and window allowing no ventilation and when they do go out to cold it strikes them more severely."[39] In January of the first year an initial outbreak of "la grippe" caused widespread sickness, primarily among the very young and very old, and "nearly the whole colony were stricken down."[40] In subsequent years the onset of cold weather continued to spawn bouts of sickness throughout the community. Susceptibility to disease did not discriminate, however. Cluff himself lost two sons to sickness between 1889 and 1892; the latter died from diphtheria while living in Provo, Utah. These and other issues weighed heavily on the minds of the colonists. Hosea Kekauoha's complaints in a letter to Joseph F. Smith in the fall of 1890 identified several sources of consternation about the climate, the lack of money, and the remoteness of their new home:

> I heard from Hawe [Cluff], he told me to go to the temple these days; that is the great joy of living here. However, I said to Hawe, I shouldn't go these days because it is very cold lately. There is a lot of snow here in Iosepa, and it is also very cold lately. That is the reason I was reluctant, because there are not any warm clothes to go. That is one thing; this is the second: There aren't any coins for riding the train to the temple. Those are my reasons I told to Hawe. I told him when there are some coins and some warm clothing I will go. I am requesting of you, servant of the most high God and our leader, to be patient with me....I have no doubt in this....Food is not a problem. We are continuing to work on the land with great happiness.[41]

Kekauoha complained indirectly, using deferential language, a rhetorical strategy common to Native Hawaiians.[42] Even through this culturally specific use of language, the nature of his difficulties emerges clearly. The purpose of his letter was to bring these matters to the attention of someone who might be able to do something about them.

Kekauoha's frustration with the lack of money was felt throughout the community, and it seems to have been the key complaint regarding the situation in Skull Valley. Charles William Naau[43] spoke with a representative from the Utah Territorial Governor's office in 1890 and related some of the issues he faced:

> [Naau] came to Utah three years ago, and has a wife and three children. He lives in a farm four miles north of the central business place, and the homes of other Hawaiians in Skull Valley. He said he contracted for the farm of 160 acres for which he was to pay $5,100.00 but the church authorities told him he could not own land because he was not a citizen of the United States, and the land was taken by the Iosepa Co.; but he is permitted to live there and till the soil on consideration of giving one-half the product to the Company....[H]e did not

like to live in Skull Valley and wanted to go to Salt Lake City where he could make money. I asked him if he was ordered to Skull Valley, and he said they were all ordered from Salt Lake City to this place, and that they could not go to Salt Lake City or any place very far off unless they got a permit from Manager, and added: "If the Bishop say no we got to stop...." He told of having left his island home three years ago with $1,200 in money, that he out $800.00 of this in a house and lot in Salt Lake City where he would like to live "but the President of the Church orders we must stay here in Skull Valley." When he lived in Salt Lake City, he worked on the Temple being paid $2.00 per day in tithing orders for seventy five cents on the dollar. He again mentioned his desire to go to Salt Lake City to work and get money, and added "but the President will not let me go, and the Manager watches us closely...." He concluded the conversation by saying: "I have worked here five months and have not seen as much as five cents in money."[44]

George Peters, Sam Kini, Joseph Kekuku, Sam Kinimakalehua, and others made similar complaints about the labor situation on the ranch, taking issue with the ambiguity in the price of goods at the store, the lack of transparency in tracking the number of hours worked, and the lack of freedom to travel freely between Salt Lake City and Skull Valley. By the winter of 1890 Kekuku, Samuel Ki'i, and several others had returned to Salt Lake City and were "getting $2.75 per day for mixing mortar."[45] All had made requests through the Hawaiian consul general's office that their return fare back to the islands be paid by the government.

Labor unrest on the ranch as a result of general dissatisfaction with compensation continued throughout the 1890s. "Work on a ranch varies," wrote one historian regarding labor patterns in Iosepa: "[I]n the summer there is much to do while in the winter the only labors performed are the chores and feeding and caring for livestock. Yet [in Iosepa] work was guaranteed the year round whether it was profitable for the company or not. Therefore, Iosepa's winter wages exceeded those of surrounding areas, and their summer wages were lower than those obtainable on nearby ranches."[46]

In 1892 requests for general raises in the daily wages paid by the ranch began, and they continued in a form of collective bargaining in which Native Hawaiian ranch workers proposed various alternatives to hourly wages. When these proved unsuccessful, ranch workers attempted to organize general strikes against ranch managers. These efforts were thwarted because of factionalism among workers fostered by managerial strategies that pitted teams of workers against one another. In June 1892 four men approached Harvey Cluff with a proposition that they be paid to haul hay with their own teams and be compensated per load instead of the standard daily wage of $1.50. This request began a short but consequential standoff between Native Hawaiian laborers and the *Haole* ranch managers that nearly ended in a general strike against the company. In response to the workers' initial request, Cluff offered to pay them "75 cents per load which is a good round price." The men countered with an offer to collect their daily wages in addition to a $1.50 per day fee for the use of their own teams, a proposition that Cluff indicated he would consider. The following day the four men "did not commence work." They met again with Cluff and presented two options, which negotiated hourly wages as well as a price per load, but included a provision for an eight-hour workday. Cluff countered with the demand that "the urgency of the work would govern the length of time to continue within reasonable limits, [and] when hay or grain was suffering and a little extra time was needed I expected them to assist without pay." The four men unanimously held out for an eight-hour day, with any hours worked in addition to that to include "extra pay."[47]

Cluff successfully negotiated favorable terms for the company by manipulating a division between the older and younger men on the ranch. Several of the younger men approached Cluff the following day and offered to use the company teams to haul the cut hay at seventy-five cents per load plus a fee of $1.50 per day to manage the teams, the sum of which they would presumably divide among themselves. Cluff agreed to this proposal, and they began the work immediately. After several days of hauling hay according to this arrangement, the "representative" of the four older men approached Cluff and informed him that "they were ready to commence hauling hay at my figures as soon as there was sufficient ready for hauling," but only after informing them that "they could feed their teams hay during the morning hour only." Cluff's strategy to bargain with the younger men, while at the same time withholding feed from the older men's teams, had the desired effect. Unable to earn wages or sustain their teams elsewhere, all of the ranch laborers were once again actively engaged in hauling hay, and by Cluff's estimation "working very hard." Although efforts to call a general strike of all ranch workers were hinted at at various times throughout 1892, they never materialized.[48]

Adding to the general dissatisfaction over wages on the ranch were the prospects of mineral deposits in the nearby mountains yielding profitable mining claims. In January 1893 several of the colonists in Iosepa became "caught in a little excitement over mineral prospects in the mountain just above the townsite." For several days workers abandoned the ranch in favor of blasting at various sites in nearby mountains in search of minerals, possibly gold. None of these mining claims ever produced anything, and for the majority of colonists work on the ranch at the daily wage of

$1.50 continued. Consistent with previous company policy, however, the wages were paid not in cash, but in credit at the company store. In March 1894 the issue of wages, never truly dormant, again surfaced. After advising "Lua and family not to accept the offer of Cecil Brown and forsake Zion," Cluff reported that several men had asked about a raise in wages.[49] "I told them," wrote Cluff, "that the Presidency advised the meeting of the directors during Conference to consult about raising their wages and that they would do right by them and that each one had better keep to work until time to go into Conference but they refused to do so."[50] A day later every Native Hawaiian worker on the ranch walked off the job. Despite Cluff's continued insistence that the board would "do what was right by them," the workers appealed as a group to the First Presidency of the Church, who deferred to the company's board of directors. The timing of the strike was key, as it occurred during the time when crops were being planted. The men repeatedly told Cluff that they would not resume work during planting time, because when planting was finished it would diminish their bargaining power. "The arguments of the natives were that if they assisted in putting in the crops being the most important part of farming, the Board would be so independent that they would not raise their wages, hence they withheld their services thinking to put us out a great deal."[51] In response to the strike the board introduced a system of graded wage labor, which classified workers and paid them accordingly. The highest classification received $1.50 per day, still lower than could be found on neighboring ranches or mining towns, but guaranteed year-round employment. Although this action satisfied the labor force for a time, it did not end disputes over wages. Following a request for higher wages in 1900 the company's board actually reclassified wages at a *lower* rate than previously, precipitating another strike.[52]

The issue of wages remained a challenge for the ranch until well past the turn of the century and was closely tied to the movement for repatriation to Hawai'i. Confusion over the number of hours and days worked arose in an environment where labor value was expressed in dollar figures yet cash wages were withheld. Costs for food, housing, adequate clothing, pocket money for transportation, and other consumer needs had to be negotiated between the laborers and ranch managers. While Native Hawaiian laborers in Iosepa complained that they had "not seen so much as five cents in money," church leaders like Smith characterized the workers' frustration and abandonment of the colony as "sin." Ranch manager Thomas Anson Waddoups remarked some years later that the credit system that preceded the shift to cash wages "was anything but a satisfactory arrangement either to us or them."[53]

THE MOVE FOR REPATRIATION

The earliest years of the settlement saw a split in the community, with several families living in Salt Lake City and the remainder of the Native Hawaiians living and working in Iosepa. Those living in the city continued to petition the consulate in San Francisco to be repatriated, claiming that they represented the views of many in Skull Valley who were too afraid to speak openly about their situation. It was a trying time for both groups. William Kinney wrote to McKinley at his San Francisco office in January 1891:

> There are a great many more at Skull Valley who want to return but who are all right-as long as they remain under the church and who can therefore wait until spring or until the government concludes to send for them. But the 13 natives in Salt Lake cannot wait-they are already living on charity. Dr. AB Carter in his way east lately left $100 with me to be spent for the natives owing to the death of two of their children....I certainly hope you will find the means to send them home without waiting further orders from home. These natives clearly come under the head of destitute Hawaiians.[54]

Several months later money was appropriated for many of these individuals to return to Hawai'i, and throughout the remainder of 1891 several families availed themselves of the opportunity.

Church officials moved quickly to respond to the flurry of reports and defend themselves against charges of mistreatment in the colony. An article was published in the *Deseret News* in November 1890 to counter the report of A. B. Carter, a well-respected physician from Hawai'i whose unflattering account of the conditions in Skull Valley was reprinted in several western newspapers, including the *Denver News*. The editors of the *Deseret News* claimed that Carter's account was "either partly or wholly fictitious" and offered an alternative version of both Native Hawaiian immigration into Salt Lake City and the decision to relocate the community to Skull Valley. Initially, the article contended, the community in Salt Lake City was "well satisfied and other natives followed them." Their removal was based solely on the lack of sufficient employment prospects; however, as "it soon became apparent that they would not rise above ordinary laborers, unless some better opportunity than this city was afforded them." The supposed concern over the Hawaiians' status as "ordinary laborers" was confusing, because that was their primary occupation in Iosepa. The rumors of dissatisfaction and the move to apply for repatriation, the article stated, had come primarily from one man, whose animosity toward the colonization project stemmed from the fact that he "had been excommunicated for improper conduct." Regarding the condition of the Iosepa community, the editor stated:

> There is no destitution in Skull Valley. Some of those who have returned were improvident and spent more that their income, so that they ran behind their brethren in the possession of "creature comforts." But they have all been supplied with necessaries and some luxuries through the kindness of the Elders having the matter in charge.... The Hawaiians, we learn, are doing very well and are contented and prosperous.[55]

The editor's assertions about the colony's "prosperous" condition were verified by other observers, based on the quality and volume of the company's agricultural production, as well as the potential of the property in relation to the surrounding area.[56] In addition, although several Native Hawaiian families continued to organize their return to Hawai'i, by January 1891 at least three other families had decided to remain in Salt Lake City, "gain[ing] their livelihood by work such as hod-carriers and the like, and now that building has stopped they told me they had promise of such food and support as they needed from the Mormon Church, drawing their provisions from the Tithing House."[57] Together with "two or three families from the Skull Valley Settlement...they all agreed in representing the colony in very fair condition; they said to the best of their knowledge and belief, there were none who wished to return to the mother country at this time."[58] Scarcely a week later, however, Kinney sent six people to San Francisco to be returned home.

At Kinney's request the church responded to both the public accusations and the official investigations by the Utah territorial government and the Hawaiian government. President Woodruff wrote a letter to Kinney in April 1991 attempting to explain the situation from the church's perspective:

> We feel deeply obliged to you for the pains you have taken to write to us upon this subject and to give us the opportunity to explain our position so that we may not appear in a wrong light to Her Majesty's Government, the Queen of Hawaii. [It is] altogether incorrect and without the least foundation in truth for these people or any others to convey the idea that we have used any influence to restrain [the Hawaiians] from returning.... We think it can be truthfully stated that there has been no encouragement given to the native Hawaiian people of our faith to emigrate to this country. For many years many of them have been urging our Elders to arrange affairs so that they could come; but there has been a feeling of reluctance entertained by us concerning their coming as we know how great a trial it might prove to them to live in a climate and in surroundings such as ours .... The most that can be said in regard to our influencing these people to

remain is that our people have encouraged them, inasmuch as they come here, to make the best of their situation and to stay, assuring them that if they applied themselves to their labors they would soon be in a position of comfort and relative independence.[59]

Woodruff also explained (presumably based on information given to him by Cluff or Joseph F. Smith; he did not speak Hawaiian) that Peter Kealaka'ihonua, who was on Kinney's list of Hawaiians wishing to return to the islands, in fact did not want to return to Hawai'i, nor did anyone else in the colony.

What emerges from these contradictory accounts is a divided community conflicted by their desire to fulfill the religious obligations that began their journey but disillusioned with the realities of their adopted homeland. Kinney recognized this and found himself in the frustrating position of mediating among the Native Hawaiian community, the Church of Jesus Christ of Latter-day Saints, and the Hawaiian consulate in San Francisco. Torn by indecision, Native Hawaiians in Utah vacillated between committing to the harsh realities of their new home and grabbing hold of the opportunity to return to the familiar life and landscape of Hawai'i. Referring to a group of seven Native Hawaiians "that originally wanted to go" but changed their minds at the last minute, Kinney remarked, "What made them change their mind was a mixture (I think) of love for relatives that were in Skull Valley, and the dread of going to the Mormons' hell which had been promised them if they went back on Utah altogether and returned to the Islands." In addition, Kinney was informed that "they believed that the desire to return was prompted of the Devil and would if yielded to result in disaster (pains) to themselves, that God would be displeased with them for turning back, and that they would be punished for it." These were charges that Woodruff explicitly denied.[60]

The question of religious obligation weighed heavily on the Native Hawaiian colonists. Both Joseph F. Smith and Harvey Cluff linked Iosepa with the gathering of the Saints to Zion in the last days, a connection that many in the community seem to have internalized. Cluff responded to the widespread desire of the Native Hawaiian settlers to abandon Iosepa by counseling both individuals and the community as a whole against leaving Skull Valley. The centrality of the gathering in the religious lives of the Saints at Iosepa was articulated unequivocally by Joseph F. Smith in personal communications with community members. Smith equated disobedience, laziness, and abandonment of the colony with a rejection of the larger project of building Zion. In addition, he articulated the belief that Native Hawaiians were Lamanites and that their gathering to Zion fulfilled biblical prophecy. "[The Hawaiians] arrived in the land of their ancestors, their legacy," wrote Smith in a letter to Kealohapauole Kaholoakeahole. "Therefore, they are not foreigners in a foreign land, rather on the birth sands of their ancestors."[61] News of the complaints about wages, the climate, and other restrictions in Iosepa reached Smith via the popular press as well as through letters from old friends from his days as a missionary in Hawai'i, many of whom had settled in Skull Valley. Many petitioned Smith directly with their issues; others complained about the lack of faith in their neighbors. Smith's responses, in nearly every case, straddled genuine compassion for the hardships endured by his friends and a resolute firmness against abandoning the colony or maligning its leaders. "Too bad," Smith wrote to Moses Nakuaau in October of 1890, "for the people who revert to sin. They tremble and their hearts will beat quickly and they will fall into the fire. However, we are pleasant with them because they do not know the things they do."[62] In response to Hosea Kekauoha's concerns over the lack of money and sufficient clothing to ward off the cold, Smith replied, "Be patient and continue to work hard in the land, and you will soon receive all of the things that you need.... First we are tried, and after we are blessed."[63] Smith expressed his feelings regarding those who left the colony and returned to Salt Lake City in 1890 in a letter to Samuel Kinimakalehua, after being notified that several of the original deserters desired to return to Skull Valley. "Oh! The uselessness of wavering! The firm faith in the religion of Christ is truly beautiful."[64]

Like Joseph F. Smith, Harvey Cluff actively discouraged the Saints at Iosepa from abandoning Skull Valley and returning to Hawai'i, invoking the religious obligation of gathering to Zion to defend his position. In March 1894 Cluff "advised Lua and family not to accept the offer of Cecil Brown to return to the Islands and forsake Zion,"[65] advice that came, not coincidentally, in the midst of tense negotiations between labor and management on the ranch regarding wages and other forms of compensation. Cluff's dual role as ranch manager and mission president once again blurred the line between the sacred and secular in managing the lives of the colonists. In August of the same year Cluff wrote that many of the Native Hawaiian Saints were "especially excited over a letter from the Hawaiian Consul residing at San Francisco offering to pay the fare of all who wished to return to their Island home. They viewed it as a command from their government to return and felt under obligation to obey."[66] The following Sunday Cluff addressed the Saints during religious services and encouraged them not to leave. "I talked upon the gathering of the Saints and the benefits to those who remained faithful and showed the Hawaiian Saints that they were under the dominion of the Church and not the Hawaiian Government."[67]

Cluff's exhortations had the desired effect, and many gave up their designs to return to Hawai'i.

Several days later Cluff addressed the First Presidency of the Church regarding the matter, an indication that the offer to return to Hawai'i posed a serious threat to the colony's future. The First Presidency agreed to permit all who wished to return to do so as soon as they saw fit and to maintain "good feelings" with all who left the colony. Cluff informed the community that there was no "desire to block the way to their return to the Hawaiian Islands. The road was open and free to be traveled [by] them as by white folk."[68] Cluff's need to remind the Native Hawaiian Saints of their freedom and the First Presidency's decision to "permit" community members to leave Skull Valley indicates at least some measure of control over their personal freedom. Regardless of the control that company managers and ecclesiastical leaders held over the colonists, the decision to remain in Iosepa rested squarely with the Native Hawaiian Saints, most of whom decided to stay in Skull Valley rather than return to Hawai'i, even in the face of fully funded repatriation offers from their government.

As colonists continued to request funds for repatriation, the question of the Native Hawaiian colony in Skull Valley remained an issue in the eyes of the Hawaiian legislature. Cecil Brown, a representative of the Republic of Hawai'i, made several offers to Native Hawaiian families in Skull Valley to pay their return fare if they desired to leave Utah and return home.[69] Ultimately most of the Native Hawaiians in Skull Valley chose to stay out of a sense of religious obligation and duty, even under trying circumstances.

LEPROSY IN IOSEPA

Leprosy hung like a dark cloud over the Native Hawaiian community throughout the 1890s. In the middle of the decade an outbreak of leprosy in the community brought the attention of Utahns to the little-known and isolated "Kanaka Ranch." Progress in building the Iosepa community was periodically reported to church members in the *Deseret News*, primarily through short reports submitted by ranch manager and mission president Harvey Cluff. It is impossible to know how widely read these reports were outside of the Salt Lake Valley's Mormon population, but it seems fair to assume that the existence of the small Native Hawaiian ranch was relatively unknown among residents of Salt Lake and the surrounding communities. While the citizenship debate in 1889 had commanded the attention of a broad cross section of Salt Lake City and northern Utah residents, once the Native Hawaiians had been removed from the city, reports on their activities were sparse and directed primarily toward church members.

Nevertheless, the fact that the specter of leprosy had arisen at the time the Hawaiians were relocated meant that any new outbreak would guarantee a good deal of public attention to Native Hawaiians in the Salt Lake Valley.

According to historian Dennis Atkins, prior to 1896, the year Utah became a state, the territorial government had almost no involvement in the life of the Iosepa settlers. State involvement was minimal even in subsequent years. "The Colony was the creation and responsibility of the Church of Jesus Christ of Latter-day Saints."[70] The town remained unincorporated under state law until 1908.[71] However, in 1896 rumors of an outbreak of leprosy in Iosepa spread after a neighboring rancher noticed "white scabs" on the arms, legs, and face of a young Native Hawaiian girl named Bessie Peters. Peters was occasionally employed washing clothes and caring for the rancher's young children. At the behest of the rancher, "the Tooele County physician made an examination of all the residents there, and discovered three cases of leprosy."[72] For the afflicted residents, this discovery meant quarantine under severe restrictions: "These lepers were moved to a house built about one and a half miles from the town, and were quarantined there. A flag pole was set up, and the inmates would raise a flag to signify that something was needed from the settlement. When this flag was seen to fly, someone would immediately go to administer to their wants. At intervals they received treatment from a doctor, but in time they all died."[73]

At least three individuals were afflicted with leprosy at this time, and Bessie Peters died on June 25 of that same year, at the age of seventeen. Another woman with leprosy, Hannah Mahoe, was forty-six years old when she was diagnosed in 1896; she died several years later. The third person known to have contracted leprosy was John Kauleinamoku. He eventually succumbed to the disease in 1899. All were buried in the small Iosepa cemetery. Buried next to John was his wife, Kapukini Kauleinamoku. Her grave is silent as to the date of her death, and it is unclear whether she, like her husband, succumbed to leprosy, or if she outlived him. The reality of the disease hung over the settlement in the 1890s and beyond, a grim reminder of one of the reasons for their initial isolation.

Public reaction to the new outbreaks of leprosy in Iosepa was swift and severe. A series of sensationalist articles appeared in the *Salt Lake Tribune* as well as the *Salt Lake Herald* in 1896. On June 4 the *Tribune* ran an article that stated: "The spread of leprosy in the Kanaka settlement in Skull valley has so excited the people of Tooele County that the county court has decided to take steps to quarantine the lepers and prevent the spread of the disease." The article also suggests that the first to be diagnosed was Kauleinamoku, and that it was not until the disease was reported to have spread to two other residents that a group of Tooele citizens petitioned the county court to investigate the situation and create a quarantine plan.[74] Two weeks later the *Salt Lake Daily Herald* ran a story as a follow-up to a similar announcement, this time including a detailed history of the "Kanaka Ranch," including pictures and identifications of several other Iosepa residents the author claimed were infected. Of particular interest is the supposedly ethnographic content of the four-page article, much of which attempts to equate the "customs" and "practices" of "Kanakas" with the spread of leprosy in Iosepa.

The sensationalist nature of the stories warrants analysis for the glimpse they provide into public sentiment toward the Native Hawaiian settlers. The subtitle of the front-page headline read, suggestively, "Unfortunate Victims of This Most Revolting Disease Living Together Only Seventy Miles from Salt Lake City." "It is common knowledge," the writer stated,

> all over the western portion of Tooele county that leprosy exists at the Kanaka ranch and all with whom I talked did not hesitate to express their indignation that such a condition was permitted to continue. The situation was denounced as a crying shame, and a disgrace to the authorities of the county of Tooele. Although there are those who contend that leprosy is not contagious, except under certain conditions, which shall be left nameless, the most intelligent of the people, both in Grantsville, and at the settlement, are a unit in agreeing that it is, and base their observations in that respect upon the personal knowledge they have acquired from long contact with the people who are infected.[75]

After listing the names of the "Kanakas" thought to have leprosy, names which, the reporter assured readers, "are common property all over the settlement, and even at Grantsville," the article condemned the "indiscriminate fashion" in which the "Kanakas" live, bathe, eat, and sleep together; young, old, man and woman alike. This behavior, the article asserted, went a long way to explain the spread of leprosy in the settlement. The article concluded with the following suggestion:

> After reviewing the matter impartially, as has been the case in this instance, it appears as if there is but one course to pursue. The authorities should select a committee of competent medical men-men of learning or repute, not farmers or cattlemen-and send them to settlement with instructions to make a thorough examination of every Kanaka in the settlement. None should be permitted to escape this ordeal: all should be thoroughly tested. Every person showing signs of leprosy should be taken away from the place at once. And wherever they go there should be extreme care that no offspring should be born to those who are

afflicted. It is a crime to permit beings afflicted with leprosy to perpetuate their species. After they shall have been deported to the place selected, the usual sanitary precautions should be indulged in relative to the place they occupied.[76]

Although few of these draconian and reactionary policies were adopted by state officials to deal with the problem of leprosy in Iosepa, measures to address the situation remained in place at the turn of the century. The call for soliciting the opinion of "competent medical men" as opposed to "farmers or cattlemen"—a not so subtle dig at the published opinions of ranch manager Harvey Cluff on the issue—apparently carried weight with both citizens and public officials. Dr. E. W. Lowell, a leper specialist (as his occupation was listed on the 1900 census), "was permitted to try his skill on the three lepers in the hospital at the colony" and was furnished room and board in Iosepa. Perhaps Lowell remained to certify that the disease had not been transmitted to others, but his ineffectiveness at treating Kauleinamoku led to his discharge by Cluff shortly afterward.[77] After Kualeinamoku's death in 1899, the saga of leprosy in Iosepa, the memory of which certainly tainted the community and its people for the remainder of its days, eventually came to an end.

A GROWING COMMUNITY

As a counterpoint to the grim years between 1890 and 1900, the turn of the century brought improvements to both the economic fortunes of the company and life in the colony. Cluff retired from management exhausted and disillusioned, but was lauded for his service by both church leaders and community members.[78] In 1902 Thomas Anson Waddoups, who had recently returned from a mission to Hawai'i, was called as both mission president and plantation manager. Although the colony faced financial challenges under Waddoups as it had under Cluff, conditions improved dramatically. In 1907 a railroad spur line and telegraph service at nearby Timpie station allowed for greater connection to surrounding communities. Economic upturns in the livestock market made the ranch more prosperous. The company invested in a water system, which provided fresh water for drinking and cooking. Home lots in Iosepa were available for purchase. The town infrastructure was improved, and residents were more acclimated to the seasonal temperature and weather changes. The paternalistic structure of the ranch operation, although still defended ecclesiastically, was mitigated by concessions to a more organized and experienced labor force. Although the community remained overwhelmingly Hawaiian, Samoan and Maori converts who migrated to Utah in small numbers joined the Iosepa settlers in Skull Valley. In 1911 Iosepa won a statewide award for "Cleanest Townsite."[79] By 1914 the plantation managers were negotiating loans for an expansion of the livestock operations into sheep ranching, an endeavor well suited to the region's sparse vegetation. Interviews with residents in subsequent years elicited fond memories of Iosepa in the decade between 1905 and 1915. In an interview with his grandson, William Kauaiwikaulakalani Wallace, John Broad remembered: "We never had any problem at the ranch. Everything was real nice, [we] had plenty of water and we had our farm under irrigation . . . we raised our own crops and we had one of the best—watermelon, squash, corn, potato, and cabbage, and all those things you know, we raised everything there without any problem at all. It was all good."[80]

The economy in the western United States stabilized somewhat after the turn of the century, the result of a combination of stable wheat prices and the expansion of the railroad infrastructure, which connected formerly remote locales in the West to global markets. In Utah especially, statehood brought increased federal spending on infrastructure and a flurry of capital investment, much of it in mining.[81] The Iosepa Agricultural and Stock Company benefited from an economic climate that brought higher prices for cattle, sheep, and agricultural products. The number of cattle raised and sold by the company, as well as general agricultural production, steadily increased after 1902, and by 1915 "Iosepa was on a firm economic foundation and paying off financially."[82]

Life at Iosepa improved dramatically following the eradication of leprosy. A healthier economic climate allowed a more profitable Iosepa Agricultural and Stock Company to invest in infrastructure that improved the living conditions of the colony. A new water system was installed to replace the old system of collecting spring and stream water from open irrigation ditches after Waddoups's wife contracted typhoid fever after drinking impure water. The new system "divert[ed] the water from six or seven mountain streams and several springs into huge cement bottom canals and gathered together. From that point the water could be distributed for irrigation, municipal, and power purposes."[83] Instead of having to collect and purify water from open ditches for culinary purposes, water was piped into homes for culinary use and to fire hydrants for municipal safety.[84] The ability to pipe water directly to homes also inaugurated beautification efforts, which included planting shade trees on the large residential lots and the town's streets. At a price tag of over a quarter of a million dollars, the water system, completed in 1908, created better living conditions and indicated the company's hopeful outlook for the future of Iosepa.

The advent of cash wages was an additional concession to residents and company employees. Although in his memoirs Waddoups referred to a bookkeeping system that "provided that the men would be individually credited with the work they performed on the ranch and in turn would be charged for whatever they purchased,"[85] widespread dissatisfaction with this system was rampant, and communication between workers and managers about their economic standing was a source of contention. The scrip system replaced this, but it also proved unsatisfactory. Often the ranch's lack of cash on hand made money unavailable for colonists who wished to travel to Salt Lake City or elsewhere. The advent of cash wages "was much more satisfactory to all concerned" and mitigated against colonists leaving the ranch to pursue seasonal labor elsewhere; they remained by choice rather than coercion.[86]

Many of the improvements in general living conditions were made possible not through the efforts of the company but as the result of regional development. Transportation and communications infrastructure shrunk the distances between Iosepa and nearby communities during the first decade of the twentieth century just as the development of Tooele County brought more travelers through Iosepa, the largest town in Skull Valley. Around 1905 the Utah Nevada Telephone Company ran a telephone wire into Iosepa from Timpie, fifteen miles north. At the same time Iosepa received its first post office, eliminating the need to travel to Grantsville to send and receive mail. A stage line was contracted to carry passengers from Iosepa to the Western Pacific Railway Company train station at Timpie, which was the nearest train stop on a line completed in 1907. The line ran from Salt Lake City to San Francisco and provided a "great convenience," which with the advent of cash wages "put us right in town."[87] The added conveniences of transportation and communication infrastructure also provided opportunities for older children to attend high school in nearby Grantsville and brought the town closer to medical facilities.

Better communication and transportation translated into expansion of the ranch's commercial endeavors. By 1911 the ranch had increased its acreage under cultivation through land purchases and had taken advantage of an expanding livestock market,[88] a move that Cluff had envisioned as the future of the colony more than a decade before. The ranch produced higher volumes of hay, but instead of selling it used it to feed its own stock, which it purchased and transported to Skull Valley via railroad. This model proved "very profitable" and provided enough cash for the ranch to cover "expenses plus the payment of the workmen."[89] The collective efforts of the ranch management, workers, and colonists were impressive enough to prompt J. Cecil Alter, Utah State historian, to rave:

Perhaps the most successful individual colonization proposition that has been attempted by the "Mormon" people in the United States is the Hawaiian colony at Iosepa.... [T]oday the several hundred folks there have water in their houses just the same as we have in Salt Lake City, and a power plant will some time give them electric lights. Their school and meetinghouses are as good as the best...at a recent annual celebration...Lorenzo D. Creek, a government official from Washington, who was studying the Indians in Tooele County at the time, rose before the great, Hawaiian, uniformed audience, after having been shown all over the place, and with much feeling said: "My friends, if this is a sample of Mormon colonization work, the best thing the government of the United States could do, would be to assist them in every way possible."[90]

The market for livestock, especially sheep, prompted the company to try to acquire additional land in the valley for grazing between 1909 and 1911.[91] The population of the town grew to approximately two hundred, and although it remained overwhelmingly Hawaiian, included Samoan, Maori, and Tahitian church members, which reflected the efforts of the church's missionary activity in the Pacific. By 1910 "Iosepa was enjoying cultural aspects of life comparable to any other community of its size in Utah."[92] Between 1905 and 1915 especially, Iosepa prospered.

COMMUNITY SOCIAL LIFE
The nearest town to Iosepa was Grantsville, thirty miles away (the railroad station at Timpie was just a station that served the nearby towns, and not a town itself). This meant that community life in Iosepa, within the context of work, home, and religious life, was often the sum total of all social relations, in the absence of frequent trips outside the valley. Social life in Iosepa was centered on the small community who resided in the town and worked for the ranch. Aside from the *Haole* ranch manager and mission president and a small group of hired hands, the majority of the community was made up of Native Hawaiians. Because church leaders selected former missionaries to Hawai'i as ranch managers and mission presidents, nearly everyone in the town spoke Hawaiian on a daily basis, although English was spoken well by most of the community members. Because of its relative isolation, especially prior to 1905, community life in Iosepa was insular in the sense that there were few opportunities for community members to interact with outsiders. In this aspect Iosepa was much like many small Mormon villages and farming communities scattered along the Wasatch Front.[93] Even following improvements that made it easier for residents of Iosepa to travel to neighboring communities and communicate with

friends and loved ones, social life in Iosepa, like many Mormon communities, was centered on religious activities and gatherings. Weekly church meetings, trips to semiannual general conferences in Salt Lake City, and the annual Pioneer Day celebrations are examples of community social life centered around religious worship. Music was also an important part of life in Iosepa, and singing groups from the community enjoyed popular appeal and performed widely in nearby communities. Community members also made efforts to integrate traditional foods and activities into their daily lives.[94] Iosepa remained until its demise a community that creatively blended Mormon and Native Hawaiian cultural practices in the isolated desert of the American West.

Like other small Mormon communities in the early twentieth century, the fact that community life centered on church activities and associations in Iosepa created in effect "a small theocracy."[95] The power of the church was even more apparent in Iosepa because of the blurring of ecclesiastical and economic authority. The board of directors of the Iosepa Agricultural and Stock Company reported directly to the First Presidency of the Church. Because Iosepa was organized ecclesiastically as a mission and not a branch or a ward, the ranch manager also served as mission president and bishop. This was true throughout the twenty-eight-year history of the colony, and the difficult nature of maintaining good social relations in the face of such ambiguity was widely recognized. Thomas Waddoups hinted at the problematic nature of social relations: "I would like to record some of the difficulties we had [in Iosepa]. We of course were presiding over the people in a church capacity and trying to teach them in Church on Sunday after having scolded them in the fields during the week in order to get them to do the work they were assigned. This of course created a situation, the difficulty of which can be readily understood."[96] In terms of management, however, the arrangement ultimately favored the company, because criticism of the management translated directly into criticism of ecclesiastical leaders, risking the potential loss of church fellowship and social ostracism. Despite these difficulties, many Iosepa residents remembered their relationships with mission presidents and ranch managers in Iosepa fondly.[97]

Another difficulty of community social life in Iosepa throughout its history was marriage. Marriages in Iosepa were expected to occur within a community that at its peak reached only 228 people. Prior to 1900 the population in Iosepa hovered between 75 and 100 people. While many remote and isolated farming communities faced similar issues, Iosepa settlers were counseled by church leaders against marrying white Mormons from neighboring communities. In a 1970 interview, former resident John Broad stated: "During our stay at that place, we were forbidden, and we were taught that the Hawaiians should marry Hawaiians, the haoles should marry haoles.... That instruction was given to us by Brother Waddoups, William Waddoups, and his older brother, Anson Waddoups.... They gave us such instruction because the haole land was to perpetuate haoles, and the Hawaiians to breed Hawaiians. They were not to be mixed, these races were not to be mixed. That was the rule they gave us on that land."[98] The policy made finding an "acceptable" companion for marriage difficult for community members, who were also encouraged not to leave Skull Valley.

Iosepa was not completely isolated from surrounding communities, however, and as the population grew after the turn of the century the need for education and medical care helped forge connections with the closest towns. Primary and secondary education took place in Iosepa in a one-room schoolhouse and was presided over primarily by women who came from outside the community to teach, presumably in English. As in most small farming communities, school was scheduled in a way that accommodated farm and ranch labor as much as possible. High school age students left the community and attended high school in Grantsville while boarding with Mormon families.[99] Medical care was another issue. For many years there was no doctor in Iosepa, and medical needs had to be addressed by a doctor in Grantsville, who would be called in times of medical emergency but was often hampered by poor weather or roads.[100]

Major community celebrations and events in Iosepa were often organized around religious holidays. Throughout Iosepa's history the largest event was the annual celebration of Pioneer Day, "the main day of each year," commemorating the day that the first Iosepa settlers entered Skull Valley on August 28, 1889.[101] Pioneer Day was a major holiday for Mormons throughout Utah, but for the rest of them was held on July 24 and commemorated the entry of the first wagon trains into the Salt Lake Valley in 1847. In larger Mormon communities, including Salt Lake City, Ogden, and Provo, Pioneer Day was a major event that included parades, oratories from church and community leaders, and historical pageants. Pioneer Day in Iosepa was equally significant and occasioned visits from church leaders who had been missionaries in Hawai'i, politicians, as well as residents of neighboring ranches and communities, including the Gosiutes residing in Skull Valley some fifteen miles south of the town. Feasting, fireworks, dancing, music, and "cultural performances" marked the event, and preparations were often begun weeks in advance as news reached Iosepa of potential attendees.[102] Generally a three-day celebration, Pioneer Day centered around religious services, which were often presided over by a visiting church official. Pioneer Day celebrated the narratives of early settlers in Utah, "pioneers" to the Salt Lake Valley. These narratives emphasized devotion to the church and the sacrifices made by Mormon settlers to "gather to Zion" and "build the Kingdom of God." Pioneer Day celebrations linked Iosepa with Mormons throughout Utah and retold a shared narrative of sacrifice that ironically began not with the early Native Hawaiian settlers in Salt Lake City but with their removal to Skull Valley.

Native Hawaiian settlers in Iosepa participated in activities that simultaneously created a feeling of cohesion within the larger Mormon community and highlighted the gulf that separated them in the minds of white Mormons. Outside of Iosepa racism against Native Hawaiians mirrored the experiences of many other "minority" peoples settling in Utah, including Chinese, Japanese, and eastern Europeans who migrated to west after the turn of the century. The church's semiannual general conferences, at which the whole population of the church was addressed by recognized leaders, occasioned travel to Salt Lake City each year in April and October. Native Hawaiian Saints from Iosepa were among those who traveled to Salt Lake City to hear the conference addresses. One of the purposes of the general conference was (and is) to "sustain" church leaders, including the prophet and president, the apostles, and other church authorities, as "prophets, seers, and revelators," a significant religious act in that members publicly affirm their allegiance to church leaders as God's chosen servants called to lead the church and its members. In addition, these semiannual meetings provide opportunities for church leaders to discuss doctrines and practices of the church, often set against the context of contemporary events, and introduce or reinforce changes in Mormon doctrine or practice. However, while the activities associated with conference contributed to the maintenance of Mormon identity within the community, other aspects of religious worship in Salt Lake City reinforced the outsider status of the Native Hawaiian community. General conferences often took place over the course of three days, making it necessary for travelers from remote areas of the Great Basin to secure lodging, either in hotels or with local church members, for the period of time they spent in Salt Lake City. While many travelers from Mormon communities along the Wasatch Front boarded in the homes of host families in Salt Lake City, Native Hawaiian families were unwelcome in the homes of white church members in Salt Lake and were forced to camp in people's yards and even on sidewalks during their trips to the city. Despite this fact, the semiannual general conferences of the church remained an important religious event for Native Hawaiian church members, who made every effort to attend.[103]

At the height of Iosepa's prosperity the community was dealt a devastating blow. In 1915 President Joseph F. Smith assembled the members of the community and announced that a temple was to be built in Lāʻie, Hawaiʻi. He urged Native Hawaiian community members in Iosepa to leave Skull Valley and offered to pay for anyone who could not afford it to return to Hawaiʻi. It is unclear how strongly Smith urged the settlers to return to Hawaiʻi, but several residents asserted that the reason they left was to obey Smith's counsel.[104] Many in fact wished to remain in Iosepa, but were told by Smith that the next generation of church leaders would not be as well disposed as he to look after their needs.[105] Those who had purchased home lots or owned property in Iosepa sold their property and possessions back to the Iosepa Agricultural and Stock Company and used the funds to pay for travel back to Hawaiʻi. Transportation arrangements were made from Salt Lake City to Honolulu. Between 1915 and 1917 families slowly began to get their affairs in order and prepare for the journey to Hawaiʻi. For some this was a return to a homeland they had not yet seen. By the summer of 1917 Thomas Waddoups had hired white laborers to work on the ranch. In the fall of that year the ranch was sold to the Deseret Livestock Company, a subsidiary corporation of the church, for $150,000. The meeting house, schoolhouse, barns, and homes in Iosepa were torn down and the lumber reused to build sheep sheds for the expanding livestock raising operations in the valley. Some of the houses were moved intact onto other ranches owned by the Deseret Livestock Company.[106] By 1945 there was little recognizable in Iosepa besides the fire hydrants, sidewalks, and a few worn-down structures. The cemetery was overgrown.

All but the four Hoʻopiʻiaina brothers and a few members from another family returned to Hawaiʻi. The decision to leave the town that they had worked so hard to build was not easy, but it highlights the role of religion in the fate of the community. Resident John Broad stated: "The most important reason we left Iosepa to come back to Hawaiʻi was because we were advised by the Prophet Joseph F. Smith."[107] Some, however, did not wish to leave, "but once the movement got underway nearly all were swept along."[108] According to Alf Callister, a rancher who was present when the majority of the settlers left the colony, "When the wagons were loaded and ready to leave for the Timpie railroad station which was fifteen miles to the north of Iosepa, the women and some of the men refused to ride in the wagons and were determined to walk the distance to the railroad. They followed the wagons on foot and with tears running down their faces, they kept looking back at their homes, uttering Goodbye Iosepa, Goodbye Iosepa."[109] Although several people from Iosepa returned to Lāʻie, others relocated elsewhere in Hawaiʻi, claiming homesteads on the Big Island, Kauai, and in Honolulu.[110] Those who returned to Lāʻie were given home lots and work on the church-owned plantation, but dissatisfaction over lower wages and homesickness for Iosepa were common. In 1917 Bessie King wrote to her grandmother after they left Iosepa and moved to Lāʻie:

Dear Grandma, I am very sorry to tell you that I didn't get to see you before we left home the snow was deep we had a cold ride until over the station. O, I was so homesick I wanted to go back again...on the 9th we got on the steamer O that ship how it did rock it made us all sick the first day after wards we was all right. Got to Honolulu on the 15 of January had a good dinner in the afternoon [then left] for Laie on the auto. Papa saw some of his nieces but Grandma talk about rain, it rained nearly every day since we got here. O we like Laie pretty fare I gess [sic] later on I [will] like it better but I still don't forget Iosepa. Papa and Roay have started to work this week, the only thing is lower wages than what we have at Iosepa. There's some old folks still living [that] said they are very proud of you and Grandpa King for taking Papa and Mother out there to receive good blessings until they return to the Islands again.[111]

One explanation for this attachment to a foreign and seemingly hostile landscape, beyond the obvious physical and emotional investment, is a lingering notion of the gathering of Israel. Even after the church had abandoned the concept in the period between 1890 and 1915, the notion of Zion as a specific place lingered in Mormon consciousness.[112] For a people with a strong attachment to a narrative renewed annually through religious ritual and symbolism, moving away from this represents a contradiction that goes to the core of religious experience. Historians and sociologists have argued that narrative is central to the project of ethnic identity.[113] In the first and most difficult years after Iosepa's initial establishment, letters exchanged between George Kekauoha, John Kauleinamoku, and others and Joseph F. Smith reveal a strong link with their adopted homeland and the Book of Mormon narrative. In one letter Smith states that Zion is the "true land of your inheritance," fusing religious and ethnic identity with a powerful notion of place.[114] After strong admonitions from Smith and other church leaders to "remain faithful" to this land of inheritance, leaving it behind created a contradictory situation for both religious and ethnic identity, an unacceptable narrative shift.

In a 1916 transcript of a church conference held in Lāʻie, when many of those who had left Iosepa had returned to Lāʻie, mission president and plantation manager Samuel Woolley characterized the array of responses to this dislocation:

"[Some have asked] Why didn't the Lord show us to this in our own country, that they were going to build a temple. We would not have come up here. We would have waited." Some were doubtful.... Some of them want to return, and some are returning.... Five families are returning. Some don't want to return. They say, "We are acquainted here, and want to stay here to fulfill the scriptures," saying that the "house of the Lord [temple] will be built in the tops of the mountains." Therefore they are permitted to return if they so desire. It has been proclaimed by the servant of the Lord, that if they want to return, and have the means to return, the earth is free to them. Therefore, it is up to them.[115]

The narrative shift within Mormonism away from the gathering took on an added sense of importance for those who, unlike so many other Mormon migrants in the Great Basin, faced actual physical removal from the landscapes that had nourished them, where they had buried the remains of their ancestors. The desire of community members to return to Iosepa represents a marked contrast from the first decade of the colony, when church leaders employed the doctrine of the gathering to keep the community intact in the face of widespread discontent. The cultural transitions that Mormonism faced in response to existential challenges in the years between 1890 and 1930 took on an uncomfortable immediacy for the Native Hawaiian settlers in Iosepa. In 1917 presumably none could have imagined the dramatic resurgence of Native Hawaiian and Pacific Islander communities in the Great Basin half a century later. Many might have seen it as the fulfillment of a prophecy they felt was unrealized in the early twentieth century.

CONCLUSION

Iosepa was established in Skull Valley according to economic and ecclesiastical principles that blended Mormonism's United Order communities with the economic model the church developed on its sugar plantation in Laie. The joint stock company structure of the Iosepa Agricultural and Stock Company was a common response to the political pressures of the Edmunds Tucker Act of 1887, but the wage labor model reflected the development of Lā'ie's profit structure. Iosepa was essentially run as a branch of the Hawaiian Mission of the Church of Jesus Christ of Latter-day Saints and shared the paternalistic goals of the mission for Native Hawaiian converts. This blend of sacred and secular authority remained at the core of the colony's model for its entire twenty-eight-year history. Life in Iosepa was difficult for the first ten years, as national depressions, disease, racism, and labor conflict tore at the fabric of the small community. Improvements in the economy, transportation, communications, and public infrastructure transformed the community into a place that more closely resembled other small Mormon settlements in the Great Basin in the early years of the twentieth century. An infusion of cash and concessions to a more experienced labor force mitigated some of the tension between labor and management between 1905 and 1915. Although racism toward community members hardly abated, life improved dramatically, and the prospects for the community's survival were strong.

In 1915 Joseph F. Smith's offer to repatriate the Native Hawaiian settlers after he announced that a temple was to be built in Lā'ie was interpreted by community members as a commandment from a prophet of God, and the vast majority of the community left Utah to return to Hawai'i, despite strong emotional attachments to the community that they had worked so hard to build. In this sense the Native Hawaiian community in Utah fell victim to the cultural transitions in Mormonism that deemphasized the doctrinal necessity of the gathering. Race was again an important factor in the fate of the community; none of the thousands of other immigrant converts who had gathered to Utah in the nineteenth century were encouraged to repatriate. Although several community members remained in Utah, and one refused to leave Skull Valley until his death in 1964, those who returned to Hawai'i were provided lots in Lā'ie and work on the plantation, though many returned to live on homestead lands on Hawai'i.[116] The Iosepa Agricultural and Stock Company sold its holdings to the Deseret Livestock Company in 1917.

CHAPTER 5

"As a Testament to the Faith of These Ancestors of Ours"

Iosepa in Public Memory

The Ho'opi'iaina family arrived in Skull Valley, Utah, in the spring of 1893. The family of four consisted of the father, John Ka'ili Ho'opi'iaina I, his wife, Antonia, and their sons, John II and Benjamin Kalani. Before John Sr.'s death in 1906 the family had three more sons: Neely, Akoni, and Peter. After John's death Antonia married John Nawahine, and the couple had a daughter. In 1915 the announcement was made that a temple would be built in Lā'ie, and President Joseph F. Smith counseled the inhabitants of Iosepa that they should return home. He offered to pay the travel expenses of anyone who could not afford the cost. Although many in the community wished to stay, "once the movement got under way nearly all were swept along."[1] Even after all others in the community had left for Hawai'i, John's five sons decided to stay in Utah, having "done some homesteading" and acquired land in Iosepa and Murray, just south of Salt Lake City. The boys and their mother spent the winters in Murray and Salt Lake City's Swede Town and the summers in Iosepa. In 1926 the Deseret Livestock Company, a land management company owned by the Church of Jesus Christ of Latter-day Saints, took possession of the old Iosepa ranch and severed the family's access to water in the valley.

The brothers all married and had children. Two of Akoni's marriages ended in divorce. He moved out to Iosepa permanently, taking up residence in a small cabin near the town site, long after the homes of his friends and family had been torn down by nearby ranchers to make fence posts. He mined several claims, hiked the hills and mountains, and farmed his land, battling both the Deseret Livestock Company and the Bureau of Land Management for access to water for his crops. Akoni died in 1968. He was buried in Iosepa cemetery, the first interment there since the town was abandoned in 1917. His love for Iosepa never faded.

Akoni's nephew Malu, who was born in Iosepa in 1915, worked in salvage yards until 1945, when he began his own salvage business with a Model A Ford and $500. By 1950 Malu's company, Intermountain Steel and Supply, had grown to a $250,000 per year business with five new trucks, two cranes, a machine shop, and 15,000 square feet of retail space.[2] Most of the children, grandchildren, and great-grandchildren of the Ho'opi'iaina brothers live in and around the Salt Lake and Utah Valleys. Many visit Iosepa regularly, and Cory Ho'opi'iaina, a businessman who lives in the Salt Lake area, has spent countless hours presiding over the Iosepa Historical Association and making improvements to the gravesite area, including a covered pavilion, restrooms, and a full-service kitchen. He recently oversaw the project to run water and a new road to the site to accommodate the growing number of attendees at the annual Memorial Day commemorative activities.

On November 3, 2001, the *Iosepa*, a fifty-seven foot, double-hulled *wa'a kaulua* (double-hulled voyaging canoe) was launched for the first time in the waters off Hukilau Beach in Lā'ie, Hawai'i. The *wa'a* was carved by master carvers Tuione Pulotu and Kawika Eskaran for the Jonathan Napela Center for Hawaiian Language and Cultural Studies at Brigham Young University Hawai'i, a program named after Jonathan Napela, the prominent Native Hawaiian who was one of the first converts to the Mormon Church in Hawai'i and the first Native Hawaiian Saint to visit Salt Lake City. The ceremonies surrounding the *Iosepa*'s launch included dance performances from representatives of the Samoan, Tongan, Hawaiian, Maori, and Tahitian communities of Lā'ie. The presentation of gifts was elaborate and included "fine [woven] mats, koa bowls, Hawaiian quilted pillows, two roasted pigs, baskets of taro and baskets of young green coconuts, breadfruit, bananas, watermelons and pineapples, plus fresh-baked French bread and cooked breadfruit."[3] The logs to build the gigantic twin hulls were selected, felled, and shipped to Hawai'i from Fiji's upland forests. Construction was truly a Lā'ie community effort, with school and church groups as well as community members spending time at the building site working or providing home-cooked meals for the workers. Nainoa Thompson, captain of the *Hōkūle'a*, Hawai'i's famous voyaging canoe, visited the site often. At the launch he commented that "Tuione [Pulotu] has built more than a canoe; he's built a community. Look around you today, you see the whole Pacific."[4]

The most important part of the launch was naming the vessel. Iosepa is a well-known name in Lāʻie; there are many descendants of Skull Valley's original settlers living in the village, and Iosepa Street, named for the home lots given to the Hawaiians when they returned from Utah to Lāʻie in 1915, runs through the middle of town. William Kauaiwiulaokanali Wallace III, director of the Jonathan Napela Center and captain of the *Iosepa*, explained that the *waʻa*'s name "came to him in a dream about his grandparents, who sold all their possessions to attend the Mormon temple in Utah where they lived in a colony with other Hawaiians and Polynesians, named Iosepa." Wallace felt that the *waʻa*, like the colony, brought together many of the cultures from the Pacific and that the name "would be a good testament to the faith of these ancestors of ours."[5]

This chapter addresses the collective memory of Iosepa, defined through the history-making efforts of both descendants of Iosepa settlers and the diasporic community of Pacific Islanders in the Great Basin who gather each year on Memorial Day to honor the memory of the abandoned colony. It is primarily through the efforts of these two communities that Iosepa's history is linked with the diasporic community of Pacific Islanders in Utah today. These are the communities that work to keep the memory of Iosepa alive and construct that memory in a way that communicates the connection between the history of the Skull Valley community and the experience of Pacific Islander Mormons in Utah today. This collective remembering of Iosepa as a community of Latter-day Saint pioneers in Zion, whose sacrifices mirror those of the pioneers before them, has been adopted by many Pacific Islander Saints in the Great Basin as they seek to negotiate ethnic, racial, and religious identities in the modern West. I argue that this process of remembering, and remembering in a certain way, has established Iosepa as a sacred space even for those Pacific Islander Saints who are not descended from Iosepa settlers. The act of remembering is collective in the sense that it is constructed. Memory is not simply a matter of recalling information stored somewhere in our heads; it is created and articulated in the context of social interaction. Collective memory is created and articulated in a variety of ways, from commemorative activities such as pageants and historical reenactments to defining places as "historic" by erecting monuments or issuing official proclamations. Collective memory is articulated in both the public and private spheres, as governments, private historical associations, and other entities take action to memorialize particular places and events in certain ways. Constructing collective memory is part of the process of articulating the narratives that define peoples and communities.[6] Articulating these shared narratives around an event or place helps individuals and communities create a "sense of history," defined by scholars as "akin to what environmental psychologists describe as a sense of place—not quite territoriality... but a sense of locatedness and belonging. Sensing history, we explore fundamental questions concerning personal and group identity and our relationship to the environment."[7] A sense of history can locate us in time and space, as well as in social life. It helps us to "gain a sense of with whom we belong, connecting our personal experiences and memories with those of a larger community, region, and nation."[8]

This sense of history can be created and maintained in a variety of ways. Memories, both personal and collective; stories passed down from family and community members; and official histories (whether produced by professional historians or endorsed by public officials or recognized community leaders) all contribute to a sense of history.[9] When a community with a shared identity agrees on a particular version of the past and communicates that past to those around them, that sense of history becomes part of its collective memory. Those memories contribute to the historical narratives used to create and re-create new identities in new contexts. Creating, remembering, and agreeing on certain historical narratives (and ignoring, forgetting, and contesting others) are the primary methods by which group identities are created and maintained.[10] These narratives, in turn, can contribute to the collective memory of a later generation of people through their telling. A sense of history, when in the service of creating and maintaining ethnic identity, becomes a sense of *our* history, the story of *our* people, however that peoplehood is defined. The specific ways that Iosepa is remembered within the Pacific Islander community in Utah and Hawai'i do all of these things.

Unlike the contemporary population of diasporic Pacific Islanders in Utah, many of the original settlers in Iosepa had explicitly religious reasons for leaving their homes and settling in Utah. John Kauleinamoku, Jonatana Napela, Solomana Pi'ipi'ilani, and others whose stories have been told in previous chapters embraced the gathering as a central tenet of the Mormon religious experience and eagerly journeyed to Zion, as did Mormon converts from Europe and the eastern United States. Religious motivations also explain why Iosepa was abandoned at the height of its success; Native Hawaiian Mormons heeded the counsel of the prophet Joseph F. Smith, the man after whom the community was named, to abandon Iosepa and return to Hawai'i. And the collective memory of Iosepa, defined largely by the descendants of Iosepa settlers, has emphasized an overwhelmingly religious interpretation of the community's history.

Whereas the collective memory of Native Hawaiian communities in the Pacific Northwest has focused on reclaiming an ethnic identity,[11] the collective memory of Iosepa is focused on asserting a connection to a religious narrative that strengthens ethnic and religious identity and functions as a powerful source of social capital in the Mormon culture region. This hybrid ethnic and religious identity is created in response to the experience of marginalization that diasporic communities of Pacific Islander Mormons often face in the white Mormon communities in the American West of which they are a part. The vast majority of Pacific Islander Mormons in the West did not have specifically religious or spiritual reasons for settling in Utah. Many were born there, many others' parents were born there, and the church has long distanced itself from the concept of the literal "gathering to Zion." However, within the Mormon culture region, religion and religious narratives are an important part of a regional identity and contribute to a powerful sense of belonging and attachment to Utah as a place. For Pacific Islander Mormons in Utah, the story of Iosepa provides a link to a more immediate history, providing that sense of history, sense of place, and feeling of belonging. In addition, Iosepa functions as a historical metaphor for the contemporary struggles many Pacific Islander Mormons face in today's West.

My assertion that this articulation of ethnic identity is constructed in relation to the dominant Mormon culture is not meant to suggest a lack of cultural authenticity or an inability of Pacific Islander Mormons in Utah to maintain a distinctive cultural identity apart from Mormonism. Instead, I follow the model of Pacific scholars who recognize that "a given cultural identity no longer rests on a more or less homogenous set of shared social experiences in a single location." Rather, the identities of Pacific Island peoples now "result from the various experiences of being a Pacific person in the many places in which Pacific people are now found."[12] That those words, which refer specifically to the experience of diasporic Pacific peoples in Aotearoa/New Zealand, apply equally well to the experiences of Pacific peoples in the American West is a testament to the transnational nature of the contemporary Pacific diaspora and the multiple identities created by unique social conditions in the Mormon culture region.[13]

The history of Iosepa has been preserved largely through the efforts of family historians, journalists, and historical associations made up of descendants of settlers or of Mormons concerned with preserving the history of Mormon migration to Utah in the nineteenth century. Although addressed by professional scholars, the stories told about Iosepa are more actively and vibrantly retold by parents and grandparents, and aunts and uncles, to younger family members. In addition, Iosepa is memorialized as an important site by historical associations, whose efforts are made legitimate by official recognition from politicians, community leaders, and religious leaders. This chapter relies on evidence from a variety of sources that tell Iosepa's history, including records of the Iosepa Historical Society, newspaper articles, documentary films, television news programs, cultural institutions, oral histories, and interviews. These various versions of Iosepa's history are created with a public audience in mind, whether that audience is Pacific Islanders or non-Pacific Islanders, Mormons or non-Mormons. The narratives they contain are intended to create a collective memory of Iosepa, a history with a variety of purposes: to foster an appreciation of the faith and dedication of Mormon "pioneers" in the Salt Lake Valley in the nineteenth century, to connect Pacific Islanders with the larger pioneer narratives of Utah and the West, and to demonstrate the persistent and pernicious specter of white racism toward Pacific Islanders past and present. In years to come the history of Iosepa will remain vibrant and relevant, even in the absence of trained scholars, thanks to the efforts of those who work to define and preserve the collective memory of Iosepa in the Great Basin region and beyond. The efforts of community members to create and disseminate their own historical narratives have been, and will continue to be, the most important and lasting contribution to the history of places like Iosepa.[14]

THE CHURCH OF JESUS CHRIST OF LATTER-DAY SAINTS IN THE PACIFIC

In 2001 a report from the US Census Bureau gathered statistical data about Native Hawaiians and Pacific Islanders in the United States. It revealed that the vast majority, 73 percent, of Native Hawaiians and Pacific Islanders living in the United States at the turn of twentieth century resided in the West. Two states, Hawai'i and California, boasted the largest populations of Pacific Islanders. Hawai'i led the way, with Pacific Islanders making up 9.4 percent of the total population. Despite large numbers of Pacific Islanders, as a percentage of total population this group made up only 0.4 percent of California residents. In Utah, Pacific Islanders make up 0.7 percent of the total population, making it the second largest concentrated population of Pacific Islanders in the country.[15] This unusually high percentage of Pacific Islanders in Utah has its roots in the long-term missionary presence of the church in the Pacific, specifically in the Polynesian island groups of Samoa and Tonga, and in the targeted educational opportunities that the church has provided for its members in the Pacific.

From the 1950s through the present, the Church of Jesus Christ of Latter-day Saints has provided educational opportunities for its members in the Pacific Islands that have facilitated their migration to the United States. This was most certainly not the original intention of church leaders.

However, economic and political realities in the region that promoted over-seas migration dovetailed with church educational programs that provided educational visas to Pacific Islander members, resulting in large numbers of Pacific Islander Saints moving permanently to the western United States and establishing a large community in Utah. Even in the early twentieth century the most prominent and cohesive Pacific Islander communities in the United States had direct ties to the church. The completion of the Lā'ie temple, the same event that prompted Iosepa's citizens to abandon their community and return to Hawai'i, also prompted a migration of Samoan Latter-day Saints to northeastern O'ahu to be close to a temple. This small community of Samoans remained relatively static, however, until after World War II. Many Samoan Saints settled in the village around the same time as Native Hawaiian Saints returning from Iosepa. By 1929 approxi-mately 125 Samoans lived in Hawai'i. Almost all, if not all, were Latter-day Saints living in Lā'ie. By 1950 some 463 Samoans lived in Hawai'i, with about half that number residing in Lā'ie. By 1952 nearly 1,300 Samoans had arrived in Hawai'i, most of whom were non-Mormon. Approximately 300 people from this group, most of whom were not Mormon, joined fam-ily members in Lā'ie.[16] For the remainder of the decade and into the early 1960s the Church of Jesus Christ of Latter-day Saints provided opportu-nities for Samoan and Tongan church members to emigrate to the United States, primarily on educational visas or as labor missionaries. The open-ing of the Church College of Hawai"i in 1955 and the Polynesian Cultural Center in 1963, both of which were located in Lā'ie, facilitated this emi-gration. Most Samoan and Tongan Latter-day Saints who migrated in the 1950s and 1960s were educated in the church's secondary schools in those countries, Pesega and Mapusaga in Samoa and Liahona on Tonga.

Hawai'i was certainly not the church's first mission in the Pacific, although it soon became recognized as something of a headquarters for the church's efforts and presence in the region. This designation was cemented with the completion of the Lā'ie temple in 1919, the dedication and open-ing of the Church College of Hawai'i, and the opening of the Polynesian Cultural Center. But the church remained an active presence throughout the Pacific, especially in places where missionaries had arrived before the end of the nineteenth century. This included all the Polynesian islands, and the by the end of World War II the church had established large congrega-tions in Tonga, Samoa, Tahiti, and New Zealand. The order of the estab-lishment and location of the church's missions in the Pacific is as follows: Hawai'i in 1850, Aotearoa/New Zealand in 1854, Samoa in 1888, Tonga in 1891, and French Polynesia in 1892. Latter-day Saint missionaries in New Zealand established themselves largely among the Maori population and succeeded in building congregations throughout the country well before the turn of the twentieth century. In Samoa, Tonga, and Tahiti, however, the earliest missions were abandoned and reestablished later. The first two missionaries to Samoa were two Native Hawaiian men, Kimo Pelio and Samuela Manoa, sent from Iosepa on Lāna'i by Walter Murray Gibson, where they were largely forgotten following Gibson's excommunication from the church. They worked to gain a small group of converts there and were overjoyed at the arrival of missionary John Dean and his family in June 1888. Two months later a Native Hawaiian missionary, C. K. Kapule, arrived in Samoa. Over two decades had passed since the arrival of Manoa and Pelio, and the few pleas they had made via mail for additional missionaries had gone unanswered. With the arrival of additional missionary couples in subsequent months and years, the Church of Jesus Christ of Latter-day Saints in Samoa continued to grow.

The Tongan mission also made a false start. The first Latter-day Saint missionaries arrived in Tonga in July 1891 and found a country in the midst of intense religious and political turmoil. In 1885 King George Tupou, together with a Wesleyan minister named Shirley Baker, had formed an offshoot of the Wesleyan Church named the Free Church of Tonga. By order of the king, the Free Church became the official church of the Tongan kingdom. Committed Wesleyans resisted the notion of coerced conversion and were persecuted by the Tupou, until in 1890 the British high commissioner in Fiji deported Baker and restored the guarantee of religious freedom enshrined in Tonga's 1875 Constitution. The first Latter-day Saint missionaries arrived approximately one year later, and after an audience with the king received permission to preach in the kingdom. By 1897 they had only gained sixteen converts. Church leaders in Salt Lake opted to close the ailing mission. The growth of the church in nearby Samoa, however, provided resources, and in 1907 the mission president in Samoa reopened the Tongan mission. Over the next three decades the fortunes of the mission waned (Mormon missionaries were effectively outlawed between 1922 and 1924) until a visit from apostle George Albert Smith. Smith visited Latter-day Saint congregations throughout Tonga and met with Queen Salote, the reigning monarch, speaking to her of "the importance of Tongans' heritage of descendants of Lehi and Israel" and the connections between Native Americans and Pacific Islanders. After his return to the United States, he sent a Book of Mormon and a Navajo woven blanket as gifts to the Queen.

The two events that most profoundly affected the growth of the church in the Pacific were World War II and the construction of the church's primary and secondary schools. World War II was a watershed event throughout

Oceania, both for nations that experienced fighting on their own soil and for those that endured a "peaceful occupation" by a foreign power. In both Samoa and Tonga the massive influx of US military personnel meant that both countries were flooded with American currency and consumer goods, as well as American films, music, and magazines. In both countries US servicemen outnumbered the local population during the occupation years. New Zealand also experienced a large influx of American troops, which certainly bolstered the number of Latter-day Saints, but nothing like on the scale of the massive cultural, economic, and political influence Samoa and Tonga experienced. The seeds of discontent with an agrarian, subsistence economy and lifestyle were sown throughout the Pacific during the war, and Samoa and Tonga met this disruptive force head on. In Tonga the war spurred the church's growth indirectly. Nervous about such an unprecedented foreign influence, the chiefs and monarchy strictly applied the quota system for foreign missionaries that had been in place for decades. Unable to obtain visas for foreign missionaries, the church expanded its practice of calling Tongan missionaries to proselytize in the country. This policy had two major effects. First, it created a cadre of strong and committed local leaders who in later years would rise to fill church leadership positions throughout the country. Second, it fostered an indigenized Tongan Mormonism that allowed Tongan Saints to negotiate their own culture with a centralized Mormon hierarchy, whose expectation of strict adherence to established church principles often conflicted with certain aspects of Tongan culture. In Samoa the war also severely curtailed the number of foreign missionaries, providing an opportunity for Samoans to preach in their own country. In 1946 a group of local missionaries baptized more than three hundred converts, a mission record. And in the years after the war a move toward local leadership for congregations began to take shape, even when the percentage of foreign missionaries increased.

Like other Christian denominations in the Pacific, the Church of Jesus Christ of Latter-day Saints worked to promote education for its members, establishing primary and secondary schools in Hawai'i, Samoa, Tonga, and New Zealand. The Church College of New Zealand, located near Hamilton, operated from 1958 to 2010. In Samoa and Tonga primary and secondary schools run by the church, most of which were established prior to World War II, are still operating. These schools, located adjacent to chapels and temples in both Samoa and Tonga, act as feeder schools to the church educational system's flagship institution in the Pacific, Brigham Young University Hawai'i. Graduates from Liahona High School in Tonga and Pesega High School in Samoa, and a small percentage of graduates from Church College of New Zealand, go on to acquire educational visas to the United States while they attend Brigham Young University Hawai'i. A smaller number continue on to graduate studies at Brigham Young University in Provo, Utah, or at other American universities. The church puts a high premium on education for members in the Pacific region, and through the Polynesian Cultural Center (PCC) creates a way for Pacific Islander church members to obtain an education while incurring a minimum of personal debt, provided they work at the PCC while they attend school. The church, through its network of schools in the Pacific and the opportunities that it provides for higher education for Pacific Islander members in Hawai'i and Utah, has provided one avenue of migration in the larger Pacific diaspora to the United States.

THE PACIFIC DIASPORA IN THE UNITED STATES

This movement of Pacific Islander Latter-day Saints to the United States must of course be viewed within the larger context of the twentieth-century Pacific diaspora of which it is a part. The modern diaspora to the United States gained momentum in the years immediately after World War II. Although Native Hawaiians had previously resided in the western United States, it was only after the end of the Second World War that non-Native Hawaiian Pacific Islanders began to arrive in the United States in earnest. The one exception happened to be the small community of Samoan Saints in Lā'ie, who had migrated there in the 1920s to be closer to the newly completed temple. Following annexation to the United States in 1898 and the passage of the Organic Act in 1900, Hawai'i became a US territory, and Native Hawaiians became citizens of the United States. Following the Berlin Conference of 1889, the Samoan islands of Tutuila and Aunu'u became unincorporated territories of the United States.

Large-scale migration of Pacific Islanders after the war began slowly at first and increased steadily and rapidly after 1965. During these years what began as a movement of primarily Native Hawaiians expanded to include Samoans, Tongans, Fijians, Marshall Islanders, Pohnpeians, Chamorros, and others. There were a variety of reasons for the exponential increase in the number of emigrants from Pacific Island nations during this period, compared to the dearth of migrants from this region in previous decades. World War II transformed Oceania, and even island nations that did not experience actual fighting served as hosts to an array of foreign, mostly American, troops. These foreigners left a lasting impression on the people who lived there, not only because of the roads, bridges, and airstrips they built, but also because of the flood of jobs, dollars, and consumer products that poured into island towns and villages. This glimpse of the emerging world of capitalist consumer culture, and opportunities to earn the cash needed to participate, proved a tempting proposition for a younger generation of Pacific Islanders. Agricultural work suffered a predictable loss of prestige. At the same time, population growth also increased steadily, contributing to a shortage of arable land and and dearth of employment opportunities in Pacific Islander communities both rural and urban. When opportunities for employment or education visas, or in the case of those Pacific nations like Samoa, Guam, and the members of the Trust Territories of the Pacific, military service, presented themselves, those who were eligible seized them. In 1965 the US Congress passed the Immigration and Nationality Act, creating opportunities for Pacific Islanders to join family members who were already living in the United States, as well as opening up opportunities for people from a larger number of Pacific Island nations to emigrate. The condition of the global economy and access to US education and work visas largely determined the pace and volume of Pacific Islander migration to the United States from the late 1960s through the 1990s. The numbers continued to increase. By the 1980s multigenerational communities of Pacific Islanders were common, with a younger generation who were not migrants but citizens. Several scholars have linked the growth of the Church of Jesus Christ of Latter-day Saints in Tonga to the educational opportunities that the church has historically provided to people in these communities, although such an explanation would not account for the high rates of member retention in Tonga.[17]

Efforts by Pacific Islanders to maintain distinct cultural identities across generations in the diaspora have been studied extensively. And certainly not all of the many Pacific Islanders living in the Salt Lake and Utah Valleys today engage in the same process of constructing and negotiating ethnic, cultural, and religious identities. Many Pacific Islanders in Utah are not Mormon. But for Latter-day Saint Pacific Islanders in Utah, specific narratives that conflate race, ethnicity, culture, and religion have their origin in historical and religious narratives peculiar to Latter-day Saint theology. Speculation about the origin of Pacific Islanders, specifically Polynesians, was common among Mormon leaders as early as the mid-nineteenth century.

Today the official church position on Polynesian origins is that Polynesians are descendants of the Semitic peoples who settled the American continents and whose story is purportedly related in The Book of Mormon. Some of the earliest Latter-day Saint missionaries in the Pacific speculated, sometimes publicly, on the connection between Native Americans and Polynesians, and others proclaimed that Polynesians were in fact "Lamanites." George Q. Cannon, Lousia Pratt, and other Latter-day Saint missionaries in the Pacific all made statements or private observations to this effect. At the dedication

of the Lāʻie temple in 1919, Heber J. Grant made an unequivocal pronounce-
ment that the people of the Pacific Islands (and it can be assumed he was
referring specifically to Polynesians) were "Lamanites." In his dedicatory
prayer he stated, "We thank thee that thousands and tens of thousands of
the descendents of Lehi, in this favored land, have come to a knowledge of
the Gospel."[18] Joseph F. Smith made similar unequivocal statements while
speaking to a group of Maori Saints visiting Salt Lake City. In the years that
followed scholarship on the origins of Pacific Islanders went in the opposite
direction, citing the overwhelming evidence that the island archipelagos of
Oceania were settled in a series of migrations from the west, not the east.[19]
However, on a tour of the Pacific in 1976 that began in Hawaiʻi, Church of
Jesus Christ of Latter-day Saints prophet and president Spencer W. Kimball
ended any speculation about the church position on Polynesian origins in
a series of addresses given at Brigham Young University Hawaiʻi, Church
College of Western Samoa in Apia, Church College of New Zealand, and
Liahona High School in Nukuʻalofa, Tonga. In each address Kimball referred
specifically to passages in The Book of Mormon that mention a shipbuilder
and his followers who sailed north and were never heard from again. In
Samoa, Kimball stated that "we have a great congregation of people in the
South Seas who came from the Nephites.... The Lord knows what he is
doing when he sends His people from one place to another.... You have
been scattered. And now you are being gathered."[20]

THE CENTENNIAL: DEFINING IOSEPA IN COLLECTIVE MEMORY

The year 1989 was important for the descendants of Iosepa settlers. It
marked the one-hundredth anniversary of the Native Hawaiian settlers'
arrival in Skull Valley on August 28, 1889. The Iosepa Historical Society
(IHS), an organization formed in 1978 by descendants of the original
Iosepa settlers, planned the commemorative festivities for the centennial.
For several years IHS volunteers worked feverishly to prepare for the centennial celebration, addressing logistical concerns about the commemorative program and fund-raising to pay for the events to take place in both
Hawaiʻi and Utah. The IHS gained access to the site from the landown-
ers and worked to have Iosepa recognized as a Utah Historical Site, which
allowed for expanded use of and access to the site for commemorative purposes. For the centennial the IHS commissioned a memorial sculpture and
monument to be placed above the restored and newly fenced graveyard.
Jan Fisher, a professor in the Fine Arts Department at Brigham Young
University Hawaiʻi, sculpted a bronze bust of a Native Hawaiian warrior
with a large feathered cap, a symbol of royalty, to sit atop a marble base

inscribed with a historical sketch of the community, the names of donors to the project, and a list of the seventy-six people buried in the graveyard. The bust faced west to look out over Skull Valley, the graveyard, and the old town site.

The centennial was recognized with an official proclamation from the state of Hawai'i, which designated August 28, 1989, as Iosepa Pioneers Centennial Day in Hawai'i. The IHS hosted a *ho'okupu* (gift) presentation at the Utah State Capitol in Salt Lake City on August 26, 1989, attended by government and Church of Jesus Christ of Latter-day Saint leaders. It featured speakers and performances by Pacific Islander cultural and historical associations from Hawai'i, Samoa, and New Zealand. The centennial festivities, which spanned four days, included a dedication of the monument by Gordon B. Hinckley, then first counselor of the First Presidency of the Church and later prophet. In his remarks Hinckley stated: "[The Iosepa settlers] came willingly and with appreciation in their hearts. They worked diligently and faithfully, and they left reluctantly.... This was not the desert we see today. This was once a beautiful community and a part of a large mosaic of communities that our people established all over the West, in Utah, Arizona, Idaho, Nevada, and California; 500 communities, at least. And among them stood Iosepa as a gem, a paradise, brought from the islands of the Pacific to the desert of the West."[21] Hinckley linked Iosepa with the "mosaic of communities" established by Mormon colonizers throughout the West. Iosepa was thus given official inclusion in the Mormon pioneer story, a story central to Mormon identity in the Great Basin and beyond. Absent in this tribute to the settlers' diligence and faith, however, were racial exclusion and ostracism. Hinckley's address established connections to a historical project important in the social lives of many Mormons in the Great Basin: the identification with Utah's "pioneer heritage." Mormons in Utah and elsewhere annually celebrate July 24, the day the first Mormon settlers entered the Salt Lake Valley, as "Pioneer Day," and many Mormons proudly commemorate their own genealogical ties to pioneer families through historical pageantry, historical reenactments, and public celebrations.[22] In 2006 alone there were thirty-two news releases from the Church of Jesus Christ of Latter-day Saints regarding the pioneers or celebrations of Pioneer Day, an average of nearly three per month.[23] A press release from July 21, 2006, announcing the annual Pioneer Day commemorative concert is representative of the language and sentiment surrounding annual Pioneer Day commemorative celebrations:

Members of The Church of Jesus Christ of Latter-day Saints celebrate Pioneer Day to remember not only the arrival of the pioneers in Salt Lake, but the sacrifice the early members of the Church made for their religion. Gordon B. Hinckley, president of the Church, said in 2001: "We must never allow recognition of their trials, of their sacrifices, of their tenacity, of their faith and their prayers in establishing this great community to lapse or be forgotten.... In all of our celebrations of the 24th of July, let us never forget it. Let us remember with gratitude and reverent respect those who have gone before us, who paid so dear a price in laying the foundation for that which we enjoy this day."[24]

The commemorative activities take on various forms each year. Mormon youth groups stage historical reenactments of pioneer treks across America's central plains in period dress, pushing handcarts and walking behind covered wagons.[25] The church has gone to great expense to purchase lands and develop historic sites to tell the stories of the triumphs and hardships of emigrant companies crossing the plains.[26] Pioneer Day is commemorated annually with an array of church-sponsored events, including concerts, pageants, addresses, and historical reenactments throughout Utah. Church publications, including *Ensign* magazine, regularly publish articles on the history of the pioneer trek west across the plains to the Salt Lake Valley. Descendants of nineteenth-century Mormon settlers in the Great Basin take pride in this "pioneer heritage." Historical organizations like the Sons and Daughters of Utah Pioneers, which work to foreground a specific historical experience and define the collective memory of it in Utah, are much like thousands of others that exist elsewhere in the United States.[27]

For Mormons the "pioneer trek" has assumed a near mythical quality and provides a narrative foundation for Mormon peoplehood couched in the language of faith, sacrifice, and the evidence of God's hand in the lives of his children. In addition, the story of the Mormon trek westward is linked to biblical narratives and connects early Mormon settlers to the people of Israel. Historian Jan Shipps argues that: "The parallel between the Mormon trek and the biblical exodus needs to be remembered... for it is the key to the pioneer experience. Just as the original designation of the Saints as chosen was a repetition of God's paradigmatic act in choosing Abraham's seed, so the Mormon trek renewed the force of God's election of the Mormons in precisely the same way that the miraculous departure from Egypt and the journey through the wilderness and into the Promised Land renewed the identity of the Hebraic tribes as the citizens of His elect nation."[28]

In addition to offering a defining event for Mormons as a people, the story of the pioneer trek also established the Salt Lake Valley as the promised land, the chosen place for God's people to build his kingdom. Just as tracing one's ancestors to these early pioneers links church members directly to the very nearly mythical pioneer generation, it simultaneously links them to a specific place and establishes a seemingly incontrovertible link between a people (the Mormons) and a place (Utah) that endures despite the church's move away from the concept of the literal gathering.[29]

The IHS worked diligently to make the historical connection between the journey of Native Hawaiian Saints east and those who crossed the plains west. References to the Native Hawaiians settlers as "pioneers" in IHS correspondence, ephemera, and commemorative events were common in the years prior to the centennial, and they remain so now.[30] Leading up to the centennial, newspaper coverage of the annual celebrations reflected this emphasis on pioneer heritage. In 1987 the *Church News* published an article about Iosepa titled "Iosepa Expresses Faith of Polynesian Pioneers."[31] It documented the Memorial Day festivities that took place that year and the visit of Gordon B. Hinckley to Iosepa. Contemplating Hinckley's visit, the article stated: "Iosepa reflects an expression of faith, obedience to counsel, and devotion to the Lord by the Polynesian pioneers more than ease, comfort, and nice things."[32] A decade later the *Salt Lake Tribune* published an article titled "Polynesians Honor *Their* Pioneers: Islanders Made Colony in Utah."[33] At the 1989 centennial fireside,[34] local historian and journalist Donald Rosenberg recited a brief synopsis of Iosepa's history to the crowd assembled at the Temple Square assembly hall:

In 1865 the Church bought a large tract of land at Laie, Oahu, in an attempt to establish another gathering place. However, the Hawaiians still had a burning desire to come to Utah.... By 1889, about 75 Hawaiians had gathered in North Salt Lake in the area which is known as Becks Hot Springs.... By this time, 40 years after the Pioneers entered Utah, the colonization of communities along all the mountain streams had already taken place. There was no place for the South Sea Islanders to go and settle as a group, which they desired to do. The need developed for a permanent place where they could obtain year round employment and again enjoy living their own customs and cultures.... Much speculation has come forth as to the reason why Iosepa was closed and abandoned. But to me, the most reasonable and logical reason is that Joseph F. Smith, then President of the Church, after one of his trips to the islands, announced that a Temple was to be built in Hawaii, and suggested, or may have suggested, that the people return to their homeland to help with the building of the Temple and the work therein. Leaving was accompanied with much mixed emotion, on one hand, the feeling of anxiety in returning to their Homeland after being gone for so many years, and their desire to help build the Temple. On the other hand, there was reluctance and regret in leaving a town which had been their home for 28 long years, and by that time, most had been born in Iosepa and knew no other life.... [W]hen the wagons were loaded and ready to leave for the Timpe [sic] railroad, fifteen miles to the north, the women refused to ride in the wagons, and were determined to walk the distance to the railroad. They followed the wagons on foot and with big tears running down their faces, they kept looking back at their homes and uttering, "Goodbye, Iosepa, Goodbye, Iosepa."[35]

Rosenberg's emphasis on certain aspects of Iosepa's history at the expense of others is revealing. His retelling of Iosepa's story testifies to the religious motivations behind Iosepa's beginning and end, but obscures the racism directed at the Native Hawaiian community that became increasingly strident in the spring and summer of 1889 and remained so throughout the community's twenty-eight-year history. Although many Native Hawaiian and Pacific Islander Mormons acknowledge racism as a factor in the removal of the Native Hawaiian community to Skull Valley in 1889,[36] it is obscured in the popular memory of Iosepa in Utah and has little place in public presentations of the community's history.

The reason for this is at least partly the concerns of the community of Native Hawaiian and Pacific Islander Mormons in Utah today. To most observers the connection between the actions of European and American converts gathering to the west and Native Hawaiian converts gathering to the east seems obvious. However, it was the lack of continuity between past and present Pacific Islander communities in Utah that many descendants worked to combat. Pacific Islanders have become a highly visible minority population in the Salt Lake Valley and neighboring communities as the numbers of Pacific Islanders in the western United States has grown since 1960. West Valley City, in the western Salt Lake Valley, is second only to Honolulu in places with a population of 100,000 or more Pacific Islanders. Salt Lake City is fourth, behind Hayward, California. Although there are several states with larger aggregate populations of Pacific Islanders, the Salt Lake Valley boasts the largest concentration of Pacific Islanders in the American West, outside of Honolulu.[37]

Pacific Islanders in Utah rely on formal and informal community organizations to maintain a connection to their home islands and to a specific idea of "traditional" culture. Pacific Islander and Native Hawaiian cultural centers have sprung up in Salt Lake City and Provo. There are a number of Polynesian dance groups, and families run catering businesses that specialize in serving Polynesian or "local" Hawaiian food and providing "local style" entertainment. Perennial Hawai'i state high school football champion Kahuku High School often plays preseason exhibition games with high school teams in Salt Lake City and West Salt Lake Valley that also boast a large percentage of Polynesian players. "Polys," slang for Pacific Islanders that is used widely throughout Utah, has been appropriated by many Pacific Islanders as a self-referential term. Disturbing to many Utahns of all ethnic backgrounds is the rise of violent gang activity in Salt Lake City, a trend that has come to be associated largely with Pacific Islanders as well as Asian Americans, Latinos, and Chicanos. Pacific Islander–based gangs, have garnered a great deal of public and media attention because of the high percentage of Pacific Islanders in Utah who are Mormons compared to other Pacific groups. Pacific Islander community leaders have worked hard to counter the negative association between Pacific Islanders and street gangs.[38]

Stressing the continuity between Pacific Islander communities past and present is an important way to counter the perceived "newness" of Pacific Islanders by whites in Utah. In addition, continuity provides Pacific Islanders with a narrative that emphasizes a deep attachment to place that combats a feeling of placelessness and alienation that some believe contributes to antisocial or criminal behavior in diasporic Pacific Islander communities. The story of Iosepa in many ways provides this continuity between historic and contemporary Pacific Islander Mormon communities in Utah. Iosepa has all of the symbolic elements necessary to stand as a historical metaphor for the lived experiences of Pacific Islanders in Utah today. It also contains all of the symbolic elements of the classic pioneer story so pervasive in Mormon public memory. Faith and sacrifice, hardships and struggle, obedience and devotion to church leaders—all of these elements are present, and they establish the settlers of Iosepa as the "Polynesian Pioneers" of the nineteenth century and diasporic Pacific Islanders in Utah as their figurative, if not literal, descendants. The public memory created around Iosepa links the Pacific Islanders of Utah today with the Mormon pioneers of the past and legitimizes their presence in today's Utah. In a newspaper article on the problem of gang violence, the story of Iosepa was invoked as an integral part of the Pacific Islander experience in Utah: "In Skull Valley, the abandoned settlement of Iosepa has become a pilgrimage site for Mormon Polynesians from across the West. Each Memorial Day, a celebration here attracts some 2,000 people.... In a strange way, despite its troubled history and tragedy, Iosepa has become a refuge for Polynesians. It's their own place tucked in the hills, where they can watch over the barren, shimmering valley below. It's a place to start over and renew." One man who travels to Skull Valley several times each year remarked that coming to Iosepa is "a way of us never forgetting that our people were here."[39]

Images on programs from the Iosepa centennial celebrations demonstrate how the organizers incorporated the pioneer narrative and central authority of Mormonism into public memory of Iosepa. The program for the Iosepa Historical Society's Ho'okupu presentation, put on as part of the

1989 centennial festivities, featured an iconic image of a Polynesian voyaging canoe. The significance of the voyaging canoe in Polynesian culture cannot be overstated. The Hawaiian Renaissance of the 1970s was spurred in large part by the efforts of Nainoa Thompson, a Hawaiian navigator who, with his crew, constructed a traditional Polynesian voyaging canoe, the *Hokulea*, and sailed it from O'ahu to Tahiti. The traditional Pacific methods of celestial navigation, lost for generations, were resurrected, and Thompson and his crew traveled to Micronesia to solicit the help of an elderly man who still knew the principles of navigation that allowed Pacific Islanders to traverse the vast expanses of the planet's largest body of water and settle the Pacific Islands. The voyage from Hawai'i to Tahiti once again linked two Polynesian cultures and offered a convincing challenge to academic theories that Oceanian archipelagos were settled through accidental discovery and drift voyages, which ignored evidence from Pacific Islander oral accounts of settlement. The voyage of the *Hokulea* demonstrated conclusively that Oceanian sailors were able to make planned and deliberate voyages that both colonized and connected archipelagos throughout the Pacific. The use of a Polynesian voyaging canoe in an iconographic representation of the Iosepa settlement emphasizes a Polynesian link to a pioneer heritage that defines early Mormonism. The journey from Nauvoo, which the Mormons left following the murder of their first prophet and president, Joseph Smith Jr., remains an important narrative for Mormons.[40] It was a defining event in the making of an isolated religious community in the American West and fostered the notion of the "gathering of the scattered tribes of Israel in the latter days." For many modern Mormons the expulsion from Nauvoo and the subsequent journey of the pioneers across the plains to the Sale Lake Valley have become the event around which all narratives of group identity solidify. For this reason, modern Mormons attach a special significance to the ability to trace one's ancestry to original settlers of the Salt Lake Valley. This bit of cultural capital is often extended; it is not uncommon to hear modern Mormons refer to themselves as being of "pioneer stock" (regardless of where they might live), meaning that they can trace their ancestry either to the original settlers of the Utah territory or to a colonizing mission sent by Brigham Young to the farther reaches of the Great Basin in the nineteenth century.

The social power of this idea is difficult to overstate in terms of both individual faith and group identity, and the rhetorical power of the pioneer narrative is most evident in its reliable invocation in talks given by Church of Jesus Christ of Latter-day Saint leaders at semiannual general conferences, in manuals for Sunday school instruction in individual wards and stakes, and in the numerous reenactments of the pioneer trek across the

Great Plains that take place in wards and stakes all over the United States each summer. As the Church of Jesus Christ of Latter-day Saints has grown internationally, the pioneer narrative is most often told as an analogy, with members in countries where the church is new referred to as the "pioneers" of their homes, communities, and nations. In a general conference address given by Gayle M. Clegg in April 2004 titled "The Finished Story," she relates the poignant tale of her husband's great-grandfather, who emigrated from England in the nineteenth century and lost his wife during the journey across the plains to the Salt Lake Valley. In asking herself whether she could have maintained her faith and devotion in the face of such hardship, she equates his experience to those of newly baptized members of the church in Africa, who have themselves become "everyday pioneers walking forward, joining a new church, leaving behind centuries of traditions, even leaving behind families and friends."[41] The idea that new converts to the church are living an experience analogous to that of nineteenth-century pioneers crossing the plains and settling new lands is a common theme voiced by church leaders in the last decade and a half.

For Pacific Islander Saints, the journeys that ended in Iosepa, beginning in the 1870s and continuing nearly until the dissolution of the settlement, provide a parallel "pioneer heritage" connecting Pacific Islanders to a larger defining narrative in Mormon history. The image of the Polynesian voyaging canoe represents the continuing voyage of discovery by diasporic Pacific Islanders. It celebrates the metaphorical voyage and thus establishes an image of Pacific peoples not as exiles, but as voyagers, explorers, and settlers of new lands. In addition, the image of the canoe represents a culturally specific interpretation of a historical event that links multiple communities to a broader historical narrative within the context of Mormon history. In celebrating the centennial of Iosepa, descendants of its settlers used specific imagery that created not an analogous connection to nineteenth-century pioneers, but a literal connection that emphasized a dual heritage spanning Latter-day Saint and Pacific Island culture and history.

The connection between the historical and contemporary Pacific Islander communities in Utah through Iosepa is a nearly ubiquitous theme, from newspaper accounts to documentary films. A recent documentary, *The Polynesian Gift to Utah* (Kathleen Weiler, 2004), investigates the growth of the Pacific Islander population in the state and the connections of many Pacific Islanders in Utah to the Mormon Church. The documentary reflects the importance of Iosepa and the pioneer narrative to the Pacific Islander community in Utah today. In a section of the film relating the history of the Iosepa settlement, one interviewee states: "To Hawaiians the Iosepa experiment is very meaningful...

We may not have direct ancestors, but to know that they were Hawaiians that came here to a very strange land and settled in Skull Valley gives me a feeling of pride...[they] paved the way for others coming to Utah.... Because of the pioneer efforts here and going back to the islands, the legacy goes on. They were the pioneers and we are in some ways living what they went through."[42] The sentiments articulated here reveal much about the role of Iosepa's history in the lives of Pacific Islanders with no direct connection to Iosepa other than the cultural connection in the Pacific. Articulating the role of Iosepa settlers as pioneers creates continuity between Pacific Islander communities past and present and mitigates the very real challenges of being perceived as a new minority ethnic group by the dominant culture. Iosepa functions as a historical metaphor for the lived experience of all sorts of Pacific Islanders in Utah today.

MEMORIAL DAY—"WE COME HERE TO BE HAWAIIAN"

Each year Memorial Day brings hundreds of families in cars, campers, and trucks to Skull Valley to participate in the commemorative festivities hosted and organized by the Iosepa Historical Society. Approximately half a mile northeast of the former Iosepa town site, Jan Fisher's proud-faced bust of a Native Hawaiian warrior, sitting atop an engraved granite memorial, looks out austerely over Skull Valley. Below the memorial flowers, leis, and US and Hawai'i state flags adorn the fenced-in Iosepa cemetery. Behind the cemetery a large covered pavilion provides shade for those sitting in chairs and visiting while they enjoy the soft falsetto voices and the sounds of the ukulele and guitars from the nearby stage. To the east of the stage lies a set of stairs leading up to a large kitchen, with hot and cold running water and a generator for power.

Yellow polo shirts identify the board of directors of the IHS, most of whom work feverishly preparing food, directing new arrivals to vacant campsites, visiting with neighbors, and amiably chatting with visiting journalists and photographers. On either side of the pavilion and kitchen families lounge in tents and campers, preparing their own food, laughing, visiting, and playing music. Children run back and forth catching lizards, hiking the steep hills behind the pavilion, and playing tetherball under the pavilion. The weekend's events include a flag ceremony; craft workshops on making *ipus*, candy leis, and flower wristbands; and fishing in the nearby pond. Saturday night centers around the luau, complete with *lau lau* (steamed pork or chicken wrapped in kalo leaves) and *kalua* pig cooked in an *imu* (underground oven). In the absence of *hali'i* (banana stumps) to place over the *imu*'s red hot rocks, a small group of workers leaves in two trucks to gather watercress from a mountain spring high above the site, one of the same springs that provided water for the people of Iosepa during the settlement's heyday. On Saturday night attendees are entertained by performances from visiting hula halau and other Polynesian performance groups. The following Sunday includes a potluck lunch following a Mormon "testimony meeting" religious service. To help fund such a grand annual gathering T-shirts are sold, adorned with slogans such as "Iosepa Ku'u Home Aloha" (Iosepa My Beloved Home), "Iosepa Polynesian Pioneers," and "Sorry, I don't speak Spanish, I'm Samoan."

Memorial Day at Iosepa draws crowds as impressive in size (often as many as one thousand people) as they are eclectic. Though many attendees are descendants of Iosepa settlers, many others represent the large and growing community of Pacific Islanders in Utah and other areas of the West; some are white Utahns with some connection to the islands, either through marriage, experience as missionaries, or casual friendships and associations. Representatives of the Sons and Daughters of Utah Pioneers, a major financial contributor to the Memorial Day festivities, are there as well. The reasons that each attendee has for spending the holiday weekend in dusty Skull Valley, often enduring clouds of mosquitoes, snakes, rain, cold, and wind even in late May, vary. Some are visiting and tending their ancestors' graves; others enjoy a comforting slice of contemporary island culture with a decidedly pan-Pacific flavor. Regardless of their motivations, Iosepa has become a place that Pacific Islanders in the West have invested with meaning and cultural significance.

For descendants of Iosepa settlers, the migration of Native Hawaiians east to the Salt Lake Valley and back again retains all of the mythic elements of peoplehood and place, of hardship and sacrifice. William Kauaiwiulaokalani Wallace III, whose grandparents left Iosepa in 1915, refers to the exodus out of the valley as "our trail of tears." This narrative has been embraced by many contemporary Pacific Islanders in the Salt Lake Valley who participate in the celebrations at Iosepa on Memorial Day. Although this has created some generally unstated tension between Native Hawaiian descendants of Iosepa settlers and others who see Memorial Day in Skull Valley as a much-needed dose of "local flavor" in Utah life, representatives from the various Pacific Islander communities see in each other a common set of experiences. Commenting on the planned programs for the 2006 Memorial Day celebration, one interviewee remarked that "we need to focus more on the history of the pioneers who came to this place. There is not much talk of the history, and a lot of the Pacific Islanders here have no idea what this place is really about."[43] There is, however, a larger shared sense of "what this place is really about." For all participants, Iosepa is experienced as a place made relevant through collective memory and the historical narratives that help make sense of and contextualize present day realities for Pacific Islanders in Utah.

Annual Memorial Day celebrations are a reminder that one important way that Iosepa is defined in collective memory is through place. Regardless of individual views about how the history of Iosepa is presented and perceived each year at the gatherings, each participant experiences the landscape and surroundings of Iosepa as a historical site with a great deal of meaning and personal significance. Some feel commitment to the site because it is the resting place of their ancestors' remains. As the place of interment for the bones of ancestors, Skull Valley will always be a sacred place for the Native Hawaiian descendants of Iosepa settlers. Lionel Broad, who left Iosepa as a young child in 1915, stated: "I feel haunted by the spirits here. Hawaiians have a feeling that the dead are dead, they're buried, but their spirit is still alive."[44] Regarding the designation of burial sites as sacred places to Native Hawaiians, Edward Ayau writes: "*Nā iwi* [bones] are placed in the ground to eventually become part of *Haumea* (Earth), thereby insuring a place for the bones forever. Most importantly, *nā iwi* impart the *mana* [spiritual power] of the deceased to that ground.... The entire area therefore becomes sacred with *mana*."[45] Iosepa was a historically significant place to Native Hawaiians in Utah long before the Iosepa Historical Society began its campaign to raise awareness of the history of Pacific Islanders in Skull Valley. The Native Hawaiian settlers at Iosepa demonstrated their attachment to Skull Valley through the obvious anguish that they felt when the town was abandoned in 1915.

This connection to Skull Valley is perhaps best explained in the Native Hawaiian concepts expressed by the following terms: *kama'aina, hānau, hānai,* and *'iwi.* Like many Hawaiian words, they can be used as both noun and verb, and often the meanings in both uses are connected. *Kama'aina,* literally a child of the land, can imply in many respects the concepts of *hānau* (birth), *hānai* (to raise up or to feed), and *'iwi* (literally bones). The question "Na wai e ho'ola i na 'iwi?" or "Who will care for one in death?" demonstrates the importance of the bones as cherished objects to be revered and cared for after death.[46] The land at Iosepa raised (*ua hānai*) families and individuals. Their relationship to it, birth and death on it, and placement of sacred bones (*na iwi*) in it established Iosepa settlers as *kama'aina* to that place, children of that land that had fed them and nurtured them, where they had placed the *piko,* or umbilical cord, of their children and the *'iwi* of their dead. This spiritual and physical connection with the land emphasizes the importance of place. It is not interchangeable with other places, but is invested with meaning through the cycles of life, death, and rebirth. For the original settlers, to abandon this land was in all senses tragic. "It was sad, it was sad to leave this place," remembered Lionel Broad. "When we left, I was riding in the last wagon. All the women walked, from here to Timpie station, crying, they didn't want to leave this place."[47] For the descendants of those settlers, the obligation to care for the remains of their ancestors animated efforts to preserve the site and commemorate the community's history and legacy.

The efforts of all who work to remember Iosepa, whether they are descendants of Iosepa settlers or not, have also contributed to its significance as a place. Many who attend the Memorial Day celebrations regard the history of Pacific Islander Mormons in Skull Valley as important because of its general association with nineteenth-century Pacific Islander pioneers in Utah. For others, Iosepa derives its significance from their own memories, shaped by their experiences with the landscape from years of coming to Skull Valley along with the stories that they have heard, all of which contribute to the act of remembering.[48] Even without direct connection to ancestors, the experiences of these people become an important part of the collective memory of Iosepa. The historical connection between the original town and its inhabitants, the history of Mormonism in Utah, and the larger history of the Church of Jesus Christ of Latter-day Saints in the Pacific Islands are made explicit to all of those who visit and celebrate at Iosepa, as evidenced by the words engraved on the memorial above the gravesite. The appeal to a broader community of Polynesian Saints, as opposed to a community of only Native Hawaiians, is evident during the celebrations, in the coverage of the event in newspapers and television, and in the memorial. Attendees at the annual celebrations represent the Samoan, Native Hawaiian, and Tongan communities. The flags that fly over the cemetery attest to the pan-Pacific appeal of Iosepa's history.

Anthropologist Thomas Murphy argues that groups within the larger Latter-day Saint community who are considered Lamanites often appropriate the "Mormon racial doctrine" to empower themselves within the context of an overwhelmingly white, American church hierarchy. "Although Mormon doctrine is imbued with colonial metaphors and racially charged symbolism," Murphy claims, "the meanings that Mormon missionaries and converts apply to those symbols are not predetermined by Church leaders or sacred texts; rather, they reflect the interests of those actively asserting them in a particular place and time."[49] The development of a "supranational Lamanite identity" rests on the ability of Mormons who self-identify as Lamanites to draw on Mormon sacred texts that emphasize their privileged position within Mormon religious doctrine. I argue, as have others, that the same phenomenon holds true in communities of Pacific Islander Mormons.[50] Self-identification as Lamanites within the context of a sacred

historical narrative creates a religious identity that reinforces and rein-
scribes the importance of ethnic identities. Many of these communities
have interpreted this narrative to resist official church attempts to suppress
local tradition in order to encourage Native American, Pacific Islander, and
Latin American communities especially to conform to the cultural traditions of white North Americans taken as normative within mainstream
Mormon society.[51] In most cases, however, the identification of specific
peoples as Lamanites has been a top-down affair, communicated through
the church hierarchy through official discourse and referencing sacred texts
and the teaching of modern prophets.[52] And although this seems to be the
case for the designation of Pacific Islanders as Lamanites within LDS theology, Pacific Islander Saints have internalized this peculiar blend of ethnic and religious identity with the pioneer connection through Iosepa as a
means of empowering themselves in a place dominated in so many ways by
the cultural presence of the church.

There is a historical basis for this pan-Pacific ethnic consciousness.
During its twenty-eight-year history, Iosepa was home not only to Native
Hawaiians, but to a (much smaller) number of Samoans, Maori, and
Tahitians, even though the language, many of the cultural practices, and
the history of the colony's existence were overwhelmingly tied to the
church's missionary efforts in Hawai'i. This appeal to a pan-Pacific consciousness speaks more to realities facing the Pacific Islander community
in Utah today.[53] The appropriation of the term "Poly" (short for Polynesian,
a term originally used by whites in Utah to refer to Pacific Islanders) as a
self-referential description has brought Tongans, Samoans, and less frequently Native Hawaiians to recognize shared interests and even create
shared institutions for community advocacy.[54] In an interview for Kathleen
Weiler's documentary *The Polynesian Gift to Utah*, Samoan sportscaster
Alema Harrington discusses how a pan-ethnic consciousness can work to
combat prevailing racial stereotypes about Pacific Islanders:

> I think the thing about my position is that people see me just as a person and
> the color line is erased at least for a fraction of a second. And when they see
> me on the news or on Sports Beat Saturday, they say "Oh look, there's Alema
> Harrington," they don't say "Oh look, there's a Polynesian."
>
> I tell the story sometimes about being on the sidelines at a high school football
> game and one of the officials came up and asked me about my job and said "You
> do a great job. I watch you all the time. You always dress so well. You always look
> so good." And he said, " You know you better be careful. There are a lot of Tongan
> guys out here and they might steal your clothes." And for a second there I think
> he caught himself when he said it because he didn't see me as a Polynesian and

I said to him "No they won't, because they are my cousins and they wouldn't do that." And it made him think for a second, "Hey you know what, he's right. And he's a Polynesian just like they are."

And maybe the next time he sees that group of kids, he'll treat them the same way he treated me. And that's the progression that we're looking for, as far as the way that we are treated as a people. And I think that my position will help that happen, hopefully, if I continue to do the things that I'm doing, then people will treat other Polynesians better. And that's what we're looking for.[55]

Harrington's experience highlights the way that pan-ethnic consciousness in Utah has developed among Pacific Islanders when faced with discrimination or racial stereotyping by whites. In Harrington's embrace of a broader ethnic identity for Polynesian, all Tongans become his "cousins." Part of this undoubtedly stems from his realization that whites in Utah often fail to distinguish between Samoans and Tongans.

Similar examples related to Iosepa abound. The inscription on the memorial statue standing above the graveyard at Iosepa appeals to a pan-ethnic consciousness among Pacific Islanders as it connects modern-day diasporic communities to Utah and their homelands. The final paragraph reads: "The seeds of our Polynesian Pioneers bore fruit in Hawai'i—the Lā'ie Temple, Brigham Young University Hawai'i, the Polynesian Cultural Center. Holy temples stand firm in New Zealand, Western Samoa, Tonga, and Tahiti as monuments to the testimonies of the faithful Polynesian Pioneers." This simple paragraph connects the history of Iosepa not only to the pioneer narrative in Utah but to the other Mormon institutions throughout the Pacific. In this reading of Iosepa's history, it is the faith of the original settlers that led to the monumental growth and accomplishments of the church in the Pacific in the twentieth century.

Cultural performances are a major part of the celebration each Memorial Day and also reflect a pan-ethnic consciousness embraced by many Pacific Islander Mormons in Utah. In May 2007 Memorial Day celebrations included performances by Maori and Tahitian dance groups, Samoan fire knife dancers, and Hawaiian hula halau.[56] Flags sitting atop the posts on the hill above the graveyard represent six Pacific Island nations. The story of Iosepa today encompasses every facet of the Mormon experience in the Pacific Islands and Utah.

David Glassberg wrote: "Places loom large not only in our personal recollections but also in the collective memory of our communities."[57] That collective memory is renewed each year as the narrative of Iosepa is redefined through the experience of Memorial Day celebrations in Skull

Valley. It is a collective memory that is used to create a shared narrative connecting the contemporary Polynesian community of Utah to the Pacific Islander community of the nineteenth and early twentieth centuries. The annual celebrations at Iosepa reaffirm Skull Valley's importance as a historically relevant place to Pacific Islander Mormons in Utah, Hawai'i, and beyond.

EPILOGUE

Since it opened its doors in 1963, the Polynesian Cultural Center (PCC) has been the number one paid tourist attraction in Hawai'i, a state that takes those sorts of things very seriously. Founded and operated by the Church of Jesus Christ of Latter-day Saints, the PCC has become somewhat of a sounding board for both supporters and detractors of the church's attitudes about race and culture in the Pacific. Its detractors argue that the PCC perpetuates and practices the worst form of cultural commodification and essentialism, wherein poor working conditions create an environment that has been characterized as everything from a cultural theme park to a cultural sweatshop. Certainly some of these criticisms have a basis in fact. The performances in the villages and in the night show can be, and have been, alternately characterized as kitschy and essentialist, staffed by students at nearby Brigham Young University making minimum wage, clothed in "traditional" dress in a highly sexualized manner (males and females alike), and packaged as an "authentic" island experience. These critiques are quite frankly difficult to argue against in an academic environment that has systematically dismantled any notion of "traditional" or "authentic" and laid bare the blatantly colonial assumptions embedded in both of these terms. The tourist gaze at the PCC, highly sexualized and imminently profitable, is on full display.[1]

But if one were to characterize daily events at the PCC as an ongoing colonial encounter, then one would expect to find the inevitable and subtle subversions of that encounter as well. And in this vein, the PCC does not disappoint. Although the "sell out" narrative may be the easiest and most obvious accusation one can drum up, these encounters, like all colonial encounters, are far from one-sided. There has been a rejoinder to these criticisms, most often articulated by Pacific Islander Mormons, some of whom have worked at the PCC as upper-level managers as well as "cultural experts" in one of the center's villages. As one scholar with intimate knowledge of the center has noted, "The person in the Samoan village who tells jokes to the tourists in four shows daily may be exhibiting his body and playing the fool, but he is also making fun of the tourists in the subtle undertones of his patter.... [He] draws in tourist dollars that pay for other members of the Samoan village to earn degrees in business and chemistry."[2] The center has provided employment for thousands of university students from the Pacific, many of whom have gone on to graduate school or to start businesses, some in their home islands, but many somewhere else entirely. The PCC (and Brigham Young University Hawai'i) has become a central location, a way station of sorts, for Pacific Islander Mormons in the diaspora.

Because of this, it is fitting that the Lā'ie branch of the Iosepa Historical Society chose the center as the location for a monument to the settlers of Iosepa. Tucked away near a drinking fountain is an old fire hydrant from the Skull Valley settlement. It sits above a small, nondescript plaque, which reads:

> This fire hydrant once served the little community of Iosepa, Skull Valley, Utah. It stands here as a reminder of the faithful Polynesian Pioneers who migrated to Utah in the late 1800's to join the "gathering to Zion," and to be married in the temple for "time and all eternity."
>
> Iosepa (meaning Joseph, referring to Joseph F. Smith) was settled on August 28, 1889, and continued for 28 years. At its peak 228 Polynesians inhabited the little desert community. When the building of the Hawai'i Temple was announced in 1915, the Iosepa Saints moved back to their beloved Hawai'i and settled along Iosepa Street in Lā'ie.
>
> The Hawai'i Temple was the first to be built by the Latter-day Saints outside of the continental United States, a lasting monument to the faith and dedication of the Polynesian Pioneers.

There are other ways that Iosepa is memorialized at the PCC. The center also houses the *Iosepa*, the double-hulled canoe named after the Skull Valley community and one of the PCC's most popular attractions. In 2008, when Brigham Young University Hawai'i was looking for a suitable place to house the *Iosepa*, William Kauaiwiulaokalani Wallace III, director of the Jonathan Napela Center for Hawaiian and Pacific Island Studies, chose PCC as the proper spot for the *Iosepa* to reside. Wallace, raised on Moloka'i, came to BYU Hawai'i (then Church College of Hawai'i) as a student, where he met his wife, Nihipora, a Maori from Aotearoa, New Zealand. That the *Iosepa*, a *wa'a* that came to life through his vision, named after the community of Saints that nurtured the faith of his grandfather, should reside at PCC seemed fitting.

As institutions go, the Pacific Heritage Academy is a far cry from the Polynesian Cultural Center. Where the latter seeks to provide cultural entertainment in the service of higher education, the former is a charter school in Salt Lake City, opened in the fall of 2012. According to its website, the academy's mission is to serve the educational needs of the growing population of Pacific Islanders in and around the Salt Lake Valley and ultimately to serve as a model for many more such schools. The Pacific Heritage Academy is founded on a pedagogy known as "expeditionary learning," a methodology that "organizes learning around an experiential project-based approach in which students do original research and create high-quality products for audiences beyond the classroom."[3] For the Pacific Heritage Academy and its board of directors, a central part of this project-based approach will be studying Iosepa, the "first Pacific Islander community in Utah,"[4] from cultural, historical, anthropological, and archaeological perspectives. The academy will presumably be non-denominational and will expand Iosepa's narrative to include a community defined not solely within the confines of the religious history of the Church of Jesus Christ of Latter-day Saints.

The PCC's story, and its role in the lives of the many students and employees from throughout the Pacific who have passed through it, is nearly half a century old. The story of the Pacific Heritage Academy has just begun, but it may yet prove to have as lasting an impact on Pacific Islanders living in the diaspora as the PCC has. As different as these institutions are, the memory of Iosepa has become a central part of what they are. The historical memory surrounding the community, and the symbolic power that memory has for Pacific Islander Mormons in the diaspora, cannot be denied.

When I first began researching, presenting, and writing about Iosepa, I started and ended my narrative in a neat and tidy twenty-eight-year period between 1889 and 1917, the years when the town *actually* existed. And there are undoubtedly many who wish that I had stuck to that model. But the memory of Iosepa cannot be contained within those chronological boundaries. The Memorial Day celebrations, the Pacific Heritage Academy, Iosepa Street, and *Iosepa* the *wa'a kaulua*, sitting under the shade of the *hale wa'a* at PCC, or sailing from Hukilau beach in Lāie Bay southeast towards Kahana along O'ahu's windward coast—because of all of these things that surround me every day, the narrative of Iosepa, its history and its life, endures. Like Oceania and its inhabitants, it is a story that transcends imposed borders and boundaries. It simply refuses to be contained. Trying to contain it does the story of this community a profound disservice. Realizing that, I allowed the story to expand in both directions, so what I have presented here is a narrative that tries to contextualize the history of a small settlement of Pacific Islander Mormons that teetered on the cusp of the nineteenth and twentieth centuries into the larger story of Pacific Islanders in the American West. For me, and for countless others, Iosepa is part of the broader story of Pacific Islanders and their journeys east and of Mormons and their journey west. I hope I have done the story of this magnificent community justice.

I cannot make sense of the story of Iosepa without understanding the stories of Hawai'i, the American West, Mormons, missionaries, land, sugar, the gathering to Zion, and the post–World War II Pacific Islander diaspora. And so throughout this study I have made an effort to connect Iosepa to the larger currents of history that link these seemingly disparate places and subjects. The Pacific maritime trade, the discovery of gold in California, the social and political upheavals in Hawai'i, and the work of missionaries from the Church of Jesus Christ of Latter-day Saints in Hawai'i—all of these individual stories form the historical context for Iosepa. Seeing Iosepa in relation to the many other Native Hawaiian communities of the American West allows a comparative perspective that both highlights Iosepa's uniqueness and emphasizes its connections to other movements of islanders to the American West. Native Hawaiians in the "Great Basin Kingdom" of nineteenth-century Mormonism were not, as has often been portrayed in contemporary accounts and histories of Iosepa, a historical anomaly, but rather one of many diasporic communities of Native Hawaiians that included communities in Washington, Oregon, and California. Native Hawaiians in the Pacific Northwest maintained cohesive communities with a unique cultural and ethnic identity well into the twentieth century and in some cases to the present day. They were present in California, Oregon, and Washington in the late nineteenth century, and although they left a less pronounced cultural footprint, are memorialized in accounts of the day as well as the names of the places and landscapes they called home. If there is a uniqueness to Utah's Native Hawaiian and Pacific Islander community in Iosepa, it lies in the religious motivations that both created and sustained it through its twenty-eight years of existence. And those religious motivations, among the most powerful narratives that inspire human action and structure human experience, remain central to communities of Pacific Islander Latter-day Saints in the West today.

Scholars of Oceania have long grasped the significance of Epeli Hau'ofa's vision of the expanding world of Oceania. Scholars of the American West have been more conservative in their geographic definitions, seemingly a bit unsure of how Hawai'i fits into the broader story of US expansion. It has been my hope throughout this study to expand the boundaries of the American West and to bring to the forefront the movement of peoples east and west in a discussion so often focused on the movement of peoples north and south. What is essential in including Hawai'i as part of the story of the American West and telling the story of the people who have moved through it is that it reveals the broader regional connections of the West to the expanding Pacific World. The Pacific diaspora connects Salt Lake City and Los Angeles, San Francisco and Las Vegas, with Honolulu and Auckland, Sydney and Nuku'alofa. And the Church of Jesus Christ of Latter-day Saints has played a central role, however unintentionally, in the creation and maintenance of that diaspora. Revealing the role of religious narratives in creating and sustaining this diaspora, as well as the role that the historical memory of Iosepa still plays, awakens us to the ways that people make sense of their actions beyond politics and economy. To that end, the memory of Iosepa will live on, in ways that I cannot yet imagine.

NOTES

INTRODUCTION

1. Greg Dening, *Beach Crossings: Voyages Across Times, Cultures, and Selves* (Philadelphia: University of Pennsylvania Press, 2004), 1–11; Geoffrey Irwin, *The Prehistoric Exploration and Colonization of the Pacific* (New York: Cambridge University Press, 1992).
2. Jean Barman and Bruce McIntyre Watson, *Leaving Paradise: Indigenous Hawaiians in the Pacific Northwest* (Honolulu: University of Hawai'i Press, 2006).
3. Social science studies of Pacific Islands nations in the forty years following World War II overwhelmingly focused on the "development problem" in Oceania and were often focused on the general question of creating sustainable development plans while maintaining the integrity (or authenticity) of local cultures. The development of an economic model described by the acronym MIRAB (Migration, Remittances, Aid, and Bureaucracy) and the growing "brain drain" phenomenon created an alarming challenge to the goal of sustaining domestic growth in ways compatible with "traditional" cultural practices. For an overview of this literature, see Karen Nero, "The End of Insularity," in *The Cambridge History of Pacific Islanders*, ed. Donald Denoon (New York: Cambridge University Press, 1997), 439–467.
4. Epeli Hau'ofa and Eric Waddell, eds., *A New Oceania: Rediscovering Our Sea of Islands* (Suva, Fiji: University of the South Pacific, 1993), 2–15.
5. Ibid. Responses to Hau'ofa's essay are included in Hau'ofa and Waddell, *New Oceania*.
6. For studies of diasporic Pacific Islander communities that build on the theme originally developed by Hau'ofa, see Cluny McPherson, Paul Spoonley, and Melania Anae, eds., *Tangata O Te Moana Nui: The Evolving Identities of Pacific Peoples in Aotearoa/New Zealand* (Wellington, NZ: Dunmore Press, 2001); Helen Morton, *Tongans Overseas: Between Two Shores* (Honolulu: University of Hawai'i Press, 2003); Cathy Small, *Voyages: From Tongan Villages to American Suburbs* (Ithaca, NY: Cornell University Press, 1997); Paul Spickard, Joanne Rondilla, and Debbie Hippolite-Wright, eds., *Pacific Diaspora: Islands Peoples in the United States and Across the Pacific* (Honolulu: University of Hawai'i Press, 2002).
7. Morgan Tuimaleali'ifano, *Samoans in Fiji: Migration, Identity, and Communication* (Suva: University of South Pacific, 1990); Michael Lieber, ed., *Exiles and Migrants in Oceania* (Honolulu: University of Hawai'i Press, 1977); Grant McCall and John Connell, eds., *A World Perspective on Pacific Islander Migration: Australia, New*

Zealand, and the USA (Pacific Studies Monograph No. 6, Sydney, Center for South Pacific Studies, 1993).

8. Philip M. Harris and Nicholas A Jones, *We The People: Pacific Islanders in the United States, Census 2000 Special Reports* (Washington, DC: US Department of Commerce, 2005).

9. Sarah Deutsch, George J. Sanchez, and Gary Y. Okihiro, "Contemporary Peoples/ Contested Places," in *The Oxford History of the American West*, ed. Clyde A Milner II, Carol A. O'Connor, and Martha A. Sandweiss (New York: Oxford University Press, 1994), 639–670.

10. Matthew Kester, "Hawai'i and the American West: A Reassessment," *Pacific Studies* 32, no. 4 (December 2009), 467–484.

11. See especially Gavan Daws, *Shoal of Time: A History of the Hawaiian Islands* (New York: Macmillan, 1968); Ralph Kuykendall, *The Hawaiian Kingdom*, 3 vols. (Honolulu: University of Hawai'i Press, 1967); Lawrence Fuchs, *Hawaii Pono: A Social History* (New York: Harcourt, Brace, & World, 1961).

12. Richard Mackie, *Trading Beyond the Mountains: The British Fur Trade on the Pacific, 1793–1846* (Vancouver: University of British Columbia Press, 1997); J. S. Holliday, *Rush for Riches: Gold Fever and the Making of California* (Berkeley: University of California Press, 1999).

13. Daws, *Shoal of Time*; Kuykendall, *Hawaiian Kingdom*; and Patrick V. Kirch and Marshall Sahlins, *Anahulu: The Anthropology of History in the Kingdom of Hawaii* (Chicago: University of Chicago Press, 1992) all briefly mention emigration of Hawaiian men in the maritime and fur trades in association with population loss and legal restrictions by the kingdom on emigration in the nineteenth century. The Kōhala Lele Project is a database of names of Native Hawaiians who worked on foreign whaling trips; it can be accessed at http://www2.bishopmuseum.org/whaling/mainscreen.asp.

14. Elliot Barkan, "Turning Turner on His Head? The Significance of Immigration in 20th Century American Western History," *New Mexico Historical Review* 77 (Winter 2002), 57–88.

15. Jonathan Kay Kamakawiwo'ole Osorio, *Dismembering Lāhui: A History of the Hawaiian Kingdom to 1887* (Honolulu: University of Hawai'i Press, 2004); Noenoe K. Silva, *Aloha Betrayed: Native Hawaiian Resistance to American Colonialism* (Durham, NC: Duke University Press, 2004).

16. For example, see "Memoirs of Thomas Hopoo," *Hawaiian Journal of History* 2 (1968), 42–54; W. J. Illerbrun, "Kanaka Pete," *Hawaiian Journal of History* 6 (1972), 156–166,; Janice K. Duncan, "Kanaka World Travelers and Fur Company Employees, 1785–1860," *Hawaiian Journal of History* 7 (1973), 99; and Robert C. Schmitt, "Population Policy in Hawaii," *Hawaiian Journal of History* 8 (1974), 90–110.

17. Jean Barman and Bruce McIntyre, *Leaving Paradise: Indigenous Hawaiians in the Pacific Northwest, 1787–1898* (Honolulu: University of Hawai'i Press, 2006).

18. R. Lanier Britsch, *Moramona; The Mormons in Hawaii* (Lā'ie, HI: Institute for Polynesian Studies, 1989); Cynthia Compton, "The Making of the Ahupua'a of Lā'ie into a Gathering Place and an Alternative Space to Capitalism" (PhD diss., Brigham Young University, 2004); Joseph H. Spurrier, *Sandwich Islands Saints: Early Mormon Converts in the Hawaiian Islands* (Lā'ie, J. H. Spurrier,1989).

19. Evidence of this can be found in nearly every existing diary from Haole Mormon missionaries in Hawai'i and elsewhere in the Pacific. In addition, Christian missionaries in general lamented the fact that conversion to Christianity rarely included abandoning indigenous spiritual beliefs or practices.

CHAPTER 1

1. Greg Dening, *Islands and Beaches: Discourse on a Silent Land, Marquesas, 1774–1880* (Honolulu: University of Hawai'i Press, 1980); Greg Dening, *The Death of William Gooch: A History's Anthropology* (Honolulu: University of Hawai'i Press, 1995); Patrick V. Kirch and Marshall Sahlins, *Anahulu:The Anthropology of History in the Kingdom of Hawai'i* (Chicago: University of Chicago Press, 1992).

2. John Meares, *Voyages Made in the Years 1788 and 1789 from China to the North-West Coast of America*, (New York: Da Capo, 1967), xxxix.

3. Ibid., 4.

4. Ibid.

5. Samuel Kamakau, *Ruling Chiefs of Hawai'i* (Honolulu: Kamehameha Schools Press, 1992), 63–64. Kaiana's grandfather was Keawekekahiali'iokamoku, and his blood relationship to the line of Hawai'i chiefs would serve him well as he sought refuge under Kamehameha from his brother Naiolea on Kauai.

6. Ibid, 153.

7. Meares, *Voyages*, 6.

8. Ibid., 8.

9. Ibid., 5–6.

10. Ibid., 29.

11. Ibid., 209–210.

12. Meares, *Voyages*, 335.

13. Kamehameha was an *ali'i* from the Kona side of Hawai'i who, with the aid of British vessels and weapons, waged a war to consolidate his power over the whole of the Hawaiian chain. By 1810 Kamehameha had succeeded in bringing all of the islands under his control with the exception of Kauai, which was acquired through diplomacy.

14. Kamakau, *Ruling Chiefs of Hawai'i*, 153.

15. Ibid., 343.

16. Kamakau, *Ruling Chiefs of Hawai'i*, 156.

17. Richard Mackie, *Trading Beyond the Mountains: The British Fur Trade on the Pacific, 1793–1843* (Vancouver: University of British Columbia Press, 1997), 13.

18. Alexander Ross, *Adventures of the First Settlers on the Oregon and Columbia* (London: Smith, Elder, 1849), 69–70.

19. David Kittelson, "John Coxe: Hawai'i's First Soldier of Fortune," *Hawai'i Historical Review* (January 1965), 196; Mackie, *Trading Beyond the Mountains*, 16–18; TomKoppel, *Kanaka: The Untold Story of Hawaiian Pioneers in British Columbia and the Pacific Northwest* (Vancouver, BC: Whitecap Books, 1995).

20. Mackie, *Trading Beyond the Mountains*, 17.

21. Kamakau, *Ruling Chiefs of Hawai'i*, 251–253.

22. Koppel, *Kanaka*, 48.

23. Information on Naukane came primarily from Kittelson, "John Coxe." John Coxe was the name given to Naukane by his fellow crew members on his first voyage aboard the *Tonquin* in 1811. I use the name Naukane throughout this discussion, although there is evidence he used either name depending on the context.

24. The account of Thomas Hopu is taken from "Memoirs of Thomas Hopoo," republished in *Hawaiian Journal of History* 1 (1967), 42–54.

25. The War of 1812 between Britain and the United States.

26. "Memoirs of Thomas Hopoo."

27. David A. Chappell, *Double Ghosts: Oceanian Voyagers on Euroamerican Ships* (Armonk, NY: Sharpe, 1997)., 28–31.

28. F. W. Howay, "Early Relations with the Pacific North-West," in *The Hawaiian Islands: Papers Read during the Captain Cook Sesquicentennial Celebration, Honolulu, August 17, 1928*, ed. Albert Pierce Taylor (Honolulu: Archives of Hawai'i,1930), 11.

29. Ibid., 13.

30. Mackie, *Trading Beyond the Mountains*.

31. See Mackie, *Trading Beyond the Mountains*; Arthur Power Dudden, *The American Pacific: From the China Trade to the Present* (New York: Oxford University Press, 1992); Walter McDougall, *Let the Sea Make a Noise* (New York: HarperCollins, 1993); Ralph Kuykendall, *The Hawaiian Kingdom, Volume One: Foundation and Transformation, 1778–1854* (Honolulu: University of Hawai'i Press, 1938).

32. Epeli Hau'ofa and Eric Waddell, eds., *A New Oceania: Rediscovering Our Sea of Islands* (Suva: University of South Pacific Press, 1988).

33. Irwin, *Prehistoric Exploration*, 101–105.

34. Mackie, *Trading Beyond the Mountains*, 3–34.

35. Howay, "Early Relations with the Pacific North-West," 34; Kuykendall, *Hawaiian Kingdom*.

36. Howay, "Early Relations with the North-West," 11–25.

37. Lilikala Kame'eleihiwa, *Native Lands and Foreign Desires Pehea Lā e Pono Ai?* (Honolulu: Bishop Museum Press, 1992); Jonathan Kamakawiwo'ole Osorio, *Dismembering Lahui: A History of the Hawaiian Nation to 1887* (Honolulu: University of Hawai'i Press, 2002); Patrick Vinton Kirch and Marshall David Sahlins, *Anahulu: The Anthropology of History in the Kingdom of Hawaii* (Chicago: University of Chicago Press, 1992).

38. Richard H. Dillon, "Kanaka Colonies in California," *Pacific Historical Review* 24, no. 1 (February, 1955), 20.

39. Nicholas Thomas, *Colonialism's Culture: Anthropology, Travel, and Government* (Cambridge: Polity, 1994), 10–22.

40. Ibid., 73.

41. Ibid., xvii.

42. "Kanaka" is the Hawaiian term for "person" or "man" and was a moniker used by Hawaiians, foreign sailors, and other Oceanian laborers throughout the region. As an indicator of the term's widespread usage and shifting meaning, it was more recently adopted as the name of an independent New Caledonia. In the nineteenth century it was the term most often used to describe Hawaiians abroad and acquired a profoundly derogatory connotation in certain contexts. I use it only in its original context when quoting from original sources.

43. For a detailed treatment of Britain's role in the Pacific maritime trade through the Hudson Bay Company and its subsidiaries, see Mackie, *Trading Beyond the Mountains*. Mackie also addresses competition between Britain and the United States for control of the Columbia River trade region. For the definitive history of Hawaiian sojourners and settlers in the Pacific Northwest prior to the twentieth century, see Jean Barman and Bruce McIntyre Watson, *Leaving Paradise: Indigenous Hawaiians in the Pacific Northwest, 1787–1898* (Honolulu: University of Hawai'i Press, 2006). For an overview of the whaling industry in the Pacific, see G. A. Mawer, *Ahab's Trade: The Saga of South Seas Whaling* (New York: St. Martin's, 1999).

44. Koppel, *Kanaka*, 59–64.

45. Ibid., 27, 32.

46. Ibid., 15–18.

47. Barman and Watson, *Leaving Paradise*, 62.
48. John K. Townsend, *Narrative of a Journey Across the Rocky Mountains to the Columbia River* (Philadelphia: Henry Perkins, 1839), 185; quoted in Mackie, *Trading Beyond the Mountains*, 199.
49. Koppel, *Kanaka*, 47.
50. Ibid., 17–18.
51. Mackie, *Trading Beyond the Mountains*, 55, 159–167.
52. Ibid., 164–165.
53. The most detailed treatment of Native Hawaiian labor and settlement in the Pacific Northwest is Barman and Watson, *Leaving Paradise*.
54. Dudden, *American Pacific*, 14.
55. Ibid., 13–16.
56. Dudden, *American Pacific*, 15; Mackie *Trading Beyond the Mountains*.
57. Briton C. Busch, "Whalemen, Missionaries, and Practice of Christianity in the Nineteenth Century Pacific," *Hawaiian Journal of History* 27 (1993), 99–100.
58. Richard Henry Dana, *Two Years Before the Mast* (New York: The Heritage Press, 1947), 51.
59. Ibid., 145.
60. Ibid., 125.
61. Walter Griffith Pigman, *The Journals of Walter Griffith Pigman*, ed. Ella Stanley Fawkes. (Mexico, MO: Walter G. Staley, 1942), 42.
62. Richard A. Greer, "California Gold-Some Reports to Hawai'i," *Hawaiian Journal of History* 4 (1970), 153–173.
63. "California," *The Polynesian*, June 25, 1848.
64. "Gold Fever," *The Polynesian*, July 9, 1848.
65. Oscar Lewis, *Sutter's Fort: Gateway to the Gold Fields* (Englewood Cliffs, NJ: Prentice Hall, 1966), 10–13.
66. Greer, "California Gold-Some Reports to Hawai'i," 164.
67. Ibid.
68. Richard H. Dillon, "Kanaka Colonies in California," *Pacific Historical Review* 24, no. 1 (1955), 17.
69. Prentice Mulford, *Life by Land and Sea* (New York: F. J. Needham, 1889), 136.
70. Susan Lee Johnson, *Roaring Camp: The Social World of the California Gold Rush* (New York: Norton, 2001).
71. David Chappell, *Double Ghosts: Oceanian Voyagers on Euroamerican Ships* (New York: Sharpe, 1997).
72. Fredrik Barth, "Ethnic Groups and Boundaries," in *Theories of Ethnicity: A Classical Reader*, ed. Werner Sollors (New York: New York University Press, 1996), 294–324.
73. Jonathan Kamakawiwo'ole Osorio, *Dismembering Lāhui: The Hawaiian Kingdom to 1887* (Honolulu: University of Hawai'i Press, 2002).
74. For the role of capital in western economic development and geographical transformation, see William Robbins, *Colony and Empire: The Capitalist Transformation of the American West* (Lawrence: University Press of Kansas, 1994). I also borrow cautiously from the argument for inclusion of Hawai'i in the broader narrative of the American West found in John Whitehead, "Hawai'i: The First and Last Far West," *Western Historical Quarterly* 23, no. 2 (May 1992), 153–177. Though I agree with Whitehead's argument that Hawai'i, by virtue of American presence there in the early years of the nineteenth century and the process of colonial development, should be considered part of the West, I am concerned that inclusion in

the broader narrative of western American history obscures the contemporary struggle for Hawaiian sovereignty and the very unique position of Hawaiians and their islands in relation to the US government.

75. James B. Allen and Glen M. Leonard, *The Story of the Latter-Day Saints* (Salt Lake City: Deseret, 1976), 204.

76. Ibid., 204–207.

77. Ibid., 207–215.

78. Quoted from the *Doctrine and Covenants*, 133: 7–8.

79. Leonard Arrington, Feramorz Y. Fox, and Dean L. May, eds., *Building the City of God: Community and Cooperation Among the Mormons* (Urbana: University of Illinois Press, 1992), 2.

80. Ibid., 12–13.

81. Allen and Leonard, *Story of the Latter-day Saints*, 292–293.

82. Ibid., 254, 270–272.

83. Leonard Arrington, *Great Basin Kingdom: An Economic History of the Latter-day Saints, 1830–1900* (Salt Lake City: University of Utah Press, 1993); David L. Bigler, *Forgotten Kingdom: The Mormon Theocracy in the American West* (Spokane: Arthur H. Clarke, 1998).

84. Quoted in Michael N. Landon, ed., *The Journals of George Q. Cannon, Volume 1: To California in '49* (Salt Lake City: Deseret, 1999), 1.

85. Ibid., 2–6.

86. Kenneth N. Owens, *Gold Rush Saints: California Mormons and the Great Rush for Riches* (Norman: University of Oklahoma Press, 2005), 32–33.

87. Even after their arrival in San Francisco, Brannan was assured that California would be the final place for the Mormons to settle. See Owens, *Gold Rush Saints*, 50–51.

88. Quoted in Owens, *Gold Rush Saints*, 51.

89. Ibid., 52–53.

90. Norma Baldwin Ricketts, *The Mormon Battalion: U.S. Army of the West, 1846–1848* (Logan: Utah State University Press, 1996), 5.

91. Ibid., 159.

92. Ibid., 188–189.

93. Ibid., 193–197, Sutter quoted on 203.

94. Theresa Gay, *James Marshall: The Discoverer of California Gold, a Biography* (Georgetown, CA: Talisman, 1967), 190.

95. Ricketts, *Mormon Battalion*, 190.

96. For a detailed look at the demographics of California's early mining communities and the social world they created, see Johnson, *Roaring Camp*.

97. Arrington, *Great Basin Kingdom*, 64–95.

98. Ibid.

99. Ibid., 66.

100. George Q. Cannon, *The Journals of George Q. Cannon*, ed. Michael L. Landon (Salt Lake City: Deseret, 1999), 77–82.

101. Richard W. Lotchin, *San Francisco, 1846–1856: From Hamlet to City* (Urbana: University of Illinois Press, 1997), 5.

102. R. Lanier Britsch, *Moramona: The Mormons in Hawai'i* (Lā'ie, Hawai'i: Institute for Polynesian Studies, 1989), 3.

103. "California Mission Journal History," Wednesday, September 25, 1850.

104. Britsch, *Moramona*, 4.

CHAPTER 2

1. "Hawaiian House of Nobles and Representatives," *Penal Code Session Laws* 1850, section 1, 154.
2. It should be noted here that even though emigration decreased as a result of legislative restrictions, the population of Hawaiians continued to decline throughout the nineteenth century due to continued epidemics, primarily smallpox.
3. Laurie F. Maffly-Kipp, "Looking West: Mormonism and the Pacific World," *Journal of Mormon History* 26, no. 1 (Spring 2000), 44–45.
4. Hōkūlani Kamakanikailialoha Aikau, "Polynesian Pioneers: Twentieth Century Religious Racial Formations and Migration in Hawai'i" (PhD diss., University of Minnesota, 2005).
5. Samuel Kamakau, *Ruling Chiefs of Hawai'i* (Honolulu: Bishop Museum Press, 1991); David Malo, *Hawaiian Antiquities (Mo'olelo Hawai'i)* (Honolulu: Bishop Museum Press, 1971); John Papa I'i, *Fragments of Hawaiian History* (Honolulu: Bishop Museum Press, 1963).
6. Lilikalā Kame'eleihiwa, *Native Lands and Foreign Desires: Pehea Lā E Pono Ai?* (Honolulu: Bishop Museum Press, 1992), 33–40, 70–79.
7. Ibid., 67.
8. Hiram Bingham, *A Residence of Twenty-one Years in the Sandwich Islands* (Hartford, CT: Huntington, 1849).
9. Kame'eleihiwa, *Native Lands and Foreign Desires*, 154.
10. Kauikeaouli represented a powerful faction of Hawaiian chiefs that actively opposed adopting Christianity and challenged Ka'ahumanu's power and authority as the favored wife of Kāmehameha.
11. Patrick V. Kirch and Marshall Sahlins, *Anahulu: The Anthropology of History in the Kingdom of Hawai'i* (Chicago: University of Chicago Press, 1992), 76.
12. Ibid.
13. Ibid., 47.
14. George Q. Cannon, address delivered at Hooperville, Utah, June 27, 1881, in *Journal of Discourses* (Liverpool, UK: F. D. and S. W. Richards, 1854), 22.
15. Lawrence W. Flake, *George Q. Cannon: His Missionary Years* (Salt Lake City: Bookcraft, 1998), 59–60. Protestant missionaries from New England arrived in Hawai'i in 1820 and developed strong relationships with high-ranking Hawaiian chiefs and government officials, and they exerted considerable influence over the social and political life of the islands in many regions. See Kame'eleihiwa, *Native Lands and Foreign Desires*; and Jonathan Kamakawiwo'ole Osorio, *Dismembering Lāhui: A History of the Hawaiian Nation to 1887* (Honolulu: University of Hawai'i Press, 2001).
16. Journal of Phillip B. Lewis, Tuesday, September 9, 1851, Archives, Joseph F. Smith Library, Brigham Young University Hawai'i.
17. R. Lanier Britsch, *Moramona: The Mormons in Hawai'i* (Lā'ie, Hawai'i: Institute for Polynesian Studies, 1989), 14–15.
18. Hōkūlani Kamakanikailialoha Aikau, "Polynesian Pioneers: Twentieth Century Religious Racial Formations and Migration in Hawai'i" (PhD diss., University of Minnesota, 2005), 99.
19. Ibid. 100.
20. Thomas Murphy, "From Racist Stereotype to Ethnic Identity: Instrumental Uses of the Mormon Racial Doctrine," *Ethnohistory* 46, no. 3 (Summer 1999), 451.

21. Much of the account of Christ's visit resembles the accounts in the Gospels of the New Testament, including the Sermon on the Mount, the Beatitudes, the calling of Apostles, etc.

22. *The Book of Mormon: Another Testament of Jesus Christ* (New York: Doubleday, 2004).

23. For a discussion of the origins of racial thinking in the early American republic with reference to Africans, see Winthrop Jordan, *The White Man's Burden: The Historical Origins of Racism in the United States* (New York: Oxford University Press, 1974). Robert F. Berkhofer Jr. discusses theories of Native American origins in terms of Christian cosmology in *The White Man's Indian* (New York: Vintage, 1979), 34–38.

24. *The Book of Mormon*, 2 Nephi 20–25.

25. Jordan, *White Man's Burden;* Berkhofer, *The White Man's Indian.*

26. David L. Bigler, *Forgotten Kingdom: The Mormon Theocracy in the American West* (Spokane: Arthur H. Clarke, 1998), 63–85.

27. Ethan Yorgasen, *Transformation of the Mormon Culture Region* (Urbana: University of Illinois Press, 2005).

28. Michael Hicks, "Noble Savages," in *Mormons and Mormonism: An Introduction to an American World Religion*, ed. Eric Eliason (Urbana: University of Illinois Press, 2001), 180–181.

29. Bigler, *Forgotten Kingdom*, 63–64.

30. Ibid., 65.

31. See Aikau, "Polynesian Pioneers," 98–111. The terms that have been used to classify Pacific Islanders since the early twentieth century—Polynesian, Micronesian, and Melanesian—have legitimately come under such scrutiny as to reveal them to be all but useless. More recent scholarship that stresses the connections rather than divisions among all the peoples of Oceania (a contested concept in and of itself) has all but ended these "cultural" categories. See Donald Denoon, ed., *The Cambridge History of the Pacific Islanders* (New York: Cambridge University Press, 1997), 8–9, 69–70. See also Russell T. Clement, "Polynesian Origins: More Word on the Mormon Perspective," *Dialogue* 13, no. 4 (Winter 1980), 88–98.

32. Quoted in Flake, *George Q. Cannon*, 63–64.

33. Aikau, "Polynesian Pioneers," 100.

34. Ibid., 44.

35. The most detailed treatment of the history of the Māhele from a Native Hawaiian perspective can be found in Lilikalā Kame'eleihiwa's *Native Land and Foreign Desires.*

36. Osorio, *Dismembering Lāhui*, 44–47.

37. Ibid., 49.

38. Quoted. in Ibid., 66.

39. Ibid., 44–60.

40. "Ka Mookuauhou o Panana Hiamololi," Hawai'i State Archives, Honolulu, HMS G64.

41. Journal of Ephraim Green, Tuesday, April 25, 1853, Archives, Joseph F. Smith Library, Brigham Young University Hawai'i.

42. For a discussion of Kaleohano and Napela and their activities with the early Mormon missionaries, see Joseph H. Spurrier, *Sandwich Islands Saints* (Hong Kong, 1998), 215–259. Edith Kawealoha McKinzie, in *Hawaiian Genealogies, Extracted from Hawaiian Language Newspapers, Volume 1* (Lā'ie, Hawai'i: Institute for Polynesian Studies, 1983), relates the genealogy of both men. For a discussion

of Hawaiian cultural patterns of marriage and kinship as they relate to social power, see Kame'eleihiwa, *Native Lands and Foreign Desires*.

43. Fred E. Woods, "An Islander's View of a Desert Kingdom: Jonathan Napela Recounts His 1869 Visit to Salt Lake City," *BYU Studies* 45, no. 1 (2006), 25–26.
44. Mormons were frequently barred from public meeting houses and forbidden to preach in some districts although technically free to do so under Hawai'i's Constitution. Both Ephraim Green and Philip B. Lewis record many incidents in their diaries. Green in particular notes the arrest of a Hawaiian convert, Uaua, for "baptising on Sunday."
45. Journal of Ephraim Green, Thursday, April 7, 1853.
46. Fred Woods, "The Palawai Pioneers on the Island of Lanai, Hawai'i," *Mormon Historical Studies* 5, no. 2 (Fall 2004), 8–11.
47. It is interesting to note that monies from Brigham Young's Perpetual Emigration Fund, which were being used to fund the emigration west of thousands of converts from England, were never considered for relocating Hawaiian converts or those from other mission areas in the Pacific, despite a more pressing need on the part of the Pacific Islander converts for assistance.
48. Fred Woods, "The Palawai Pioneers on the Islands of Lanai, Hawai'i," 5.
49. Ibid., 26.
50. Cynthia D. Woolley Compton, "The Making of the Ahupuaa of Laie into a Gathering Place and Plantation: The Creation of an Alternative Space to Capitalism" (PhD diss., Brigham Young University, 2005).
51. Woods, "The Palawai Pioneers on the Island of Lāna'I,"9–10.
52. Brigham Young to Parley P. Pratt, August 19, 1854, Church Historical Department, Salt Lake City, Utah, 1–2.
53. Arrington, *Great Basin Kingdom*, 50–51.
54. Quoted. in Woods, "The Palawai Pioneers on the Island of Lāna'I,"9.
55. Quoted in Woods, "The Palawai Pioneers on the Island of Lāna'I,"11.
56. Edward Leo Lyman, *San Bernardino: The Rise and Fall of a California Community* (Salt Lake City: Signature, 1996), 296–300.
57. Aikau, "Polynesian Pioneers," 137.
58. Jonathan Napela to Kamehameha III, Hawai'i State Archives, Honolulu.
59. Quoted in Woods, "The Palawai Pioneers on the Island of Lāna'I,"13.
60. Woods, "The Palawai Pioneers on the Island of Lāna'i," 14–17; Raymond Clyde Beck, "Iosepa, Hawai'i's Zion," Archives, Joseph F. Smith Library, Brigham Young University Hawai'i, 40–42.
61. Beck, "Iosepa, Hawai'i's Zion," 44–45.
62. Beck, "Iosepa, Hawai'i's Zion," 46–48.
63. Journal of Ephraim Green
64. Woods, "The Palawai Pioneers on the Island of Lāna'i," 17–18.
65. See Compton, "The Making of the Ahupua'a of Lā'ie," 23–81.
66. Aikau, "Polynesian Pioneers," 138.
67. Britsch, *Moramona*, 63–74.
68. Lance Chase, "Life in Early Lā'ie, 1850–1880" (paper presented at the annual meeting of the Mormon Pacific Historical Society, May 8–9, 1981, Lā'ie, Hawai'i). Transcript of address in the records of the Mormon Pacific Historical Society, Archives, Joseph F. Smith Library, Brigham Young University Hawai'i.
69. For a specific treatment of land tenure in Lā'ie after the Māhele and throughout the plantation era, see Jeffrey S. Stover, "The Legacy of the 1848 Māhele and

Kuleana Act of 1850: A Case Study of Lā'ie wai and Lā'ie molo'o Ahupua'a, 1846–1930" (master's thesis, University of Hawai'i, August 1997).

70. E. S. Craighill Handy, Elizabeth Handy, and Mary Kawena Pukui, *Native Planters in Old Hawai'i: Their Life, Lore, and Environment* (Honolulu: Bishop Museum Press, 1972).

71. Compton, "The Making of the Ahupua'a of Lā'ie," 23.

72. Ibid., 11–22.

73. Carol A. McClennan, "Foundations of Sugar's Power: Early Maui Plantations, 1840–1860," *Hawaiian Journal of History* 29 (1995), 34.

74. Kirch and Sahlins, *Anahulu*, 101–107.

75. McClennan, "Foundations of Sugar's Power," 44–45.

76. Membership records indicate that many Native Hawaiian converts chose not to gather in Lā'ie between 1865 and 1880. *Records of the Hawaiian Mission, All Islands*, Archives, Joseph F. Smith Library, Brigham Young University Hawai'i.

77. Transcript of letter from George Nebeker, Wednesday, October 14, 1867, reprinted in Andrew Jenson, *History of the Hawaiian Mission of the Church of Jesus Christ of Latter-day Saints, Volume 4, 1861–1885*, Pacific Islands Room, Joseph F. Smith Library, Brigham Young University Hawai'i.

78. Jenson, *History of the Hawaiian Mission*, Friday, April 6, 1866.

79. Compton, "The Making of the Ahupua'a of Lā'ie," 23–37.

80. Lance D. Chase, "The Hawaiian Mission Crisis of 1874: Character as Destiny," in *Temple, Town, and Tradition: The Collected Historical Essays of Lance D. Chase* (Lā'ie: Institute for Polynesian Studies, 2000), 16.

81. Ibid., 20.

82. Robert Stauffer, *Kahana: How the Land Was Lost* (Honolulu: University of Hawai'i Press, 2004), 90.

83. Chase, "The Hawaiian Mission Crisis of 1874," 19–21.

84. Stauffer, *Kahana*.

85. Ibid., 124–125.

86. Ibid., 125–129.

87. Ibid.

88. Ibid., 87–89.

89. The "rebels" who went to Kahana from Lā'ie petitioned Brigham Young regarding their situation, which resulted in Mitchell's release from his calling as mission president as well as their welcome back into the church as full members.

90. Jenson, *History of the Hawaiian Mission*, Sunday, October 14, 1866.

91. Richard D. Poll, "Utah and Mormons: A Symbiotic Relationship," in *Mormons and Mormonism: An Introduction to an American World Religion*, ed. Eric A. Eliason (Urbana: University of Illinois Press, 2001), 164–179.

92. Compton, "The Making of the Ahupua'a of Lā'ie," xxi.

93. Stauffer, *Kahana*, 92–143.

CHAPTER 3

1. Richard White, *"It's Your Misfortune and None of My Own": A New History of the American West* (Norman: University of Oklahoma Press, 1991), 183.

2. For a discussion on the centrality of wage labor in the American West, see Patricia Nelson Limerick, *The Legacy of Conquest: The Unbroken Past of the American West* (New York: Norton, 1987), 97–101. Also see Melvyn Dubofksy, "The Origins of Western Working Class Radicalism, 1890–1905," 131–154. For a discussion of the West's connection to global commodities markets, especially in relation

to agricultural production and the preponderance of wage labor, see Harriet Friedman, "World, Market, State, and Family Farm: Social Bases of Household Production in the Era of Wage Labor," *Comparative Studies in Society and History* 20, no. 4 (October 1978), 545–586.

3. Ethan Yorgason, *Transformation of the Mormon Culture Region* (Urbana: University of Illinois Press, 2005).

4. White, *"It's Your Misfortune and None of My Own"*, 181.

5. Early Native Hawaiian settlers in the Pacific Northwest experienced a gradual erosion of their economic, political, and social status as larger numbers of Americans settled the region. As a consequence, many chose to settle north of the 49th parallel in British Columbia to avoid the increasingly exclusionary racial policies of the US government after 1846. See Jean Barman and Bruce MacIntyre Wilson, *Leaving Paradise: Indigenous Hawaiians in the Pacific Northwest, 1787–1896* (Honolulu: University of Hawai'i Press, 2006), 162–190.

6. Napela's letter to Young is reprinted in its entirety in Fred Woods, "An Islander's View of a Desert Kingdom: Jonathan Napela Recounts His 1869 Visit to Salt Lake City," *BYU Studies* 45, no. 1 (2006), 22–34. The article also includes a brief biography of Napela. For references to Napela's agricultural operations on Maui and his interactions with early Mormon missionaries, see George Q. Cannon, *My First Mission* (Salt Lake City: Juvenile Instructor Office, 1879); journal of Ephraim Green, Archives, Joseph F. Smith Library, Brigham Young University Hawai'i.

7. Andrew Jenson, *History of the Hawaiian Mission of the Church of Jesus Christ of Latter-day Saints, 1861–1885*. Pacific Islands Collection, Joseph F. Smith Library, Brigham Young University Hawai'i; journal of Harvey H. Cluff, microfilm copy, Joseph F. Smith Library, Brigham Young University Hawai'i.

8. Leonard Arrington, "On Writing Latter-day Saint History," in *Voyages of Faith: Explorations in Mormon Pacific History*, ed. Grant Underwood (Provo, UT: Brigham Young University, 2000), 7.

9. For a detailed treatment of the vision of Mormonism's leaders for a theocratic empire in the West, see especially Klaus J. Hansen, *Quest for Empire: The Political Kingdom of God and the Council of Fifty in Mormon History* (East Lansing: Michigan State University Press, 1967), and David L. Bigler, *Forgotten Kingdom: The Mormon Theocracy in the American West, 1847–1896* (Logan: Utah State University Press, 1998).

10. Jenson, *History of the Hawaiian Mission, 1861–1885*, Monday, October 3, 1864.

11. Ibid., Tuesday, April 8, 1889.

12. Ibid., Wednesday, April 9, 1872.

13. Ibid., 224.

14. Jon Kamakawiwo'ole Osorio, *Dismembering Lāhui: A History of the Hawaiian Nation to 1887* (Honolulu: University of Hawaii Press, 2002), 193.

15. Journal of Harvey H. Cluff, microfilm copy, Archives, Joseph F. Smith Library Brigham Young University Hawai'i.

16. *Deseret News*, July 26, 1873.

17. *Deseret News*, June 2, 1876. The *Deseret News* often published news delivered by mail from many of its missions and remote settlements, alerting Salt Lake Valley residents to upcoming events associated with the work of the Church abroad. Hence the news of the impending arrival of Hawaiian Saints emigrating to Utah with William King.

18. *Deseret Evening News*, December 7, 1879.

19. *Deseret Evening News*, May 13, 1879; July 31, 1882.

20. *Deseret Evening News*, November 22, 1884.

21. *Deseret Evening News*, April 23, 1888.

22. *Deseret Evening News*, April 8, 1889.

23. *Deseret Evening News*, April 12, 1889.

24. Limerick, *Legacy of Conquest*, 260.

25. "Local Items," *Utah Reporter*, April 26, 1870, 4.

26. "White or Chinese: Saltair Wants to Know Which It Is to Be in Park City," *Park City Mining Record*, January 24, 1903.

27. Don C. Conley, "The Pioneer Chinese in Utah," in *The Peoples of Utah*, ed. Helen Papanikoulas (Salt Lake City: Utah State Historical Society, 1976), 254–271.

28. Gunther Peck, *Reinventing Free Labor: Padrones and Immigrant Workers in the North American West, 1880–1930* (New York: Cambridge University Press, 2000).

29. Limerick, *Legacy of Conquest*, 260.

30. Matthew Frye Jacobson, *Barbarian Virtues: The United States Encounters Foreign Peoples at Home and Abroad, 1876–1917* (New York: Hill and Wang, 2000), 141–142.

31. The schooner *Fairy Queen*, for instance, was in 1873 under the command of a master named Raaiana, and its crew consisted of seven Hawaiian seamen: Kaniela Rupanihi, John Kahula, Kekahu, Hopenopeno, Peni, Keaho, and Keikaikai. The following year the same schooner's crew consisted of eighteen Hawaiians, and in 1875, eleven Hawaiians, all different than the first group. The schooners *Leahe* and *Haleakala* out of Honolulu also consisted of mostly Hawaiian crew members. VFM 532, Manuscripts Collection, G. W. Blunt White Library, Mystic Seaport Museum, Inc.

32. "Kanaka Party," *Deseret Evening News*, April 11, 1860.

33. Kerri Inglis, "A Land Set Apart: Disease, Displacement & Death at Makanalua, Molokai" (PhD diss., University of Hawai'i, 2004), 75.

34. Inglis, 73–81.

35. *Book of Mormon*, 1 Nephi: 13–14.

36. "General," *Deseret Evening News*, October 21, 1868.

37. Inglis, "A Land Set Apart," 85–86.

38. Ibid. 87–91.

39. "Narrow and Illiberal Policy," *Deseret Evening News*, February 17, 1869.

40. *Daily Corinne Reporter*, April 12, 1873.

41. "Local and Other Matters," *Deseret Evening News*, February 23, 1870.

42. "The Sandwich Islands Social Situation," *Deseret Evening News*, April 4, 1873.

43. "Hawaiian Lepers," *Deseret Evening News*, April 25, 1873.

44. "The Leprosy," *Deseret Evening News*, April 6, 1888.

45. "Hawaiian Lepers," *Deseret Evening News*, April 25, 1873.

46. "Infanticide in the Hawaiian Islands," *Valley Tan*, January 25, 1860, 3.

47. *Deseret Evening News*, December 8, 1869.

48. "By Telegraph," *Deseret Evening News*, July 20, 1881.

49. "Missionary Messages," *Ogden Standard Examiner*, January 9, 1885, 1.

50. "Sandwich Islands Mission," *Ogden Standard Examiner*, September 16, 1881, 2.

51. "The Spotted Boy-Kanaka Immigration," *Salt Lake Tribune*, April 24, 1883, 2.

52. D. W. Meinig, "The Mormon Culture Region: Strategies and Patterns in the Geography of the American West," *Annals of the Association of American Geographers* 55, no. 2 (June 1965), 191–220.

53. Leonard J. Arrington, *Great Basin Kingdom: An Economic History of the Latter-Day Saints, 1830–1900* (Cambridge, MA: Harvard University Press, 1958), 352.

54. Ibid., 352. See also Thomas Alexander, *Mormonism in Transition: A History of the Latter-day Saints, 1890–1930* (Urbana: University of Illinois Press, 1996).

55. Ian Haney-Lopez, *White by Law: The Legal Construction of Race* (New York: New York University Press, 1996), 37. Evelyn Nakano-Glenn argues that racism is an ideology that underlies foundational ideas of American citizenship and that the idea of "fitness" for citizenship was intimately tied up with the categories that defined whiteness across the United States. *Unequal Freedom: How Race and Gender Shaped American Citizenship and Labor* (Cambridge, MA: Harvard University Press, 2002).

56. "Kanakas as Citizens," *Deseret Evening News*, June 8, 1889.

57. Haney-Lopez, *White by Law*, 49–77.

58. *In re* Kanaka Nian, Supreme Court of Utah, 6 Utah 259, 21 P. 993 (1889).

59. Ibid.

60. A blurb in the *Salt Lake Tribune* on 6 June 1889 revealed that in fact judges Zane and Huntr had admitted Native Hawaiians as citizens in October of 1884, prior to the 1887 Chinese Exclusion Act.

61. "Kanakas as Citizens."

62. "The Kanaka Applicants," *Salt Lake Tribune*, June 2, 1889.

CHAPTER 4

1. Donald Meinig, "The Mormon Culture Region: Strategies and Patterns in the Geography of the American West, 1847–1964," *Annals of the Association of American Geographers* 55, no. 2 (June 1965), 191–220.

2. Leonard J. Arrington, *Great Basin Kingdom: An Economic History of the Latter-Day Saints, 1830–1900* (Cambridge, MA: Harvard University Press, 1958), 210–211.

3. Thomas Alexander, *Mormonism in Transition: A History of the Latter-day Saints, 1890–1930* (Urbana: University of Illinois Press, 1996), 15.

4. Ibid.

5. Alexander, *Mormonism in Transition*.

6. Andrew A. Jenson, "Iosepa Colony: Tooele County, Utah," Church Historical Department, Salt Lake City, Utah.

7. Alexander, *Mormonism in Transition*, 201.

8. Typical Mormon "villages" followed a distinctive pattern of spatial and social organization long recognized by social scientists and cultural geographers interested in communities throughout the American West. Lowry Nelson, *The Mormon Village: A Pattern and Technique of Land Settlement* (Salt Lake City: University of Utah Press, 1952); Richard V. Francaviglia, *The Mormon Landscape: Existence, Creation, and Perception of a Unique Image in the American West* (New York: AMS Press, 1978); Richard H. Jackson, *Cultural Geography: People, Places, and Environment* (St. Paul, MN: West Publishing, 1990).

9. Cynthia Woolley Compton, "The Making of the Ahupua'a of Lā'ie into a Gathering Place and an Alternative Space to Capitalism" (PhD diss., Brigham Young University, 2005).

10. For an excellent description of the social life of multiethnic communities on Hawaiian sugar plantations, see Ronald Takaki, *Pau Hana: Plantation Life and Labor in Hawai'i, 1835–1920* (Honolulu: University of Hawai'i Press, 1983). For the role of the Hawaiian legal system in enforcing labor contracts in Hawai'i, see

Sally Engle Merry, *Colonizing Hawai'i: The Cultural Power of Law* (Princeton, NJ: Princeton University Press, 2000).

11. Nelson, *The Mormon Village*.

12. Thomas A. Waddoups, "The Iosepa Agricultural and Stock Company," December, 1956, 1, Archives, Joseph F. Smith Library. Brigham Young University Hawai'i, Lā'ie.

13. Journal of Harvey H. Cluff, 1889–1896, microfilm copy, Pacific Islands Room, Joseph F. Smith Library, Brigham Young University Hawai'i, 1.

14. Ibid., 1.

15. Ibid., 2–4.

16. Ibid., 7.

17. Journal of Harvey H. Cluff, 23.

18. Arrington, *Great Basin Kingdom*, 383–384.

19. Ibid. Most of the other joint stock companies were associated with colonizing ventures outside the Wasatch Front. One went to Canada, another to Mexico, and another to western Wyoming. Only one other joint stock venture was established near Salt Lake City.

20. Nelson Knight, "This Old House: The John Henry and Marie Kaoo Makaula House," *The Capitol Hill Neighborhood Council Bulletin* 47 (March 2005), 1–2.

21. "Articles of Incorporation," Iosepa Agricultural and Stock Company, Tooele County Courthouse, Tooele, Utah, 12.

22. Dennis Atkins, "A History of Iosepa: The Utah Polynesian Colony" (master's thesis, Brigham Young University, 1958), 10–11.

23. Ibid., 24–26.

24. Ibid., 26–27.

25. Ibid., 33–37.

26. Nelson, *The Mormon Village*; Arrington, *Great Basin Kingdom*.

27. Armand Mauss, *All Abraham's Children: Changing Mormon Conceptions of Race and Lineage* (Urbana: University of Illinois Press, 2003).

28. Compton, "The Making of the Ahupua'a of Lā'ie."

29. Journal of Harvey H. Cluff.

30. "The Iosepa Colony," *Deseret News*, December 29, 1894, 26.

31. Atkins, "A History of Iosepa," 27.

32. Journal of Harvey H. Cluff.

33. Joseph F. Smith to Kalawainui Kealohapauole, July 16, 1890, in Richard E. Turley Jr., ed., "Joseph F. Smith Incoming Correspondence, 1855–1918," in *Selected Collections from the Archives of the Church of Jesus Christ of Latter-day Saints*, Brigham Young University Hawai'i Archives and Special Collections.

34. The Hawaiian government's focus on distressed sailors for repatriation aid reflected the high percentage of Native Hawaiians working in American maritime industries. However, funding for Native Hawaiians stranded or otherwise "indigent," whether in western North America or in the Pacific Islands, was available only selectively. Cited in "Appendix A: Indigent Hawaiians in Utah and Samoa," in *Report of the Minister of Foreign Affairs to the Hawai'i Legislature, Session of 1892* (Honolulu: Leiali'i Publishing, 1892).

35. William Kinney to D. A. McKinley, June 22, 1889, in *Records of the Foreign Office and Executive*, Series 404, "Hawaiian Officials Abroad," Hawai'i State Archives.

36. Ibid., June 26, 1889.

37. Ibid., June 29, 1889.

38. William Wallace Cluff, *The Cluff Family Journal*, microfilm copy, Joseph F. Smith Library, Brigham Young University Hawai'i, 344.

39. Journal of Harvey H. Cluff.

40. W. W. Cluff, *The Cluff Family Journal*, 344.

41. Hosea N. Kekauoha to Joseph F. Smith, October 12, 1890, in Turley, "Joseph F. Smith Incoming Correspondence."

42. Mary Kawena Pukui, *Nana i ke kumu* (Honolulu: Hui Hānai, 1972).

43. The report described Naau as an "intelligent man" who had "seen much of the world, [having] been several years in the Arctic regions on a whaling vessel."

44. Cited in "Appendix A," in *Report of the Minister of Foreign Affairs to the Hawaii Legislature*, 61–62.

45. Ibid., 65.

46. Atkins, "A History of Iosepa," 47.

47. Journal of Harvey H. Cluff.

48. Ibid.

49. Lua and his family, in addition to two other families, arrived at the consul general's office almost exactly one month later and were given passage back to Honolulu. Charles T. Wilder to Francis Hatch, April 13, 1894, *Records of Hawaiian Officials Abroad*, Series 404, Hawai'i State Archives.

50. Journal of Harvey H. Cluff.

51. Ibid.

52. Atkins, "A History of Iosepa," 50.

53. Thomas Anson Waddoups, "Biography of Thomas Anson Waddoups," Archives, Joseph F. Smith Library, Brigham Young University Hawai'i, 11.

54. William Kinney to D. A. McKinley, January 2, 1891, in *Records of the Foreign Office and Executive*.

55. "Our Hawaiian Colony," *Deseret Evening News*, November 20, 1890.

56. *Report of the Minister of Foreign Affairs to the Hawaii Legislature*, 73.

57. Ibid., 74.

58. Ibid.

59. Wilford Woodruff to William Kinney, April 10, 1891, in *Records of the Foreign Office and Executive*, Series 404, "Hawaiian Officials Abroad," Hawai'i State Archives.

60. *Report of the Minister of Foreign Affairs to the Hawaii Legislature*, 78.

61. Joseph F. Smith to Kealohapauole Kaholoakeahole, May 22, 1890, in Turley, *Selected Collections*.

62. Joseph F. Smith to Moses Nakuaau, October 8, 1890, in Turley, *Selected Collections*.

63. Joseph F. Smith to H. N. Kekauoha, October 21, 1890, in Turley, *Selected Collections*.

64. Joseph F. Smith to Sam. M. Kinimakalehua, December 8, 1890, in Turley, *Selected Collections*.

65. Ibid.

66. Journal of Harvey H. Cluff.

67. Ibid., August 5, 1894.

68. Ibid., August 12, 1894.

69. Ibid.

70. Atkins, "A History of Iosepa," 27.

71. Ibid.

72. Vestil J. Harrison, "Life Sketch of Thomas Anson Waddoups," Archives, Joseph F. Smith Library, Brigham Young University Hawai'i.

73. Ibid.

74. "Leprosy in Tooele County," *The Salt Lake Daily Tribune*, June 4, 1896, 7.
75. "Leprosy in the Kanaka Settlement," *The Salt Lake Herald*, June 20, 1896, 1.
76. Ibid., 6.
77. W. W. Cluff, *The Cluff Family Journal*, 369.
78. Journal of Harvey H. Cluff.
79. Waddoups, "Biography of Thomas Anson Waddoups," 13–15.
80. William Wallace III, interview by John Broad, Kenneth Baldridge Oral History Collection, Archives, Joseph F. Smith Library, Brigham Young University Hawai'i.
81. Richard White, *"It's Your Misfortune and None of My Own": A New History of the American West* (Norman: University of Oklahoma Press, 1991), 241–258; Elroy Nelson, "The Mineral Industry: A Foundation of Utah's Economy," *Utah Historical Quarterly* 31, no. 3 (Summer 1963), 178–196.
82. Atkins, "A History of Iosepa," 37–40.
83. Ibid., 52.
84. Ibid.
85. Waddoups, "Biography of Thomas Anson Waddoups," 11.
86. Ibid.
87. Ibid., 14.
88. William Barrell to Joseph F. Smith, October 9, 1913. Scott G. Kenney Collection, L. Tom Perry Special Collections, Brigham Young University.
89. Waddoups, "Biography of Thomas Anson Waddoups," 14.
90. "Latter Day Colonization by Latter-day Saints," *Deseret Evening News*, December 16, 1911.
91. Barrell to Smith.
92. Atkins, "A History of Iosepa," 77.
93. Nelson, *The Mormon Village*.
94. Journal of Harvey H. Cluff; see also Edna Hope Gregory, "Iosepa: Kanaka Ranch," *Utah Humanities Review* 2, no. 1 (1948), 3–9. Benjamin Cluff, president of Brigham Young Academy, former missionary to Hawai'i, and brother to Harvey Cluff, often wrote his brother to request "permission" for some of the laborers at Iosepa to leave the ranch to give musical performances at church activities in Provo and other areas of Utah Valley. Benjamin Cluff Papers, L. Tom Perry Special Collections, Brigham Young University.
95. Nelson, *The Mormon Village*, 34.
96. Waddoups, "Biography of Thomas Anson Waddoups," 16.
97. Clinton Kanahele, interview by John Broad, June 13, 1970. Manuscripts Collection, Brigham Young University Hawai'i Archives.
98. Ibid.
99. Waddoups, "Biography of Thomas Anson Waddoups," 14.
100. Ibid., 13.
101. Ibid., 17.
102. Cluff, *Cluff Family History*, 84–85; Atkins, "A History of Iosepa," 58–60.
103. Dawn Wasson, interview with author, March 3, 2007.
104. Wallace interview by Broad.
105. Ella Brunt Kamauoha interview with Edwin Kamauoha, Hawai'i, March 1958, quoted in Atkins, "A History of Iosepa," 80.
106. Waddoups, "Biography of Thomas Anson Waddoups," 17.
107. Wallace interview with Broad.
108. Cuma Sorensen Ho'opi'iaina, "Ho'opi'iaina Family History," in *Iosepa*, Archives, Joseph F. Smith Library, Brigham Young University Hawai'i.

109. Ibid.
110. Journal of William Waddoups, Archives, Joseph F. Smith Library, Brigham Young University Hawai'i.
111. Bessie King to unknown, January 26, 1917, Lā'ie, Hawai'i, typescript copy, Archives, Joseph F. Smith Library, Brigham Young University Hawai'i.
112. Alexander, *Mormonism in Transition*.
113. Stephen Cornell, "That's the Story of Our Life," in *We Are a People: Narrative and Ethnicity in Constructing Ethnic Identity*, ed. Paul Spickard and Jeff Burroughs (Philadelphia: Temple University Press, 2000), 41–55.
114. Joseph F. Smith to K. Kealohapauole May 26, 1890, in Turley, *Selected Collections*.
115. Samuel E Woolley, regular annual, April 8, 1916, 81. Quoted in Compton.
116. Cuma Sorensen Ho'opi'iaina, "Ho'opi'iaina Family History."

CHAPTER 5

1. Cuma Sorensen Ho'opi'iaina "Ho'opi'iaina Family History," in *Iosepa*, Archives, Joseph F. Smith Library, Brigham Young University Hawai'i.
2. "Personalities," *Intermountain Industry Magazine*, November 1951, 27–30.
3. Bob Krauss, "Lā'ie Launches Icon of Community Pride," *Honolulu Advertiser*, November 4, 2001, A6.
4. Ibid., A22.
5. Teena Shapiro, "BYU-Hawaii Sets Sail in Classroom on Canoe," *Honolulu Star-Bulletin*, November 1, 2001.
6. See David Glassberg, *Sense of History: The Place of the Past in American Life* (Amherst: University Press of Massachusetts, 2001); Roy Rosenzweig and David Thelen, *Presence of the Past: Popular Uses of History in American Life* (New York: Columbia University Press, 1998).
7. Glassberg, *Sense of History*, 6–7.
8. Ibid.
9. Glassberg, *Sense of History* offers a collection of essays that link a sense of history to a sense of place as he investigates the ways that various communities and organizations create history. In "Memory and American History," *Journal of American History* 75 (March 1989), 1117–1129, David Thelen focuses on similar projects for creating collective memory around historical events.
10. Stephen Cornell, "That's the Story of Our Life," in *We Are a People: Narrative and Multiplicity in Constructing Ethnic Identity*, ed. Paul Spickard and Jeff Burroughs (Philadelphia: Temple University Press, 2001), 41–55.
11. Jean Barman and Bruce McIntyre Watson, *Leaving Paradise: Indigenous Hawaiians in the Pacific Northwest, 1878–1898* (Honolulu: University of Hawai'i Press 2006), 217–218.
12. Cluny MacPherson, Paul Spoonley, and Melanie Anae, *Tangata O Te Moana Nui: The Evolving Identities of Pacific Peoples in Aotearoa/New Zealand* (New Zealand: Dunmore Press, 2001), 13–14.
13. Ibid. For more on the boundaries and history of the Mormon culture region, see Donald Meinig, "The Mormon Culture Region: Strategies and Patterns in the Geography of the American West, 1847–1964," and Ethan Yorgasen, *Transformation of the Mormon Culture Region* (Urbana, University of Illinois Press, 2004), 1.
14. Michael Frisch, *A Shared Authority: Essays on the Craft and Meaning of Oral and Public History* (Albany: State University of New York Press, 1990), 179–238.

15. Elizabeth M. Grieco, *The Native Hawaiian and Other Pacific Islander Population: 2000* (Washington, DC: US Department of Commerce, Economics and Statistics Administration, US Census Bureau, December 2001).

16. Max Edward Stanton, "Samoan Saints: Samoans in the Mormon Village of Laie, Hawaii" (PhD diss., Department of Anthropology, University of Oregon, 1973).

17. John Connell, *Migration, Employment, and Development in the South Pacific*, Country Report No. 4 (Noumea: South Pacific Commission, 1984). See also K. Sudo, "Expanding International Migration by Tongan People: Strategies and Sociocultural Effects on the Homeland," in *Contemporary Migration in Oceania: Diaspora and Network*, ed. K. Sudo and S. Yoshida, JCAS Symposium Series No. 3 (Osaka: The Japan Center for Area Studies, National Museum of Ethnology 1997), 101–112; Tamar G. Gordon, "Inventing Mormon Identity in Tonga" (PhD diss., University of California Berkeley, 1988).

18. "Dedication of the Laie, Hawai'i, Temple," typescript copy, Manuscripts Collection, University Archives, Brigham Young University Hawai'i.

19. For a concise summary of the most recent scholarship on the subject, see especially Patrick V. Kirch, *On the Road of the Winds: An Archaeological History of the Pacific Islands Before European Contact* (Berkeley: University of California Press, 2000).

20. Quoted in Russell T. Clement, "Polynesian Origins: More Word on the Mormon Perspective," *Dialogue* 13, no. 4 (Winter 1980), 88–98.

21. Copy of address found in Edwin Kamauoha Collection, Archives, Joseph F. Smith Library, Brigham Young University Hawai'i.

22. For a recent analysis of re-creating nineteenth-century pioneer history through historical reenactment in Mormon communities, see Megan Sanborn Jones, "(Re)living the Pioneer Past: Mormon Youth Handcart Trek Reenactments," *Theatre Topics* 16, no. 2 (2006), 113–130.

23. "Newsroom," www.lds.org, accessed May 30, 2007, http://lds.org/ldsnewsroom/v/index.jsp?vgnextoid=62b0801111f5f010VgnVCM1000004e94610aRCRD&query=pioneer&bucket=AllNewsroomContent&maxResults=10.

24. "Church Members Remember the Sacrifice of Pioneers," Church of Jesus Christ of Latter-day Saints press release, July 21, 2007, http://lds.org/ldsnewsroom/v/index.jsp?vgnextoid=e54d22526078f010VgnVCM100000176f620aRCRD&vgnextchannel=9ae411154963d010VgnVCM1000004e94610aRCRD, May 30, 2007.

25. Jones, "(Re)living the Pioneer Past."

26. "Church Leader Gives Congressional Testimony on Martin's Cove," Church of Jesus Christ of Latter-day Saints Newsroom, May 30, 2002, accessed July 11, 2007, http://www.lds.org/ldsnewsroom/v/index.jsp?vgnextoid=b9042e636369f010VgnVCM100000176f620aRCRD&vgnextchannel=9ae411154963d010VgnVCM1000004e94610aRCRD.

27. See Glassberg, *Sense of History*, especially chapter 7, "Making Places in California" (165–202) on the formation of the Sons and Daughters of the Golden West in late nineteenth-century California. Glassberg looks at the work of historical associations made up of descendants of early California settlers and their efforts to identify their ancestors as gold rush pioneers in "early" California.

28. Jan Shipps, *Mormonism: The Story of a New Religious Tradition* (Urbana: University of Illinois Press, 1985), 122.

29. Richard D. Poll, "Utah and Mormons: A Symbiotic Relationship," in *Mormons and Mormonism*, ed. Eric Eliason (Urbana: University of Illinois Press, 2001), 164–179.

30. Edwin Kamauoha Collection, "Correspondence, 1983–1989," University Archives, Brigham Young University Hawai'i. The logo for the historical association, printed on T-shirts and ephemera, reads "Iosepa Polynesian Pioneers."

31. "Iosepa Expresses Faith of Polynesian Pioneers," *Church News*, May 30, 1987.

32. Ibid.

33. "Polynesians Honor *Their* Pioneers: Islanders Made a Colony in Utah," *Salt Lake Tribune*, May 26, 1997.

34. *Firesides* is a common colloquial term used in the Mormon Church to describe a religious address given outside the normal Sunday meetings. They often take place on Sunday evenings or during the week, can range in subject from personal histories and church history to scriptural topics, and are intended to provide an inspirational religious message.

35. "Talk Given by Donald J. Rosenberg on Iosepa, Centennial Fireside at Temple Square Assembly Hall, 7:00 pm, August 27, 1989," in Edwin Kamau'oha Collection, Manuscripts Collection, University Archives, Brigham Young University Hawai'i.

36. Charles Andrus conversation with author, 17 May 17, 2006; Dawn K. Wasson conversation with author, November 11, 2006.

37. Grieco, *Native Hawaiian and Other Pacific Islander Population*.

38. Tim Sullivan, "Gangs of Zion," *High Country News*, August 8, 2005.

39. Tim Sullivan, "Gangs of Zion," *High Country News*, August 5, 2005, 5.

40. Shipps, *Mormonism*, 109–129.

41. Gayle M. Clegg, "The Finished Story," General Conference of the Church of Jesus Christ of Latter-day Saints, April 2004, accessed August 21, 2010, http://lds.org/general-conference/2004/04/the-finished-story?lang=eng.

42. *The Polynesian Gift to Utah* (Kathleen Weiler, 2004). Transcript of documentary accessed July 1, 2007, http://www.kued.org/productions/polynesian/script/index.html.

43. Anonymous interviewee interview with author, May 21, 2006..

44. Lionel Broad interview, "Polynesian Settlement in Utah," Prime Time Access Television, Archives, Joseph F. Smith Library, Brigham Young University Hawai'i.

45. Edward Halealoha Ayau, "Native Hawaiian Burial Rights," in *Native Hawaiian Rights Handbook*, ed. Melody Kapilialoha MacKenzie (Honolulu: University of Hawai'i Press, 1991), 247.

46. Mary Kawena Pukui, *Olelo Noe'au: Hawaiian Proverbs and Poetical Sayings* (Honolulu: Bishop Museum Press, 1983).

47. Broad interview.

48. Thelen, "Memory and American History," ix.

49. Thomas Murphy, "From Racist Stereotype to Ethnic Identity: Instrumental Uses of the Mormon Racial Doctrine," *Ethnohistory* 46, no. 3 (Summer 1999), 453.

50. Ibid., "From Racist Stereotype to Ethnic Identity," 451–480; Paul Spickard, "Race, Religion, and Colonialism in the Mormon Pacific," in *Revealing the Sacred in Asian and Pacific America*, Jane Iwamura and Paul Spickard (New York: Routledge, 2002), 107–123.

51. See Michael Hicks, "Noble Savages," in *Mormons and Mormonism: An Introduction to an American World Religion*, ed. Eric Eliason (Urbana: University of Illinois Press, 2001), 180–199.

52. Leonard J. Arrington and Davis Bitton, *The Mormon Experience* (New York: A.A. Knopf, 1983), 145–160; Russell T. Clement, "Polynesian Origins: More Word on the Mormon Perspective," *Dialogue* 13 (Winter 1980), 88–98.

53. Spickard, Paul R., Joanne L. Rondilla, and Debbie Hippolite Wright. *Pacific Diaspora: Island Peoples in the United States and Across the Pacific* (Honolulu: University of Hawai'i Press, 2002), 14–15.

54. Paul Spickard and Jeff Burroughs, eds., *We Are a People: Narrative and Ethnicity in Constructing Ethnic Identity* (Philadelphia: Temple University Press, 2000), 7–11.

55. *A Polynesian Gift to Utah* (Kathleen Weiler, interview transcripts), accessed July 10, 2007, http://www.kued.org/productions/polynesian/interviews/index.html.

56. Memorial Day program, "Iosepa Festival, E wai wai ana kupuna o Iosepa, to Value the Elders of Iosepa ... May 25, 26, 27, 2007 at Iosepa." Copy in author's possession.

57. Glassberg, *Sense of History*, 19.

EPILOGUE

1. Christopher B.Balme,, "Staging the Pacific: Framing Authenticity in Performances for Tourists at the Polynesian Cultural Center," *Theatre Journal* 50 (1998), 53–70.

2. Paul Spickard, "Race, Religion, and Colonialism in the Mormon Pacific," in *Revealing the Sacred in Asian and Pacific America*, ed. Jane Iwamura and Paul Spickard (New York: Routledge, 2003), 116.

3. "Expeditionary Learning: Our Approach," accessed September 9, 2011, http://elschools.org/our-approach/what-we-do.

4. Ofa Moea'i, personal communication with author, November 14, 2011.

SOURCES CONSULTED

BOOKS, EDITED VOLUMES, AND PUBLISHED PROCEEDINGS

Adler, Jacob, and Robert M. Kamins. *The Fantastic Life of Walter Murray Gibson: Hawaii's Minister of Everything*. Honolulu: University of Hawai'i Press, 1986.

Alexander, Thomas G. *Mormonism in Transition: A History of the Latter-Day Saints, 1890–1930*. Urbana: University of Illinois Press, 1996.

Allen, James B., and Glen M. Leonard. *The Story of the Latter-Day Saints*. Salt Lake City: Deseret, 1976.

Arrington, Leonard J. *Great Basin Kingdom: An Economic History of the Latter-Day Saints, 1830–1900*. Cambridge, MA: Harvard University Press, 1958.

Arrington, Leonard J., and Davis Bitton. *The Mormon Experience: A History of the Latter-Day Saints*. 2nd ed. Urbana: University of Illinois Press, 1992.

Arrington, Leonard J., Feramorz Y. Fox, and Dean L. May, eds. *Building the City of God: Community and Cooperation Among the Mormons*. Urbana: University of Illinois Press, 1992.

Ayau, Edward Halealoha. "Native Hawaiian Burial Rights." In *Native Hawaiian Rights Handbook*, edited by Melody Kapilialoha MacKenzie, 245–273. Honolulu: University of Hawai'i Press, 1991.

Bancroft, Hubert Howe, Henry Lebbeus Oak, and A. L. Bancroft & Company. *History of the Northwest Coast*. San Francisco: Bancroft, 1884.

Barman, Jean, and Bruce McIntyre Watson. *Leaving Paradise: Indigenous Hawaiians in the Pacific Northwest, 1787–1898*. Honolulu: University of Hawai'i Press, 2006.

Barth, Fredrik. "Ethnic Groups and Boundaries." In *Theories of Ethnicity: A Classical Reader*, edited by Werner Sollors, 294–324. New York: New York University Press, 1996.

Battistini, Lawrence H. *The Rise of American Influence in Asia and the Pacific*. East Lansing: Michigan State University Press, 1960.

Berkhofer, Robert F., Jr. *The White Man's Indian*. New York: Vintage, 1979.

Bigler, David L. *Forgotten Kingdom: The Mormon Theocracy in the American West*. Spokane: Arthur H. Clarke, 1998.

Bingham, Hiram. *A Residence of Twenty-one Years in the Sandwich Islands: Or, the Civil, Religious, and Political History of Those Islands: Comprising a Particular View of the Missionary Operations Connected with the Introduction and Progress of Christianity and Civilization among the Hawaiian People*. Hartford, CT: Huntington, 1849.

The Book of Mormon: Another Testament of Jesus Christ. New York: Doubleday, 2004.

Borofsky, Robert. *Remembrance of Pacific Pasts: An Invitation to Remake History*. Honolulu: University of Hawai'i Press, 2000.

Britsch, R. Lanier. *Moramona: The Mormons in Hawai'i*. Laie, Hawaii: Institute for Polynesian Studies, 1989.

Britsch, R. Lanier. *Unto the Islands of the Sea: A History of the Latter-day Saints in the Pacific*. Salt Lake City: Deseret, 1986.

Brownlee, W. Elliot. *Dynamics of Ascent: a History of the American Economy*. 2nd ed. Chicago: Dorsey, 1988.

Busto, Rudiger V. "Disorienting Subjects: Reclaiming Pacific Islander/Asian American Religious Traditions." In *Revealing the Sacred in Asian and Pacific America*, edited by Jane Iwamura and Paul Spickard, 9–28. New York: Routledge, 2003.

Cannon, George Q. *My First Mission*. Salt Lake City: Juvenile Instructor Office, 1879.

Chappell, David A. *Double Ghosts: Oceanian Voyagers on Euroamerican Ships*. Armonk, NY: Sharpe, 1997.

Chase, Lance D. "Life in Early Lā'ie, 1850–1880." Records of the Mormon Pacific Historical Society. Archives, Joseph F. Smith Library, Brigham Young University Hawai'i, Lā'ie.

Chase, Lance D. *Temple, Town, and Tradition: The Collected Historical Essays of Lance D. Chase*. Laie: Pacific Institute/Brigham Young University Hawai'i Press, 2000.

Cluff, William Wallace. *The Cluff Family Journal*. Microfilm copy. Joseph F. Smith Library, Brigham Young University Hawai'i.

Conley, Don C. "The Pioneer Chinese in Utah." In *The Peoples of Utah*, edited by Helen Papanikoulas, 254–271. Salt Lake City: Utah State Historical Society, 1976.

Cronon, William, Jay Gitlin, and George A. Miles. *Under an Open Sky: Rethinking America's Western Past*. New York: Norton, 1992.

Dana, Richard Henry. *Two Years Before the Mast*. New York: Heritage, 1947.

Dening, Greg. *Beach Crossings: Voyages Across Times, Cultures, and Selves*. Philadelphia: University of Pennsylvania Press, 2004.

Dening, Greg. *The Death of William Gooch: A History's Anthropology*. Honolulu: University of Hawai'i Press, 1995.

Dening, Greg. *Islands and Beaches: Discourse on a Silent Land: Marquesas, 1774–1880*. Honolulu: University of Hawai'i Press, 1980.

Denoon, Donald et al, eds. *The Cambridge History of the Pacific Islanders*. New York: Cambridge University Press, 1997.

Deutsch, Sarah. "Landscapes of Enclaves." In *Under an Open Sky: Rethinking America's Western Past*, edited by George Miles, William Cronon, and Jay Gitlin, 110–131. New York: Norton, 1992.

Doctrine and Covenants of the Church of the Latter Day Saints. Kirtland, Ohio, F. G. Williams, 1835.

Dudden, Arthur Power. *The American Pacific: From the China Trade to the Present*. New York: Oxford University Press, 1992.

Eliason, Eric A. *Mormons and Mormonism: An Introduction to an American World Religion*. Urbana: University of Illinois Press, 2001.

Ellsworth, S. George. *Zion in Paradise; Early Mormons in the South Seas*. Logan: Faculty Association, Utah State University, 1959.

Lawrence W. Flake, *George Q. Cannon: His Missionary Years*. Salt Lake City: Bookcraft, 1998.

Francaviglia, Richard V. *The Mormon Landscape: Existence, Creation, and Perception of a Unique Image in the American West*. New York: AMS Press, 1978.

Frisch, Michael H. *A Shared Authority: Essays on the Craft and Meaning of Oral and Public History*. Albany: State University of New York Press, 1990.

Fuchs, Lawrence H. *Hawaii Pono: A Social History*. San Diego: Harcourt Brace Jovanovich, 1983.

Gay, Theresa. *James Marshall: The Discoverer of California Gold, a Biography*. Georgetown, CA: Talisman, 1967.

Gibson, Walter Murray, Thomas G. Thrum, and Saturday Press. *The Shepherd Saint of Lanai: Rich "Primacy" Revelations: Gathered from Various Sources and Produced in Historical Shape for the First Time in the "Saturday Press."* December 24, 1881 to January 21, 1882. Honolulu: T. G. Thrum, 1882.

Glassberg, David. *American Historical Pageantry: the Uses of Tradition in the Early Twentieth Century*. Chapel Hill: University of North Carolina Press, 1990.

Dening, Greg. *Sense of History: the Place of the Past in American Life*. Amherst: University of Massachusetts Press, 2001.

Gregory, James. "The West and Workers: 1870–1930." In *Blackwell Companion to the American West*, edited by Bill Deverell, 240–255. Victoria: Blackwell, 2004.

Grieco, Elizabeth M. *The Native Hawaiian and Other Pacific Islander Population: 2000*. Census 2000 Brief, C2KBR/01–14. Washington, DC: US Census Bureau, December 2001.

Hackett, David G., and Jan Shipps. *Religion and American Culture: A Reader*. New York: Routledge, 1995.

Handy, E. S. Craighill, Elizabeth Handy, and Mary Kawena Pukui. *Native Planters in Old Hawai'i: Their Life, Lore, and Environment*. Honolulu: Bishop Museum Press, 1972.

Haney-Lopez, Ian. *White By Law: The Legal Construction of Race*. New York: New York University Press, 1996.

Hansen, Klaus J. *Quest for Empire: The Political Kingdom of God and the Council of Fifty in Mormon History*. East Lansing: Michigan State University Press, 1967.

Harris, Phillip M., and Nicholas A Jones. *We the People: Pacific Islanders in the United States, Census 2000 Special Reports*. Washington, DC: US Department of Commerce, 2005.

Hau'ofa, Epeli, Eric Waddell, Vijay Naidu, and University of the South Pacific, School of Social and Economic Development. *A New Oceania: Rediscovering Our Sea of Islands*. Suva, Fiji: School of Social and Economic Development, University of the South Pacific in Association with Beake House, 1993.

Hereniko, Vilsoni, and Rob Wilson. *Inside Out: Literature, Cultural Politics, and Identity in the New Pacific, Pacific Formations*. Lanham, MD.: Rowman & Littlefield, 1998.

Howay, F. W. "Early Relations with the Pacific North-West." In *The Hawaiian Islands: Papers Read During the Captain Cook Sesquicentenial Celebration, Honolulu, August 17, 1928*, edited by Albert Pierce Taylor. Honolulu: Archives of Hawai'i, 1930.

Ii, John Papa, Mary Kawena Pukui, and Dorothy B. Barráere. *Fragments of Hawaiian History*. Rev. ed. Honolulu: Bishop Museum Press, 1983.

Irwin, Geoffrey. *The Prehistoric Exploration and Colonization of the Pacific*. New York: Cambridge University Press, 1992.

Iwamura, Jane, and Paul Spickard. *Revealing the Sacred in Asian and Pacific America*. New York London: Routledge, 2002.

Jacobson, Matthew Frye. *Barbarian Virtues: The United States Encounters Foreign Peoples at Home and Abroad, 1876–1917*. New York: Hill and Wang, 2000.

Jackson, Richard H. *Cultural Geography: People, Places, and Environment*. St. Paul: West Publishing, 1990.

Johnson, Susan Lee. *Roaring Camp: The Social World of the California Gold Rush*. New York: Norton, 2001.

Jordan, Winthrop. *The White Man's Burden: The Historical Origins of Racism in the United States*. New York: Oxford University Press, 1974.

Journal of Discourses. Liverpool, UK: F. D. and S. W. Richards, 1854.

Kamakau, Samuel Manaiakalani. *Ruling Chiefs of Hawaii*. Rev. ed. Honolulu: Kamehameha Schools Press, 1992.

Kamakau, Samuel Manaiakalani, Mary Kawena Pukui, and Dorothy B. Barráere. *Ka Po'e Kahiko: The People of Old*. Bernice P. Bishop Museum Special publication no. 51. Honolulu: Bishop Museum Press, 1964.

Kame'eleihiwa, Lilikalā. *Natives Lands and Foreign Desires: Pehea Lā e Pono Ai?* Honolulu: Bishop Museum Press, 1992.

Kirch, Patrick Vinton, and Marshall David Sahlins. *Anahulu: The Anthropology of History in the Kingdom of Hawaii*. 2 vols. Chicago: University of Chicago Press, 1992.

Koppel, Tom. *Kanaka: The Untold Story of Hawaiian Pioneers in British Columbia and the Pacific Northwest*. Vancouver, BC: Whitecap Books, 1995.

Kuykendall, Ralph Simpson. *The Hawaiian Kingdom*. Honolulu: University of Hawai'i Press, 1957.

Lamar, Howard. "From Bondage to Contract: Ethnic Labor in the American West, 1600–1890." In *The Countryside in the Age of Capitalist Transformation: Essays in the Social History of Rural America*, edited by Steven Hahn and Jonathan Prude, 293–326. Chapel Hill: University of North Carolina Press, 1985.

Landon, Michael N., ed. *The Journals of George Q. Cannon, Volume 1: To California in '49*. Salt Lake City: Deseret, 1999.

Lewis, Oscar. *Sutter's Fort: Gateway to the Gold Fields*. Englewood Cliffs, NJ: Prentice Hall, 1966.

Lieber, Michael ed. *Exiles and Migrants in Oceania*. Honolulu: University of Hawai'i Press, 1977.

Limerick, Patricia Nelson. *The Legacy of Conquest: The Unbroken Past of the American West*. 1st ed. New York: Norton, 1987.

Limerick, Patricia Nelson, Clyde A. Milner, and Charles E. Rankin. *Trails: Toward a New Western History*. Lawrence: University Press of Kansas, 1991.

Lotchin, Richard W. *San Francisco, 1846–1856: From Hamlet to City*. Urbana: University of Illinois Press, 1997.

Lyman, Edward Leo. *San Bernardino: The Rise and Fall of a California Community*. Salt Lake City: Signature, 1996.

Maffly-Kipp, Laurie. "Eastward Ho!" In *Retelling U.S. Religious History*, edited by Thomas Tweed, 127–148. Berkeley: University of California Press, 1997.

Malo, Davida. *Hawaiian Antiquities (Mo'olelo Hawaii)*. 2nd. ed. Honolulu: Bishop Museum Press, 1971.

Mawer, G. A. *Ahab's Trade: The Saga of South Seas Whaling*. New York: St. Martin's, 1999.

Mackie, Richard Somerset. *Trading Beyond the Mountains: The British Fur Trade on the Pacific, 1793–1843*. Vancouver: University of British Columbia Press, 1997.

Mauss, Armand. *All Abraham's Children: Changing Mormon Conceptions of Race and Lineage*. Urbana: University of Illinois Press, 2003.

McCall, Grant, and John Connell, eds. *A World Perspective on Pacific Islander Migration: Australia, New Zealand, and the USA*. Sydney: University of New South Wales, 1993.

McKinzie, Edith Kawealoha. *Hawaiian Genealogies, Extracted from Hawaiian Language Newspapers, Volume 1.* Lāʻie, Hawaiʻi: Institute for Polynesian Studies, 1983.

McPherson, Cluny, Paul Spoonley, and Melania Anae, eds. *Tangata O Te Moana Nui: The Evolving Identities of Pacific Peoples in Aotearoa/New Zealand.* New Zealand: Dunmore Press, 2001.

Meares, John. *Voyages Made in the Years 1788 and 1789 from China to the North-West Coast of America.* New York: Da Capo, 1967.

Merry, Sally Engle. *Colonizing Hawaiʻi: The Cultural Power of Law.* Princeton: Princeton University Press, 2000.

Milner, Clyde A., Carol A. O'Connor, and Martha A. Sandweiss. *The Oxford History of the American West.* New York: Oxford University Press, 1994.

Morton, Helen. *Tongans Overseas: Between Two Shores.* Honolulu: University of Hawaiʻi Press, 2003.

Mulford, Prentice. *Life by Land and Sea.* New York: F. J. Needham, 1889.

Nakano-Glenn, Evelyn. *Unequal Freedoms: How Race and Gender Shaped American Citizenship and Labor.* Cambridge, MA: Harvard University Press, 2002.

Nelson, Lowry. *The Mormon Village: A Pattern and Technique of Land Settlement.* Salt Lake City: University of Utah Press, 1952.

Nero, Karen. "The End of Insularity." In *The Cambridge History of Pacific Islanders,* edited by Donald Denoon, 259–396. New York: Cambridge University Press, 1997.

Osorio, Jon Kamakawiwoʻole. *Dismembering Lāhui: A History of the Hawaiian Nation to 1887.* Honolulu: University of Hawaiʻi Press, 2004.

Owens, Kenneth N. *Gold Rush Saints: California Mormons and the Great Rush for Riches.* Norman: University of Oklahoma Press, 2005.

Papanikoulas, Helen, ed. *The Peoples of Utah.* Salt Lake City: Utah State Historical Society, 1976.

Peck, Gunther. *Reinventing Free Labor: Padrones and Immigrant Workers in the North American West, 1880–1930.* New York: Cambridge University Press, 2000.

Pigman, Walter Griffith. *The Journals of Walter Griffith Pigman.* Edited by Ella Stanley Fawkes. Mexico, MO: Walter G. Staley, 1942.

Pomeranz, Kenneth, and Steven Topik. *The World That Trade Created: Society, Culture, and the World Economy, 1400–the Present, Sources and Studies in World History.* Armonk, NY: Sharpe, 1999.

Pukui, Mary Kawena. *Nana i ke kumu.* Honolulu: Hui Hānai, 1972.

Pukui, Mary Kawena, and Dietrich Varez. *Olelo Noʻeau: Hawaiian Proverbs & Poetical Sayings.* Bernice P. Bishop Museum Special Publication no. 71. Honolulu: Bishop Museum Press, 1983.

Quinn, D. Michael. "Religion in the American West." In *Under an Open Sky,* edited by Clyde Milner et al., 145–166. New York: Norton, 1992.

Rainbird, Paul. *The Archaeology of Micronesia.* New York: Cambridge University Press, 2004.

Ricketts, Norma Baldwin. *The Mormon Battalion: U.S. Army of the West, 1846–1848.* Logan: Utah State University Press, 1996.

Robbins, William G. *Colony and Empire: The Capitalist Transformation of the American West, Development of Western Resources.* Lawrence: University Press of Kansas, 1994.

Rosenzweig, Roy, and David Thelen. *Presence of the Past: Popular Uses of History in American Life.* New York: Columbia University Press, 1998.

Ross, Alexander. *Fur Hunters of the Far West.* London: Smith, Elder, 1855.

Scott, James C. *Domination and the Arts of Resistance: Hidden Transcripts.* New Haven: Yale University Press, 1990.

Shipps, Jan. *Mormonism: The Story of a New Religious Tradition*. Urbana: University of Illinois Press, 1985.

Silva, Noenoe K. *Aloha Betrayed: Native Hawaiian Resistance to American Colonialism*. Durham, NC: Duke University Press, 2004.

Small, Cathy. *Voyages: From Tongan Villages to American Suburbs*. Ithaca, NY: Cornell University Press, 1997.

Spickard, Paul R., and W. Jeffrey Burroughs. *We Are a People: Narrative and Multiplicity in Constructing Ethnic Identity*. Philadelphia: Temple University Press, 2000.

Spickard, Paul R., Joanne L. Rondilla, and Debbie Hippolite Wright. *Pacific Diaspora: Island Peoples in the United States and Across the Pacific*. Honolulu: University of Hawai'i Press, 2002.

Spurrier, Joseph H. *Sandwich Islands Saints: early Mormon converts in the Hawaiian Islands*, Lā'ie, J. H. Spurrier: 1989.

Stauffer, Robert H. *Kahana : How the Land Was Lost*. Honolulu: University of Hawai'i Press, 2004.

Takaki, Ronald T. *A Different Mirror: A History of Multicultural America*. 1st pbk. ed. Boston: Little, Brown, 1993.

Takaki, Ronald T. *Pau Hana: Plantation Life and Labor in Hawaii, 1835–1920*. Berkeley, Calif.: Ronald Takaki, 1983.

Thomas, Nicholas. *Colonialism's Culture: Anthropology, Travel, and Government*. Cambridge: Polity, 1994.

Tuimaleali'ifano, Morgan. *Samoans in Fiji: Migration, Identity, and Communication*. Suva: University of South Pacific, 1990.

Underwood, Grant. *Voyages of Faith: Explorations in Mormon Pacific History*. Provo, UT: Brigham Young University Press, 2000.

Walter McDougall. *Let the Sea Make a Noise*. New York: HarperCollins 1993.

White, Richard. *"It's Your Misfortune and None of My Own": A New History of the American West*. Norman: University of Oklahoma Press, 1991.

Yorgasen, Ethan R. *Transformation of the Mormon Culture Region*. Urbana: University of Illinois Press, 2004.

RESOURCES IN ARCHIVES AND SPECIAL COLLECTIONS; UNPUBLISHED MANUSCRIPTS

"Articles of Incorporation." Iosepa Agricultural and Stock Company. Tooele County Courthouse, Tooele, Utah.

Barrell, William, to Joseph F. Smith, October 9, 1913. Scott G. Kenney Collection, L. Tom Perry Special Collections. Brigham Young University, Provo, Utah.

Beck, Raymond Clyde. "Iosepa: Hawai'i's Zion." Archives, Joseph F. Smith Library. Brigham Young University Hawai'i, Lā'ie.

Brigham Young to Parley P. Pratt, August 19, 1854, Church Historical Department, Salt Lake City, Utah.

Cluff, Benjamin, Papers. L. Tom Perry Special Collections. Brigham Young University, Provo, Utah.

Cluff, Harvey H., Journal. Microfilm copy. Pacific Islands Collection, Joseph F. Smith Library. Brigham Young University Hawai'i, Lā'ie.

Green, Ephraim, Journal. Typescript copy. Archives, Joseph F. Smith Library. Brigham Young University Hawai'i, Lā'ie.

Harrison, Vestil J. "Life Sketch of Thomas Anson Waddoups." Archives, Joseph F. Smith Library. Brigham Young University Hawai'i, Lā'ie.

"Hawaiian House of Nobles and Representatives." *Penal Code Session Laws* 1850, Section 1, Hawai'i State Archives.

Ho'opi'iaina, Cuma Sorensen. "Ho'opi'iaina Family History." In *Iosepa*. Archives, Joseph F. Smith Library. Brigham Young University Hawai'i.

In re Kanaka Nian. Supreme Court of Utah, 6 Utah 259, 21 P. 993, 1889.

Jenson, Andrew. *History of the Hawaiian Mission of the Church of Jesus Christ of Latter-day.Saints, 1850–1930.* 7 vols. Pacific Islands Room, Joseph F. Smith Library Archives. Brigham Young University Hawai'i, Lā'ie.

Jenson, Andrew. "Iosepa Colony: Tooele County, Utah." Church Historical Department, Salt Lake City, Utah.

"Ka Mookuauhou o Panana Hiamololi." Hawaii State Archives, Manuscripts Collection. HMS G64.

Kamau'oha, Edwin. Edwin Kamau'oha Collection, Manuscripts Collection, University Archives, Brigham Young University Hawai'i.

Kanahele, Clinton. Interview by John Broad , June 13, 1970. Manuscripts Collection, Joseph F. Smith Library. Brigham Young University Hawai'i, Lā'ie.

King, Bessie, to unknown, January 26, 1917. Typescript copy. Archives, Joseph F. Smith Library. Brigham Young University Hawai'i, Lā'ie.

Kinney, William, to D. A. McKinley, June 22, 1889. *Records of the Foreign Office and Executive.* Series 404, "Hawaiian Officials Abroad." Hawai'i State Archives.

Kinney, William, to D. A. McKinley, January 2, 1891. *Records of the Foreign Office and Executive.* Series 404, "Hawaiian Officials Abroad." Hawai'i State Archives.

Lewis, Phillip B., Journal. Archives, Joseph F. Smith Library. Brigham Young University Hawai'i, Lā'ie.

Records of the Hawaiian Mission, All Islands. Archives, Joseph F. Smith Library, Brigham Young University Hawai'i, Lā'ie.

Records of the Iosepa Agricultural and Stock Company. Church Historical Department, Salt Lake City, Utah.

Report of the Minister of Foreign Affairs to the Hawai'i Legislature, Session of 1892. Honolulu: Leiali'i Publishing, 1892. Hawai'i State Archives.

Turley, Richard E., Jr.,ed. "Joseph F. Smith Incoming Correspondence, 1855–1918." In *Selected Collections from the Archives of the Church of Jesus Christ of Latter-day Saints.* Brigham Young University Hawai'i Archives and Special Collections.

Waddoups, Thomas A. "The Iosepa Agricultural and Stock Company." December 1956. Archives, Joseph F. Smith Library. Brigham Young University Hawai'i, Lā'ie.

Waddoups, William. *Journal of William Waddoups.* Archives, Joseph F. Smith Library, Brigham Young University Hawai'i.

Wallace, William, III. Interview by John Broad. Kenneth Baldridge Oral History Collection, Archives, Joseph F. Smith Library, Brigham Young University Hawai'i, Lā'ie.

Wilder, Charles T., to Francis Hatch, April 13, 1894. *Records of Hawaiian Officials Abroad.* Series 404, "Hawaiian Officials Abroad." Hawai'i State Archives.

Woodruff, Wilford, to William Kinney, April 10, 1891. *Records of the Foreign Office and Executive,* Series 404, "Hawaiian Officials Abroad." Hawai'i State Archives.

NEWSPAPERS

Church News (Salt Lake City, Utah).

Daily Corinne Reporter (Corinne, Utah).

Deseret Evening News (Salt Lake City, Utah).

High Country News (Denver, Colorado).
Honolulu Star-Bulletin (Honolulu, Hawai'i).
Ogden Standard Examiner (Ogden, Utah).
Park City Mining Record (Park City, Utah).
Salt Lake Tribune (Salt Lake City, Utah).
The Polynesian (Honolulu, Hawai'i).

PUBLISHED ARTICLES

Barkan, Elliot Robert. "Turning Turner on His Head? The Significance of Immigration in 20th Century American Western History." *New Mexico Historical Review* 77 (Winter 2002): 57–88.

Busch, Briton C. "Whalemen, Missionaries, and Practice of Christianity in the Nineteenth Century Pacific." *Hawaiian Journal of History* 27 (1993): 91–118.

Clement, Russell T. "Polynesian Origins: More Word on the Mormon Perspective." *Dialogue* 13 (Winter 1980): 88–98.

Dillon, Richard H. "Kanaka Colonies in California." *Pacific Historical Review* 24, no. 1 (February 1955): 17–23.

Dubofksy, Melvyn. "The Origins of Western Working Class Radicalism, 1890–1905." *Labor History* 7, no. 2 (1966): 131–155.

Duncan, Janice K. "Kanaka World Travelers and Fur Company Employees, 1785–1860." *Hawaiian Journal of History* 7 (1973): 93–111.

Friedman, Harriet. "World, Market, State, and Family Farm: Social Bases of Household Production in the Era of Wage Labor." *Comparative Studies in Society and History* 20, no. 4 (October 1978): 545–586.

Greer, Richard A. "California Gold-Some Reports to Hawai'i." *Hawaiian Journal of History* 4 (1970): 153–173.

Gregory, Edna Hope. "Iosepa: Kanaka Ranch." *Utah Humanities Review* 2 (1) (1948): 3–9.

Igler, David. "Diseased Goods: Global Exchanges in the Eastern Pacific Basin, 1770–1850." *American Historical Review* 109, no. 3 (June 2004): 693–719.

Illerbrun, W.J., "Kanaka Pete." *Hawaiian Journal of History* 6 (1972): 156–169.

Jones, Megan Sanborn. "(Re)living the Pioneer Past: Mormon Youth Handcart Trek Reenactments." *Theatre Topics* 16, no. 2 (2006): 113–130.

Kittelson, David. "John Coxe: Hawai'i's First Soldier of Fortune." *Hawai'i Historical Review* (January 1965): 194–198.

Knight, Nelson. "This Old House: The John Henry and Marie Kaoo Makaula House." *Capitol Hill Neighborhood Council Bulletin* 47 (March 2005): 1–2.

Maffly-Kipp, Laurie. "Looking West: Mormonism and the Pacific World." *Journal of Mormon History* 26, no. 1 (Spring 2000): 40–63.

McClennan, Carol A. "Foundations of Sugar's Power: Early Maui Plantations, 1840–1860." *Hawaiian Journal of History* 29 (1995): 33–56.

Meinig, D. W. "The Mormon Culture Region: Strategies and Patterns in the Geography of the American West." *Annals of the Association of American Geographers* 55, no. 2 (June 1965): 191–220.

"Memoirs of Thomas Hopoo." *Hawaiian Journal of History* 2 (1968): 42–54.

Morris, Nancy J. "Hawaiian Missionaries in the Marquesas." *Hawaiian Journal of History* 13 (1979): 46–58.

Murphy, Thomas. "From Racist Stereotype to Ethnic Identity: Instrumental Uses of the Mormon Racial Doctrine." *Ethnohistory* 46, no. 3 (Summer 1999): 451–480.

Nelson, Elroy. "The Mineral Industry: A Foundation of Utah's Economy." *Utah Historical Quarterly* 31, no. 3 (Summer 1963): 178–196.

Nomura, Gail M. "Significant Lives: Asia and Asian Americans in the History of the U.S. West." *The Western Historical Quarterly* 25, no.1 (Spring 1994): 69–88.

Schmitt, Robert C. "Population Policy in Hawaii." *Hawaiian Journal of History* 8 (1974): 90–110.

Thelen, David. "Memory and American History." *Journal of American History* 75 (March 1989): 1117–1129.

Whitehead, John S. "Hawai'i: the First and Last Far West?" *Western Historical Quarterly* 23, no. 2 (Spring 1992): 153–177.

Woods, Fred E. "An Islander's View of a Desert Kingdom: Jonathan Napela Recounts His 1869 Visit to Salt Lake City." *BYU Studies* 45, no. 1 (2006): 25–26.

Woods, Fred E. "The Palawai Pioneers on the Island of Lanai, Hawai'i." *Mormon Historical Studies* 5, no. 2 (Fall 2004): 3–36.

THESES AND DISSERTATIONS

Aikau, Hōkūlani Kamakanikailialoha. "Polynesian Pioneers: Twentieth Century Religious Racial Formations and Migration in Hawai'i." PhD diss., University of Minnesota, Minneapolis, Minnesota, 2005.

Atkins, Dennis. "A History of Iosepa: The Utah Polynesian Colony." Master's thesis, Brigham Young University, Provo, Utah, 1958.

Compton, Cynthia. "The Making of the Ahupua'a of Lā'ie into a Gathering Place and an Alternative Space to Capitalism." PhD diss., Brigham Young University, Provo, Utah, 2004.

Gordon, Tamar G. *"Inventing Mormon Identity in Tonga."* PhD diss., University of California Berkeley, Berkeley, California, 1988.

Inglis, Kerri. *"A Land Set Apart: Disease, Displacement, & Death at Makanalua, Molokai."* PhD diss., University of Hawai'i, Honolulu, Hawai'i, 2004.

Morris, Nancy J. "Hawaiian Missionaries Abroad, 1852–1909." PhD diss., University of Hawaii, Honolulu, Hawai'i,1987.

Stover, Jeffrey S. "The Legacy of the 1848 Mahele and Kuleana Act of 1850: A Case Study of the La'ie Wai and La'ie Malo'o Ahupua'a, 1846–1930." Master's thesis, University of Hawaii, Honolulu, Hawai'i, August 1997.

INDEX